ALL THE LAW IN THE WORLD WON'T STOP THEM

SHIRES PRESS

4869 Main Street
P.O. Box 2200
Manchester Center, VT 05255
www.northshire.com

ALL THE
IN THE LAW
WORLD
WON'T STOP THEM

Copyright © 2017 by GREG VEITCH

ISBN Number: 978-1-60571-349-6

Building Community, One Book at a Time
A family-owned, independent bookstore in
Manchester Ctr., VT, since 1976 and Saratoga Springs, NY
since 2013. We are committed to excellence in bookselling.
The Northshire Bookstore's mission is to serve as a resource for
information, ideas, and entertainment while honoring the
needs of customers, staff, and community.

Printed in the United States of America

All The Law in the World Won't Stop Them

To Ron,

Enjoy these true stories of Saratoga's notorious past!

Greg J. Veitch

Greg Veitch

Dedication

To all those who love Saratoga Springs and its
wonderful, amazing and notorious history

Table of Contents

Acknowledgments

On the cover of almost every book the name of the author stands alone, giving the impression that the work is the product of single minded determination to accomplish the task of completing the work. While writing a book can certainly be a lonely endeavor, the reality is that many people have an influence over the finished product. At least that was the case for me. Being a severely limited amateur writer and historian, this book would never have been written had not a multitude of people been willing to contribute to the effort.

To start at the beginning I suppose that my deep love of Saratoga Springs and appreciation of history could be traced to my parents, Michael and Gail. From an early age my parents instilled in my siblings and I a tremendous love of family and a solid connection to the place of our birth.

As a history teacher for over thirty years, a turf writer and author of two books himself, my father was the first to read a complete draft of this book. His insight and editorial suggestions made this narrative much more readable than it otherwise would have been. This first effort at polishing the finished product was indispensable in developing a readable narrative.

My father deserves special thanks for his assistance.

Leigh Hornbeck, Dave Patterson and my daughter Rachel also provided early reads of the manuscript. Each supplied valuable suggestions and commentary on the draft which led to a more well-written book than I could have accomplished on my own. Leigh and Dave in particular added specific recommendations that really added value to the finished version of this story. Donna Bates provided detailed editorial work that I am sure has saved me considerable embarrassment for my inability to properly use correct grammar and punctuation.

Without the research assistance of several individuals this book would never have been written. The Saratoga Room at the Saratoga Springs Public Library is an excellent resource for anyone looking into the history of Saratoga Springs. Teri Blasko and Victoria Garlanda at the Saratoga Room provided many leads and tips on various aspects of my research efforts. Executive Director of the Saratoga Springs History Museum, Jamie Parillo was instrumental in tracking down various photographs and other material while my visits to City Historian May Ann Fitzgerald were always productive.

Phil Steffen created the illustration of the roulette wheel for the chapter title pages. He can be reached at nicesign@hotmail.com. Cathleen Duffy provided the author photograph on the back cover. She can be contacted through her Facebook page, "Horse Whisper

Photography."

Finally, my wife Jennifer has been a constant supporter and confidant throughout this process. Without her patience and grace I would never have seen this thing through. She is a model of encouragement and understanding and always has been. Not just throughout this process but throughout the course of our lives together. It is not easy being the spouse of a police officer who moonlights as an author, but Jen makes it look easy. She is the love of my life and the most wonderful and beautiful woman I have ever known. Thank you Jen, for your support and patience over the past few years.

Introduction

This book is the end result of a long series of coincidences or divine guidance, if you believe in such things, as I do. My family's connection to Saratoga goes back six generations now. My great-great grandfather, Silas Veitch was born in Canada. He was a terrific horseman and traveled the racing circuit most of his life, riding and training racehorses throughout the United States and Canada, including at Saratoga Springs. He had five children, one of them being Sid Veitch, who had a short-lived racing career before landing permanently in Saratoga Springs. One of his sons, Donald, is my grandfather, a lifelong city resident and World War II veteran who was the Director of Urban Renewal during that time in the City's history. Don's first of five children is Michael, my father and a history teacher for 32 years at the Saratoga Springs Junior High School, longtime turf writer for the Saratogian newspaper, and author of two books on the history of horse racing in Saratoga Springs. I am the second of Mike's five children and I have lived my entire life in Saratoga Springs (except during my college years at Plattsburgh) and today, my children attend Saratoga Springs City Schools. For a while, the Veitch family owned the building that is now the excellent restaurant, The Olde Bryan Inn, and that is where the genesis of this book can be found.

One of my earliest memories from childhood is walking up the hill in High Rock Park to attend a family reunion in the mid-1970s. From where I grew up on Circular Street, we walked out our back door, across High Rock Ave and up the hill to the reunion at the Veitch home in the building that is today the Olde Byran Inn. At the family gathering, one of the men told me a tale about my great-grandfather, Sid Veitch. As I recall, the story went like this:

Sid Veitch was somewhat of a rough and tumble character. He was a horseman for a while like most of the Veitch men in those days, but he also associated with some rather shady folks. One night Sid was in a car with a couple of gangsters when they shot a guy and dumped him at the hospital. No one knew why the man was shot and left for dead, but those details weren't the point of the story, the point was to illustrate my great-grandfather's character. According to the tale, when the police came to Sid and started asking questions, he said, "I don't know who shot the poor fellow because I was in the front seat and the shooting took place in the back seat." The story was the about the unsolved murder of Adam Parillo in 1936, but I didn't know that then. I just found Sid Veitch's antics amusing, even as a young child.

I never heard much more about the murder my great-grandfather was allegedly involved in, but I never forgot the story. About 11 years after I was hired as a police officer in my hometown, I received a call from a retired detective. I had been promoted to lieutenant, assigned to the detective division and the retired detective asked me to check on an old case in the archives.

While I was there, I decided on a whim to look at the oldest case I could find, and there, on the top of the box, was a file with the words "Parillo Murder" written on it. When I started reading the reports inside I realized, this was the murder that Sid Veitch was supposedly involved with and although the case file was meager when compared to the documents produced during a murder investigation today, I found no mention of Sid Veitch anywhere.

Even though great grandpa Sid probably wasn't involved with the murder of Adam Parillo in any meaningful way, the story itself was fascinating and I started to research the crime. Eventually I put the Parillo story together and did a presentation for the Saratoga Springs History Museum. When I was done, the first words a friend said to me were, "You should write a book."

By then I knew there were a host of other stories from Saratoga's past I found just as interesting and just as incredible as the murder of a local convict. For more than one hundred years, Saratoga Springs struggled with gambling, crime, vice, and corruption. The struggle is the central premise of this work.

This book is also a detailed account of the people and places involved in the long battle between the forces of good and evil in Saratoga Springs from the earliest days of the village through 1921. It contains many names of people and places, some recognizable as national organized crime figures as well as local residents whose only connection to crime and gambling in Saratoga Springs is a single mention during an obscure raid. They are all included in this narrative, in the hope that anyone looking for a family connection to this history might find factual information, even if it is only a brief mention.

The title of this book comes directly from a quote from Richard Canfield. He was addressing a reporter during the latter part of his career as a gambler and he was asked why he thought gambling was so prevalent throughout the country, even though it was entirely illegal. Canfield told the reporter that it was his belief that the lure of the gaming tables was too much for the majority of the populace to resist. That it was an enjoyable way to pass the time for those who could afford it and that gambling, if conducted honestly, was no more dangerous to the moral fabric of the country than the stock market. During the interview Canfield explained that if men of means desired to amuse themselves by gambling at his tables, "…all the law in the world won't stop them."

The moment I read that quote it struck me as an entirely accurate description of the conditions at Saratoga Springs for well over 100 years of the town's history. Saratoga Springs always seemed to have gambling and no one seemed to stop it or care that there were laws against it. Even when arrests were made, it never seemed to matter and the battle raged throughout the history of the famous resort. Indeed, all the law in the world could not stop the gamblers and gangsters at Saratoga.

Many of the places described in this book no longer exist. Residents of Saratoga Springs, no matter how long they have called the Spa City home, may be surprised to learn of places like Willow Walk and Searing's Alley. Visitors today would probably react in disbelief upon hearing the stories contained in these pages, the stories contained within seem nothing like the small city we know today. But true Saratogians understand that we have a unique and colorful history. We are exceptionally proud of our past, warts and all. My hope is that the reader enjoys and appreciates these stories, even if they don't approve of the behavior of some of our most famous and influential residents and visitors. There is truly no place like Saratoga Springs.

The Early Gamblers at Saratoga

The gambling equipment had been secured in the jail cells for safe keeping. Superintendent of Police Thomas Sullivan had just led the most spectacular gambling raid in the history of Saratoga Springs. Everyone knew gambling had been a part of the Saratoga Springs social scene almost as long as the village had been settled. Now, it was the summer of 1919 and after a decade of law and order under Chief of Police James King, the gamblers and gangsters were back in Saratoga in a big way, trying to outmaneuver the law and having some success at that.

The gambling stuff had been confiscated during a raid at 210 South Broadway and Thomas Sullivan had given orders that the equipment was to be kept securely locked in the jail cells for the time being. Was there a safer place in all of Saratoga to store the valuable apparatus than in a locked jail cell in the bowels of the police station of the city? Superintendent Sullivan decided everything was safe enough that he could finally go home.

No sooner had Superintendent Sullivan left the station than a man of questionable morals came lurking through the police department. There was no doubt tension was in the air as the figure slunk over to the duty sergeant's desk and picked up the keys to the jail cells. The desk sergeant looked up and, recognizing Officer Edward Carroll, warned the officer that he was about to become involved in some pretty dangerous business, messing around with the evidence back in the jail area.

Officer Carroll ignored the warning from Desk Sergeant James Sullivan, brother of Superintendent Sullivan, and thought he would risk it anyway. Thomas Sullivan was out of the office just then and Rachel Brown, a notorious gangster out of New York City, and a few friends were waiting for the young officer at the back of the station.

Carroll let the gamblers in through the door to the police station on Maple Avenue and showed them to the jail cells, opened the locked cell, and watched as Brown and company made off with just as much of the stuff as they could carry. On the way out of the station the gamblers passed Officer Hugh Dorsey and the stress of the operation started to show on the faces of the criminals until Officer Carroll assured the men that Dorsey was all right and wouldn't give them any trouble.

Carroll was right; neither Dorsey or James Sullivan, who had decided to take a look at what was happening and saw the group carrying off the goods under the watchful eye of Officer Carroll, raised the alarm. James was sure to tell his brother soon, but for the time being, the brazen raid had been pulled off successfully.

The men had managed to retrieve the roulette ball, many of the chips and cards needed to play the various card games offered at 210 South Broadway, and various other articles that were easily carried by hand. What the raiding party did not manage to liberate from the police station were the larger pieces of equipment, like the wooden roulette and card tables that had been dismantled during the police raid and deposited in the jail cell with the other items. They would need to make a second trip.

Soon the men were gathered again near police headquarters, but this time they sensed that they were being watched and another brazen attack on the police station was deemed ill-advised. While Rachel Brown and crew were certainly men of action, they also knew that perhaps all the cloak and dagger play could be avoided. Other measures could be taken to secure their property and they assumed that a different approach would be just as successful as their earlier theft because they were allies with the greatest criminal mastermind of the day, Arnold Rothstein, who just so happened to also be in Saratoga at that time and also just so happened to have greased the palms of many local officials before the start of the 1919 summer season.

Five men had been arrested during the raid on South Broadway but at their initial court appearance on the night of the raid, the District Attorney, Charles Andrus, appeared before the court and flatly declared that he did not have enough evidence to proceed with charges against four of the defendants, even though the gambling apparatus had not yet been stolen from the jail. The gamblers walked away, scot-free.

After the second attempt at thievery from the police station was abandoned, Rachel Brown found a willing partner to make a motion in court before Saratoga Springs City Court Judge Michael McTygue, requesting a return of the gambling equipment based upon the theory that since the defendants had all been discharged, save one who was not arrested at the scene, then the tables and furniture were otherwise possessed legally. Judge McTygue agreed and released the remaining evidence being held in the city lock-up to Rachel Brown and partners.

Three weeks later Thomas Sullivan made another raid, this time on Circular Street and, much to his surprise, the police seized the same gambling equipment that had been stolen from them by Rachel Brown with the help of Officer Carroll!

How did Saratoga get to such a state? Sure, there had been gambling in town all along, but how exactly does a town totally surrender to criminal gangsters to the point where not only are they allowed the freedom to remove lawfully seized evidence of their crimes from within the police station itself, but then to be so audacious as to then continue right on using the stolen equipment at a different gambling den in the same city? How does the local criminal court work not for the good people of Saratoga Springs to ensure justice is done, but rather for the benefit of the most nefarious of visitors to the Spa?

The answer is complex and is rooted in the history of Saratoga Springs itself. The history of gambling, vice, corruption, and crime in Saratoga Springs reveals a village never quite able to resist the temptation of an open town, but never quite sure it wanted to go all-in on surrendering to the gamblers and gangsters either. The struggle for the conscience of Saratoga Springs lasted for well over one hundred years, see-sawing back and forth between the forces of good and the forces of evil. To seek the answer to the question, how did Saratoga Springs become such a haven for the gamblers and criminals? One should start at the beginning and follow the trail straight to the end.

No one really knows for sure the date that open gambling was established in Saratoga Springs. Fixing an exact date as to when the authorities decided to turn a blind eye to gambling in Saratoga Springs would prove elusive indeed. Common belief is that the origins of public gambling at the Spa coincided with the arrival of John Morrissey, who organized the first racing meet in 1863 before partnering with William Travers and others to open the Saratoga Race Course the following year. But the fact is that gambling was an entrenched Saratoga tradition well before John Morrissey's first visit to Saratoga Springs and his building of the magnificent Club House that stands today in Congress Park as the Canfield Casino, home of the Saratoga Springs History Museum.

Public gambling haunts in the United States (both legal and illegal) originated in the southern states of America. Wealthy plantation owners would find gambling an attractive place to spend their excess money. Gambling in private homes was widespread and considered a gentlemanly pursuit in the highest social circles, a tradition brought over from the gentlemen's clubs of old England.

The gentlemen of the southern aristocracy spread westward and northward with the expansion of the young United States in the early half of the nineteenth century as they travelled to far off vacation destinations in order to escape the oppressive summer heat of the American South. Coupled with the massive summer migration (for those who could afford it) of city dwellers to escape the oppressive humidity and squalor of places like New York, Philadelphia, and Boston, summer resorts like Saratoga Springs sprang up and welcomed the wealthiest of the American citizenry. Gambling became just one of the many leisure activities sought after and offered at places like Saratoga Springs in the 19th century.

There were generally two types of gambling dens in the United States, and Saratoga Springs, during the middle decades of the 1800's. So called, "second class" places were no frills establishments generally located in local taverns while "first-class" places were more elegant houses, modeled on the old gentleman's clubs of England usually without the British tradition of hereditary membership. Many of the early American gambling "second class" places were blatantly dishonest, particularly in the open and lawless west.

Called skinning houses or wolf dens, the games were set up exclusively to fleece unsuspecting marks brought to the game by "ropers" or "steerers." They were so-called because of their ability to "steer" naïve men, and sometimes women, from more wholesome pursuits and into the rigged games of chance managed by honest looking fellows. Most of these games didn't last long in the same place as they naturally sought to avoid attracting too much attention from authorities. Repeat visitors were rare, since the scam would only have become obvious after the sucker had been separated from his money and a return visit would be unlikely. Local people would know to avoid these "second-class" joints as they generally made no attempt to have fair play. [1]

By the late 1820's and early 1830's, relatively fair, upscale gambling houses could be found in most American cities. [2] These "first-class" houses were distinguished from the lower class hells by their generally honest play for repeat customers and local gamblers (though they were not immune from scamming an easy mark if the opportunity presented itself), availability of food and drink, the more distinguished atmosphere, and the generally higher level of wealth among the patrons.

Additionally, one could differentiate the first and second class gambling house by determining the split of the nightly profit. Second class gambling dens split the profit between the steerer, banker, and dealer. First class gambling spots were more at risk since they had an established address, so local authorities would eventually learn where they were located. The profits of a first class house would be split between the owner of the building, his employees, and local police and politicians who needed to be paid off. [3]

The gambling situation in Saratoga was no different. Eventually first and second class gambling houses would spring up in Saratoga Springs. By the time Richard Canfield was enjoying his greatest years at the Spa around the turn of the twentieth century, second class "poolrooms" and first class "clubs" would be operational throughout the village.

By the late 1830's a few billiard halls were offering games of chance and faro tables for their customers' entertainment in Saratoga Springs. [4] These places were not however, exclusive gambling places and the action was probably kept discreet by the proprietors. In his book, *Roll the Bones: The History of Gambling*, David Schwartz references the "gamblers of Park Row" in Saratoga prior to 1840. He probably refers to the gamblers from Park Row in New York City who would follow the crowds to Saratoga in the summer as there is no evidence of a "Park Row" in early Saratoga Springs.

In the office of the Saratoga Springs City Historian there is a copy of a letter written by an early resident of Saratoga Springs, Edmund J. Huling. Written about 1889, Mr. Huling describes the early gambling situation in Saratoga Springs. Huling was manager of the Saratoga Sentinel and connected with other newspapers during the middle and late decades of the 1800's. He came to Saratoga Springs in 1831 as a ten-year-old boy and his narrative provides the most credible early record of the gamblers at Saratoga Springs, well before the arrival of Morrissey.

According to Huling, during the 1830's there was a grove on Broadway across from the Chancellor of the State's residence where lawyers, arguing before the Chancellor, could hear the falling of bowling pins, the crashing of billiard balls, and the clicking of roulette balls falling into the spinning wheel. Who owned this gambling place, Huling does not say, but he does name George W. Cole as the first "boss" gambler in Saratoga Springs.

George Cole owned a place that was located at the southern end of Broadway on property that would later become the Clarendon Hotel. Cole's place had bowling, billiards, and gambling and was open during the summer season. Cole eventually sold his gambling place (probably in the late 1830's) and became a railroad ticket agent, a fact confirmed by the 1860 United States Census records. George W. Cole died in 1879 in Cincinnati at the age of 70.[5] There is no mention of Cole's operation ever being disturbed by the authorities.

Cole's time as top gambler in Saratoga Springs was followed by Joseph Vanderslice and Peter Arnot who, in Huling's narrative, soon found themselves destitute and thus moved on from their Saratoga Springs ventures. Their only importance to the history of gambling in Saratoga Springs is this mention in the Huling letter. The location of the Vanderslice and Arnot places are lost to history.

Huling tells us that Theodore M. Collar and Robert Gridley were rivals in the 1840's. Both had places near the railroad depot. Gridley's story will be recounted shortly but Collar is worth mentioning for the pretentious gambling house that he built on the north side of Division Street between Broadway and the rail station.

In 1861 Collar was a respectable member of the community, serving as vice president of Hook and Ladder Company Number 3 in town.[6] By 1867 he had been arrested and convicted of selling liquor without a license[7] along with several others in town and he died suddenly in 1874 at 54 years of age[8], leaving his operations to sons who could not manage to make a profit from their late father's business.

Reports of open gambling at Saratoga were widely circulating throughout the country by the 1850's. In 1850 one gentleman reportedly lost nearly $200,000 at the gaming tables in Saratoga Springs and attempted to settle the debt with an offer of $10,000 cash and a $100,000 bond. When that was met with a less than enthusiastic response from the winners, an agreement was made to have a third party determine the amount to be paid. To the considerable delight of the poor bettor whose luck was not running that night, the arbitrator decided that $4000 was enough for any one man to lose in a single sitting.

At about the same time, the mayor of Boston reportedly lost $32,000 after unsuccessfully playing 32 straight card games in Saratoga. [9] A man named Watson, arrested in New York City in 1859, claimed that the reason he needed to steal from his neighbor was that he had lost $17,000 in just two weeks while gambling at Saratoga. [10] The judge was not sympathetic and sent the man to The Tombs- the notorious New York City jail of that era.

In the category of "The more things change, the more they stay the same," in 1921 (62 years after the poor loser in New York City was sent to the Tombs), a Glens Falls man named John McCauley plead guilty to the charge of being a common gambler. He did so with an appeal of leniency since he had "…engaged in the business of taking bets because of the nearness of Glens

Falls to Saratoga Springs where gambling was said to be flagrant."[11] Fortunately, Mr. McCauley was spared any jail time and was sentenced to pay a $500 fine.

An article in the New York Times dated August, 23, 1853 described the Saratoga gambling situation this way:

"It is astonishing (notwithstanding the stringent state law) with what bold and unblushing effrontery GAMBLING is carried on here. The business is just as public, and much more extensive than any others. Enter either of the largest establishments near the Railroad Depot, and you will find faro, roulette, cards or almost any game, played in open sight – the parties thinking it even unnecessary to have a screen before the open door. Have they no Grand Juries here, or are there no officers sworn to execute the laws of the State?"

The two establishments mentioned by the Times' correspondent may have belonged to Ben Scribner and Robert Gridley, two of the earliest known public gambling den proprietors in Saratoga Springs. Both had places near the Railroad terminal and both paved the way for later, more extravagant, gamblers.

The Troy Daily Times in August of 1890, in an article that chronicled the early years of gambling in Saratoga Springs, fixes the year of 1829 as the date when Benjamin Scribner first opened his place in the alley across from the United States Hotel. [12] He would have been 36 years old at that date, a not unreasonable age to have established a "bank" to support a gaming room. Yet his obituary in the New York Sun on April 12, 1880, claims that Scribner played his first game of Faro in 1831.

Still others, like George Waller in his book, *Saratoga: Saga of an Imperious Era*, make the definitive statement that Scribner opened in Saratoga Springs in the year 1842. Huling makes only a brief mention of Ben Scribner, saying only that he had a small place here before going to work for Morrissey, a fact acknowledged by other sources.

"Old Scrib" as he was widely known by friends and associates, was a native of Albany, New York. Starting his working life as a hardware clerk in the state capitol of New York, he quickly discovered, as many young men of the gambling fraternity did, that he was attracted to the fast paced, exciting lifestyle of the gambler. [13]

He moved to Washington, DC, and fell in with some gamblers while working as a manager of a hotel in the nation's capital. Eventually his bankroll grew and his gambling interests expanded. He became known throughout the East Coast and players could be found at any number of Scribner-backed games in New York City, Washington DC, Philadelphia, and of course, Saratoga Springs. As a player and gambling house operator, he experienced the inevitable highs and lows of a gambler's life.

Described as physically unimposing, he was nevertheless a cold and calculating individual. [14] By the time the Civil War started, Ben Scribner was going through one of those low periods of his life. His bad fortune was helped along by a couple of con men in Detroit who managed to take $10,000 from "Old Scrib" that he had brought to that city in order to start a faro bank. The card game the Detroit men were running was crooked, but Scribner found out too late. [15] He was broke and needed his luck to turn. His salvation came in the form of John Morrissey.

A former competitor, Morrissey took on Scribner around this time as a dealer and minority partner in his gambling houses in New York and Saratoga. Included in his compensation while working for Morrissey was a fifteen per cent take from the profits of the faro tables from which he dealt. [16] From the moment he entered the employ of Morrissey, "Old Scrib" was able to remain in the game, and financially solvent, for the remainder of his life. He would become a trusted confidant of Morrissey's and became his financial man in 1870. In fact, Morrissey died in 1878 owing Ben Scribner $23,000.

Ben Scribner departed this life a wealthy man, the proceeds of his gambling endeavors netting him a final nest egg in the neighborhood of $250,000. [17] His sister, to whom he left around $84,000 of his fortune, witnessed Scribner's final gamble when she asked if he would like her to retrieve a minister to attend to him in his final hours. Scribner replied that he had been his own protector and counselor all his life and didn't intend to change on his deathbed at age 77. [18]

The aforementioned Robert Gridley was a native Saratogian and successful gambler by the 1840's. Huling describes Gridley as owning several good houses and apparently living quite well. In 1845 the society pages of the New York City newspapers mentioned the fashionable set passing time in Saratoga at the lake or playing "billiards and ten-pins at Gridley's."[19]

What is known about Robert Gridley is that he operated a billiard hall and bowling alley called the "Pavilion." The Pavilion was on Matilda Street near the corner of Division Street and ran the length of the block to Railroad Place across from the old train station. Arriving passengers on the trains, if interested in such things, could see directly into the windows of Gridley's place, where the roulette wheels were spinning.

Gridley had already been in business at the location in March of 1843 when one of the greatest fires in Saratoga Springs history burned his building, along with the entire block, to the ground. Gridley was a relatively successful gambler as competition could be described as sparse into the late 1840's. Scribner, Gridley, and maybe one or two others were the only games in town. [20]

Competition from other gambling houses would increase dramatically in the decades to follow and Gridley would eventually sell his building to two men in March 1871 for $45,000. They, in turn, would sell the property to John Morrissey in August of that same year for $36,000.[21] In later years, after Matilda Street was renamed Woodlawn Ave, Gridley's place would have an address of 9 Woodlawn Ave and locals may recall the building under the name of Capital Storage or, for those interested in games of chance, the Chicago Club.

After selling the Pavilion property (some referred to it as the Gridley Club) Robert Gridley bought a piece of land out Nelson Ave that was part of the original lot on which the Saratoga Race Course was later situated. [22] Turning away from the games of chance, Gridley invested in the property by raising trout in a series of three cascading ponds he built on the property that were fed by clear, cold spring water. [23] Numbering in the tens of thousands, Gridley trout were sold to local groceries until one spring a retaining wall of one of the ponds gave way, collapsing the next pond downhill and draining both into Lake Lonely where it was said the fishing got noticeably better in the short term. [24]

Robert Gridley was one of the early gentlemen gamblers. He was known as an honorable man despite his involvement in illegal gambling. He was a businessman, operating a grocery, raising and selling brook trout, and harvesting ice from his ponds. Unfortunately, like many gamblers, Robert Gridley saw his gambling fortune disappear and he died a poor man in the late 1890's after selling his Nelson Ave property to Spencer Trask, who incorporated the grounds into his estate known today as the famous artist retreat, Yaddo. [25-26]

If you visit the Yaddo grounds today you will pass along a road that is open to the public. The road divides two ponds. An aerial view of the grounds shows the possible outline of a third pond back toward the direction of the racetrack in an area that is not open to the public and cannot be seen from the road. There are no trout in the water today, but it is interesting to think that perhaps these three ponds once belonged to one of Saratoga Springs' original gamblers.

One other gambler of note operated in Saratoga Springs in the years before Morrissey's arrival. Christian Schaffer was a well-known and respected gambler in the second half of the nineteenth century both in Saratoga and New York City. He claimed to have polished Morrissey in the finer points of gambling when Morrissey first made his mark in the trade in New York City. [27]

It was said that Chris Schaffer dealt cards at Saratoga for 47 straight seasons and was mentioned in the society pages in the later years of his life alongside gambling fraternity notables such as Phil Dwyer, Col. Wescott of Colorado (a United States Senator), and Joe Cotton, who earned the moniker, "Papa of the Bookmakers."[28]

Although he usually dealt cards for other gambling men of the era, Schaffer's own Saratoga faro bank was open for business during the years of 1865-1870 and may have had the highest play of any gambling place during that time. He was known to pay out as much as $100,000 in a single day when the cards turned in favor of his patrons. One can assume that he would have collected as much when the cards turned in favor of the house, which, of course, it is certain that they did.

Schaffer's Saratoga club ran 24 hours per day with the employees working in shifts to keep the games running non-stop. [29] Like Gridley, Schaffer was unable to withstand the increasing competition from other gamblers and maintain an independent operation. By 1886 he was arrested in Saratoga dealing cards for another gambler and by then he was unable to bankroll his own game. [30]

Like Robert Gridley, Schaffer once amassed a small fortune in the gambling business, but ran out of money before the end of his life. His games were square and he was known as an honest gambler despite his testimony to the Lexow Commission investigating corruption in New York City that he made payoffs to police and political officials. [31]

While none of the gamblers of the early days of Saratoga Springs ever reached the level of fame and fortune that Morrissey and Canfield were to achieve, they deserve acknowledgement in this account of the gamblers at the Spa. George Cole, Theodore Collar, Robert Gridley, and the others, are names that do not dominate the historical record of gambling in Saratoga Springs but nonetheless have an important place in the soul of the "Monte Carlo of America."

Endnotes

Chapter 1

1   Schwartz, David G. *Roll the Bones: The History of Gambling*. Gotham Books, NY. 2006.

2   Ibid.

3   Ibid.

4   Asbury, Herbert. *Suckers Progress: An Informal History of Gambling in America from the Colonies to Canfield*. Dodd, Mead and Company. New York. 1938.

5   "Personals," The Saratoga Sentinel, July 17, 1879.

6   "Home Matters," The Saratogian, March 28, 1861.

7   "Local," The Saratogian, September 26, 1867.

8   "Died," The Saratoga Sentinel, November 26, 1874.

9   "Live at Saratoga," Troy Daily Times, August 30, 1890.

10 The Daily Intelligencer, Wheeling, VA, September 14, 1859.

11 "Says Saratoga Set Bad Example," The Saratogian, February 10, 1921.

12 Troy Daily Times, August 30, 1890.

13 "Ben Scribner," The Sun, April 12, 1880.

14 "The Tiger," The New Orleans Crescent, January 10, 1869.

15 "Old Scrib Laid Out," The Brooklyn Union, July 14, 1885.

16 The Daily Graphic, April 12, 1880.

17 The Sun, April 12, 1880.

18 Albany Times, February 6, 1886.

19 "United States Hotel," The Herald, August 13, 1845.

20 "Gambling at Saratoga," The Sun, July 21, 1901.

21 "HON: JOHN MORRISSEY PUCHASES PAVILLION PROPERTY," The Daily Saratogian, August 26, 1871.

22 "Where Horses Rest," The Daily Saratogian, July 1, 1889.

23   "Shorts," The Saratogian, January 29, 1874.

24   The Daily Saratogian, January 22, 1875.

25   "GAMBLING AT SARATOGA," New York Times, July 21, 1901.

26   "SARATOGA SPRINGS," Troy Daily Times, October 8, 1886.

27   Troy Daily Times, July 23, 1890.

28   "Racetrack and Mountain," Troy Daily Times, July 25, 1890.

29   "Says Byrnes Took Bribes," New York Herald, November 12, 1895.

30   "More Gamblers Arrested," New York Times, August 6, 1886.

31   Ibid.

The Constables and Night Watch

In the days of Scribner, Gridley, and Schaffer, there was no police force in Saratoga Springs. The modern police department was not officially established until April, 1887. Prior to that time a system of police constables, summer Broadway police patrols, summer detectives and night watchmen provided limited law enforcement duties for the village. A few of the larger hotels would hire New York City police officers as security for the summer but the village had no modern police department of its own.

The New York State Police was not established until 1917, while Saratoga County Sheriff's Deputies served legal paperwork and managed the jail. In times of general alarm, like the pursuit of a dangerous or escaped criminal, able-bodied men would form a posse and join with deputies and constables or even local judges or district attorneys until the emergency had been dealt with.

The night watch was an early policing system that was mainly an early warning system designed to alert the population to emergencies at night, like an outbreak of a fire, rather than a patrolling and investigative force. Night watchmen normally did not conduct investigations or perform many of the functions that police officers commonly do today, although they did round up drunk and disorderly persons and deposit them in the village lock-up when necessary.

Constables served court processes and conducted limited investigations for local courts. They were responsible for the execution of search warrants and arrest warrants issued by local courts as well as the serving of civil process papers like evictions. Constables worked per diem and were required to submit an invoice to the village police board, which would approve or disapprove of the payment for services rendered.

Services might include travel expenses for tracking down and transporting fugitives, feeding and housing prisoners, incidental expenses required for an investigation, as well as the daily pay on the dates that their services were required. In 1878, Saratoga Village Constable L.W. Van Antwerp earned only $18.00 for his services while Constable John Fryer earned $624.33 for the year. [1]

In Saratoga Springs, constables and night watchmen, and later the Broadway squad, were overseen by the Police Board, which was made up of local citizens who worked in occupations other than law enforcement and were appointed by the village president (mayor). In the middle decades of the 1800's the closing of gambling dens by local authorities would not have been the responsibility of the night watch or the constables unless directed to do so by a judge or magistrate - although the village charter of 1826 did specifically ban gambling and commanded the village trustees to enforce the gambling laws.

The system of law enforcement in the early-to-mid nineteenth century is one we would not recognize today. Typically, private citizens who found themselves victims of crime would be required to swear out a complaint before a local judge, who would then need to issue search or arrest warrants based on probable cause before any public official would take action. It was no different for so-called victimless crimes such as gambling or prostitution.

An identified, civilian complainant would be required to swear out a complaint against a vice location before a judge, who would then issue the appropriate warrant. A constable would then be charged with executing the warrant. Generally, if no citizen came forward to make a complaint regarding a gambling den, the local authorities simply did nothing, even if everyone in town knew where the action was.

How the constable system worked is illustrated by the tragic killing of a constable serving a warrant in Saratoga Springs in 1862 at a home at the intersection of Van Dam Street and Matilda Street (which is known today as Woodlawn Avenue). [2]

At that time a water-well was located near Broadway and Van Dam Street that provided drinking water for the residents of the area. A very poor family lived at the corner of Van Dam and Matilda St. by the name of Packard. John Packard lived there on the northwest corner with his wife and three adult daughters. They mainly kept to themselves with Mr. and Mrs. Packard described as elderly and possibly senile while the three daughters were considered odd, but church going ladies.

One of the daughters, Mary, was seen taking the pump handle for the well and bringing it home. The theft meant that other residents had no ability to easily obtain drinking water from the well.

Two men, Ira Hale and F.D. Wheeler, had purchased the pump handle a few years earlier and went to the Packard home in an attempt to retrieve it. Although the Packard family was inside, they refused to open the door and return the pump handle to its rightful owners. With no police department to turn to for the investigation of the theft and the arresting of the offenders, Hale and Wheeler went to Police Justice White and applied for a warrant to search the home for the pump handle.

The warrant was given to Constable L.J. Vibbard, who invited Constable William W. Mitchell to accompany him to the Packard residence. Once they arrived, they, too, were denied entry by the occupants.

After repeatedly demanding entry and stating the purpose of their visit, Vibbard and Mitchell forced the front door open. They were immediately attacked with an axe by John Packard. While the constables struggled to disarm Mr. Packard, an interior door swung open and Mary Packard shoved a pike (a long pole with a bayonet or knife attached to the end) into Constable Mitchell's stomach. During the melee the pump handle was thrown from a second story window.

Poor Constable Mitchell was critically wounded. He was brought to his home on Walnut Street in the hope he could recover from the wound. Sadly, he succumbed on May 26, 1862, at the age of 41.[3]

John and Mary Packard were tried and convicted of manslaughter for the death of Constable Mitchell. The local townsfolk raised a sum of money to send the remaining family members to relatives out of state where John and Mary joined them upon their release from prison many years later.

There can be little doubt that the job of constable was a difficult one in the mid-to-late 1800's in Saratoga Springs, as it would have been anywhere else. Policing, as we know it today, was a relatively new human phenomenon. It wasn't even until 1829 that the first organized modern police force was established in London, England, by Sir Robert Peel. It was not until 1845 that New York City Police Department was formed.

Constables of the era did not even wear uniforms. In Saratoga Springs, it wasn't until 1878 that constables appeared in uniform for the first time.[4] Constables would have been required to supply their own weapons and many armed themselves with their own private pistols while on duty. Often they had other occupations and supplemented their income with their pay from their constable duties. For example, L.J. Vibbard, a constable for many years in Saratoga who was with Constable Mitchell when Mitchell was murdered, owned a store that sold hats and furs on Marvin Row in the 1840's. [5]

The Constables of Saratoga Springs did not lack for work. Even beyond the gambling situation, crime in Saratoga Springs was not unheard of in the 1800's. Robberies, murders, and assaults on constables happened with surprising frequency. By 1858 the village was in need of a lock-up for petty criminals and those needing to be held temporarily for more serious offenses. Some of the work conducted by the early constables and policemen (they were all men) of the village might surprise residents and visitors of today's Spa City.

In August 1855, a $15,000 theft was committed at Congress Hall. A Mr. Halsey from Ithaca was staying at the hotel when he left his room unattended for a couple of hours. Although he left the room locked, the room was entered and when the theft was discovered, a general alarm was raised. [6]

A couple of shady looking characters had been noticed in town and one in particular drew the attention of a reporter for the New York Evening Post, Edward Skidmore. Skidmore, while having dinner at Congress Hall, thought he recognized a person he remembered as a burglar from New York City dining at a table nearby.

When the man got up to leave, Skidmore notified a Mr. Snyder and the two started to follow the suspicious fellow. They were joined in the pursuit by a Congress Hall employee by the name of Hathorn and continued to follow the man from Congress Hall all the way past the Columbia Hotel. There, the suspicious character was joined by two others and the three of them eventually walked into a wooded area off of Greenfield Avenue.

Hathorn put a Mr. Steele on the scent and went to get Constable L.J. Vibbard. Vibbard and Hathorn then returned to Congress Hall and waited for the trio to return. When they did, the three men were arrested, giving their names as William Henderson, George Eddy, and Abram Kingsbury. Henderson, it was said, had been well acquainted with the state prison system and had a "rascally look" about him. They were searched and found to be in possession of tools for opening doors and trunks like nippers and skeleton keys.

They were all sent to the County Jail to await sentencing, as there was little doubt they were the ones who committed the theft, Kinsgbury having been seen by a witness in the same hallway as the theft before daylight and all three having been recognized as loitering in the area of Congress Hall for three or four days before the crime. [7]

Over the years there were many constables in Saratoga. Some went on to become deputy sheriffs or, like George Blodget, joined the police department when it was formed in 1887. To be sure, many of them served with quiet distinction, but none of them likely had similar exploits as a constable as one Eugene Andrus.

Eugene Andrus was employed as a constable for the village of Saratoga Springs as well a detective for the

Delaware and Hudson Railroad during the 1880's and 1890's. One summer afternoon in 1885, Eugene Andrus was summoned to the train depot where the watchman, Nathaniel Annis, had discovered a tramp in one of the cars who refused to leave when Annis asked.

Andrus arrived on the scene and after attempting to talk the man into leaving of his own accord, finally delivered the ultimatum that he could either leave or be taken to the village lock-up. The trespasser, who gave his name as George Murphy and claimed to be on the run from some unnamed people who were trying to poison him in New Jersey, refused and so Andrus was obliged to take the man to the holding cells in the town hall. [8]

Just when Andrus and Murphy arrived on Lake Avenue, outside the doors of town hall leading to the jail, Andrus decided that he would check Murphy over for any dangerous items. In Murphy's overcoat Andrus found a piece of shoe leather and a book. The discovery of the book apparently revealed some mental instability on the part of Murphy, who declared that he allowed no one to look at the book and immediately pulled a revolver out of his pocket and fired at Andrus.

Taken by utter surprise and delayed in returning fire by the fact that he had on a long coat buttoned to the bottom, Andrus managed to draw his own gun as he fell backward into the street. Despite being hit in the right thigh and left hand, Andrus managed to fire four shots at Murphy, striking him in the abdomen and causing a serious injury to the criminal.

Officers John Fryer and George Young heard the gunfire and rushed to the scene, disarming Murphy and taking him into custody while summoning doctors Boyce and Grant to dress the lawman's wounds.

A closer examination of Murphy, who also was known by an alias of Thomas Evans, found that he was 36 years old, weighed about 160 pounds, and was missing the third finger on his left hand. His moustache and weathered face matched the description of an escaped murderer that West Virginia officers had wired to the Saratoga authorities about one week prior to the shooting fracas. Murphy denied having killed anyone although he did admit to having lived in Wheeling, West Virginia, for a time when he was employed by the railroad there.

It does not appear that it was ever determined for certain if Murphy was the escaped convict from West Virginia but one thing *was* for certain, that he was sent to Dannemora Prison for ten years of hard labor after he pled guilty to the shooting of Detective Andrus. [9]

Both Murphy and Andrus were fortunate to recover fully from their respective wounds. It was beneficial to Murphy, who spent the following ten years at hard labor in state prison, and it allowed Andrus to continue his career in law enforcement. He would need his full physical capacity five years after the shooting when he was employed as a detective for the Delaware and Hudson Railroad.

During the summer of 1890 the Delaware and Hudson railroad was having trouble on the freight train that made a midnight run from Schenectady to Delanson. The train carried fresh produce and was broken into several times. The train was a non-stop run from point to point and apparently a group of Italian day workers would jump the train for a fast ride home after working all day in Schenectady. The train did not stop exactly where the men desired, so they would pull the brakes and hop off the train where it was convenient for them.

This was exceptionally dangerous since the line from Schenectady to Delanson was a single track and a train that was stopped on the line unscheduled would be in the way of oncoming trains. A serious collision had narrowly been avoided recently and so it was that Saratoga constable Andrus was hired as a detective for the Delaware and Hudson Railroad.

One night in mid-August Andrus boarded the train as it left the Schenectady station, reaching 30 miles per hour on its midnight dash to Delanson. Andrus, one of the conductors, and one of the trainmen climbed to the top of the train and started to work their way back to the tail end of the freight cars as the train sped down the tracks.

They soon discovered three men riding the bumpers between two of the cars; each was armed with a club and defying Andrus's orders to throw down their weapons and climb to the top of the car. Being employed to put an end to the troubles on this particular train, Andrus realized mere words would be insufficient to convince the three men to surrender so, drawing his own club, Andrus jumped down between the cars, prepared to fight it out with the three men.

A desperate fight ensued between the cars of the speeding train and one of the men lost his footing and fell off the train. By the end of the fight the remaining two troublemakers had been disarmed by Andrus and were ordered to climb up the train. This time they meekly complied and were handcuffed before being turned over to the trainman for the rest of the trip.

Continuing the job, Andrus and the conductor moved further along the train and found three more riders between the cars. Once again, a fight followed a refusal by the group to peacefully climb to the top of the train, and once again one of the fellows fell off the train during the brawl and the other two gave up and were brought forward in irons. Andrus again commanded the space between the cars.

As if that had not been enough excitement for one night, Andrus moved on and discovered three more unauthorized passengers on the freight train. One of the group was a rather tall man and Andrus attempted to reach down and pull him up to the top of the train where he could be secured like the others. Only this time, the rapidly moving train hit a rough patch of track just as Andrus leaned over the side, throwing him from the speeding train. To the horror of the conductor, Andrus was tossed onto a rocky embankment.

The train was ordered stopped and it was backed up to where Andrus had been tossed. Expecting to find a broken and bruised man, the train workers found instead a smiling Andrus who appeared no worse for having been thrown from a speeding train. He apparently had managed to land on his feet and avoid any serious injury.

The train continued its journey with all the remaining trespassers alighting from the train before Andrus had a chance to get at them. The four he did manage to capture were brought to the Schenectady police lock-up and then to the county jail. [10]

Village constables like William Mitchell and Eugene Andrus are a testament to the quality of the men who policed the early years of Saratoga Springs. Their stories are not the only instances of violence, crime, and disorder in Saratoga's formative years. The lawmen of early Saratoga Springs faced many problems that we typically associate with larger, more urban areas. In addition to the summer crowds, two areas of the growing village managed to give no end of trouble to the Saratoga authorities, Willow Walk and Searing's Alley.

Endnotes

Chapter 2

1   "Town Expenses," The Saratoga Sentinel, January 23, 1879.

2   "Deplorable Affair," The Saratogian. June 6, 1862.

3   Durkee, Cornelius E. *Reminiscences of Saratoga*. 1928. Higginson Book Co. Salem.

4   "From Northern Points," The Albany Argus, May 30, 1878.

5   Daily Saratoga Republican, August 20, 1845.

6   "Great Robbery at Congress Hall," New York Times, August 8, 1855.

7   Ibid.

8   "An Insane Tramp's Act," Daily Saratogian, June 1, 1885.

9   "The June Term. Several Prisoners and Cases Disposed Of," The Daily Saratogian, June 16, 1885.

10   "Battled on the Bumpers," Gloversville Daily Leader, August 22, 1890.

Chapter 3

Willow Walk and Searing's Alley

Policing the crowds visiting Saratoga Springs from the urban areas of the country was surely a priority for local officials. Yet a couple of local areas gave law enforcement in the village no end to trouble over the years. One of these areas is today known as High Rock Avenue, but in the late 1860's and early 1870's it was known as Willow Walk. The street was known for a short time in the 1890's as Spring Avenue but received its original name for the beautiful willow trees that lined the street as it led from Lake Avenue towards the famous High Rock Spring. In the earliest days of the village, Willow Walk was known as a "lover's lane" for its picturesque setting, but by the late 1860's the area of Willow Walk (including the nearby sections of Lake Avenue and Henry Street) was referred to as the "valley of the shadow of death" by the local constables. [1]

The area was indeed a troublesome spot with many saloons and brothels lining the street. Samantha May ran a house of prostitution on Willow Walk that frequently drew the attention of the constables for the illegal selling of liquor,[2] fist fights,[3] and of course, the sex trade. [4] Austin White kept a "house of ill fame and gambling house" on Henry Street which was described in the local paper after it was raided as, "the most disreputable and vile resort in town."[5]

Even a murder was committed just around the corner from Willow Walk in 1871. In those days a saloon and boarding house stood at the intersection of Henry Street and Lake Avenue. It was called the Atlantic Shades and was owned by a man with the last name of Weeks whose son, George Weeks, tended bar there in March 1871.

On the seventh day of that month Samuel Young, the eldest son of the editor of the Saratoga Sentinel newspaper, visited the place in the middle of the afternoon and started drinking with a few other patrons. A party of about four or five men were dancing, singing, and drinking, all in good humor. Along with Young, two or three locals were joined by a couple of French Canadians, one of them going by the name Hank Husher or Huscher (it was spelled both ways in newspaper accounts of the murder.)[6] They all seemed to be getting along just fine until a teenage boy entered the saloon.

John Dugy, also a French Canadian, was 14 years old and had just moved into a house on Catherine Street. He had been sent to get a pie for dinner and went to the Atlantic Shades where Young, Husher, and the others were drinking. Dugy bought the pie from Mr. Weeks and when he turned to leave, a drunk Samuel Young made a motion toward the boy's pie. Dugy pulled it away and told Young not to touch it. Husher stepped in and accosted Young, in the name of defending his fellow Frenchman. Husher struck a blow and then kicked Young in the head after he fell to the floor. Weeks and a couple of the other patrons quickly stopped Husher from further harming Young and ejected him from the bar. Young was helped to his feet and back to his home. [7] Later that evening, Young would die from the blow to the head he suffered.

Husher was soon arrested and placed in the village lock-up. Husher tried to escape the jail by setting it on fire but the attempt was discovered and the flames suppressed before any significant damage was done or any prisoner's freedom was gained. [8] His misguided attempt to uphold the honor of his French brethren ultimately cost Husher ten years at hard labor in Clinton Prison. [9]

In 1869 the area experienced a series of violent robberies. One man, walking along Lake Avenue near Willow Walk had his money and watch stolen after being severely beaten. [10] It was the third such robbery on Lake Avenue in just a few days. But robbery wasn't the only violence on Willow Walk during the summer of 1869.

On the same day that the gentleman was relieved of his belongings on Lake Avenue, three constables had gone to the residence of the Keith family at the corner of Willow Walk and Lake Avenue to arrest the man of the house for beating his wife. Mr. Keith decided that he would rather not comply with the conditions of the warrant and fought the lawmen off for a time, stabbing Constable Esmond before finally being subdued. [11]

As bad as it may sound, perhaps the worst part about Willow Walk was not the crime, violence, and prostitution that was taking place there. The worst part about Willow Walk might have been the village lock-up that was located there from 1869 to 1871.

At that time a boarding house and saloon called the Kayderosseras Hotel stood about fifty or sixty yards from the intersection of Lake Avenue. The saloon and the jail were operated by a man named Patrick Brady. [12]

Referred to mockingly as the Willow Walk Bastille, the jail was built as an annex to the hotel on the north side of the building. Described as looking more like a "wood shed" than a secure jail facility, the lock-up had three jail cells in a twelve-by-twenty foot room. Each cell had a bunk with a mattress and a small wooden seat for the unfortunate souls required to spend the night there. The room was heated by a wood stove opposite the cells. [13]

Each cell was constructed of wooden boards with an inch or so gap between each to allow for light and air to pass. Any fresh air would have been appreciated by the prisoners as an open sewer ran below the front door of the Kayderosseras Hotel and jail, emptying into the village creek that ran along Willow Walk. Each of the cells was secured by heavy wooden doors and padlocks. A door at the rear of the jail cells led to Brady's saloon. [14]

Brady himself was no doubt a rough character. He was arrested several times during his life for being drunk and disorderly in public. He kept several English pit bulls and conditioned them to be fighting dogs. Brady trained one of the dogs to attack anyone who fought with him and stationed the dog in his saloon as additional security.

One April night in 1871 Brady managed to get drunk and attacked his wife in the saloon with a club. His guard dog immediately launched an attack on poor Mrs. Brady, biting her around the neck as Brady continued the assault with his club. A few patrons of the bar managed to come to the rescue of Mrs. Brady and pried the dog away from her, tossing it into the village creek. Undeterred, the dog returned to the fray and latched onto Mrs. Brady's legs; all the while Patrick Brady continued the assault on the helpless woman, brandishing a gun and threatening to shoot anyone who touched his dog. When the beating mercifully was finished, Mrs. Brady was hurried off to a neighbor's home to recover from her wounds while Patrick Brady retreated to a small room, locking himself inside with his dogs and a few of his firearms. [15]

Patrick Brady treated the prisoners of the Willow Walk Jail poorly, to say the least. Local authorities reported that those they placed in the jail for being drunk and disorderly were often released in a more intoxicated condition than when they went in. [16] The assumption was that since Brady was paid a fee for each person housed in the lock-up, a revolving door of drunk and disorderly persons was in his best financial interest, regardless of what was best for the community.

By 1871 when the annex of town hall was being built and the jail cells installed, the public officials and local papers were getting tired of the black eye that Brady was giving the village. The final straw came when a young woman ran away from her home in Montreal. She was located in the village in November of that year and housed in Brady's jail overnight while waiting to continue the journey back home.

Terrified, the young lady did not sleep that night and when she pleaded for some water, Brady offered her whiskey instead. The woman, Matilda Auben, made it safely home to Canada, bringing with her a terrible cold she contracted during her stay in Saratoga Springs' village jail. [17]

Even though the new jail cells in the Town Hall would not be finished for about two more weeks, the village declined to renew the lease for the lock-up with Brady at the end of November thus leaving the village without a lock up for about 15 days. Surely this must have been welcome news for local ne'er-do-wells.

One can imagine the sigh of relief from the village fathers when the new jail was opened in December 1871. Prisoners would no longer be subjected to the horrible conditions of the lock-up and the treatment of the notorious Patrick Brady. The new lock up was built in the annex to the Town Hall and is in the same place (more or less) in the building as it is today. The old jail cells on Willow Walk passed into history on December 15, 1871, when Patrick Brady had them torn down and a carriage house built in their place. [18]

The Willow Walk jail had gained a level of notoriety for the poor treatment of prisoners held there. As a point of historical accuracy, it was the third location of the village lockup. The first jail was built by Esek Cowan shortly after he arrived in Saratoga Springs around 1812. Cowen, a lawyer by trade, built a home on Congress Street (known then as West Congress Street) and built an adjoining stone structure that served for many years as the village jail. Before being torn down during the Urban Renewal era of the city, the building was used as a blacksmith's shop and later housed the Green Cave, a nightclub frequented by the African-American population of the city. [19]

It is not certain when Cowan's jail on Congress Street was abandoned as the village lock-up, but in 1858 the Saratogian reported that the wait for a new jail was over as the lock-up was to be in a building at the corner of Caroline and Putnam Streets. The June 17, 1858, edition of the Saratogian announced the new location of the jail this way:

"Lock Up. Saratoga is at last to have a 'lock up'. The decree has gone forth and the miniature prison is already erected – on Putnam Street, west side, just south of Caroline. Rogues and rummies will please take notice."

As proud as the village might have been with its new jail, and despite the tough talk from the newspaper, the Putnam Street jail was built on the cheap. In fact, within a year stories began circulating about how easy it was for prisoners to escape from the facility.

In September, 1859, the Albany Times reported that "prisoners escape as easily as they would from a rotten shad-net." Furthermore, the Albany paper suggested that the Saratoga authorities didn't mind too much that their prisoners escaped, simply as a matter of economics. If the prisoners, many of whom were petty criminals, did escape, they were unlikely to return and therefore the village was spared the expense of court proceedings and the cost of housing the offenders. That they would be free to commit crimes in other places seemed of no concern to the Saratoga authorities, suggested the Albany Times.

The Saratogian, for its part, called upon the citizens of Saratoga to remedy the situation, if for no other reason than to avoid the kind of reputation that this sort of neglect was certain to bring to the town. [20]

By 1864 efforts were being made to better secure prisoners in the village. There had yet to be established a permanent police force but Colonel Searing (the rank designating his position in the Army of the Potomac during the Civil War) did establish a police office in the Morey Building at the corner of Caroline and Putnam Streets. The police office, presumably for the use of constables and night watch officers, was located on the second floor of the building while the jail was located on the third floor. Prisoners were kept, "'snug as a bug in a rug' and quiet as comfortable, even in cold weather" until 1869 when the Willow Walk jail opened its doors. [21]

The constables and night watchmen stayed on in the Morey building until the building caught fire in 1872, making it unusable as a police office. [22] Fortunately, the annex of the Town Hall was under construction and nearing completion at the time. Police business and the housing of prisoners were soon moved permanently to the building at the corner of Broadway and Lake Avenue.

Another local hot spot for authorities was Searing's Alley. Like the Willow Walk area, Searing's Alley gave authorities all they could handle and also, like Willow Walk, the earliest history of the location gave no indication that it would end up as the hotbed of criminal activity that it eventually became.

One of the very first settlers of Saratoga Springs was Samuel Searing. Originally from Hempstead, Long Island, Samuel Searing moved to Saratoga Springs with his family at the close of the American Revolution. His grandson, William M. Searing, was a lawyer in town who, upon the outbreak of the Civil War, organized three companies for the Union Army, two from Saratoga Springs and one from Greenfield.

During the war he was promoted to the rank of Colonel in the Thirteenth Regiment and led local troops in the battles of South Mountain, Antietam, Fredericksburg, and Chancellorsville among other actions. [23]

William Searing owned property in the mid 1800's near the railroad overpass that used to cross over Congress Street. Eventually a small alley running south from Congress Street between numbers 72 and 76 Congress Street (just west of the overpass) was established and took the name of Searing's Alley.

The alley ended at the back of a barn and contained a brick tenement building that once housed many Italian immigrants and earned a bad reputation for the general conditions of the block. The October 2, 1886, edition of the Daily Saratogian, reporting an arrest in the area, described Searing's Alley as a "hive of foreigners" with police reporting that the block was a source of "constant brawls and disturbances." Furthermore, the newspaper commented, "The entire place is a stench in the nostrils of the public and the police, and should be suppressed." Another time it was said that Searing's Alley, "reeks in the filth of degraded humanity."[24]

It would take many years for conditions to improve in Searing's Alley. In 1887 a general fight broke out during a card game in the alley. Charles Varrona, Louis Serrocco, and two others were playing "casino" in Varrona's house when a dispute arose that turned violent when Varrona struck one of the other players in the head with a club. A local tough guy, Michael Lounge, joined the fray and several policemen were called upon to quell the disturbance.[25]

Lounge, a "notorious Italian ruffian" according to the local press, had a bad reputation in the village, once brutally beating a female companion and bragging that he had $100 that would get him out of any legal trouble he encountered because of his actions.[26] Whether it was the $100 or his reputation, no one cooperated with the authorities in either case against Michael Lounge and it does not appear that he spent any time in jail for his involvement with either episode.

One day in February, 1904, a resident of Searing's Alley, Dominick Sapone, a.k.a "Dominick Soap," held a party. In attendance were Arthur Deffendorf, William Wicks, Frank Mecora, and several others. By evening time everyone was thoroughly drunk and shortly before midnight Wicks and a man named John Case started a friendly match of who could slap the other's hat off.

Naturally the game turned serious and eventually Wicks, Case, Deffendorf, Meroca, and Sapone were thrashing about the room in a general free-for-all. Deffendorf and Wicks were thrown out of the house by Sapone, Mecora, and the other men present. [27]

The ejection of the two men from the Sapone home was not enough for Mecora, however, and he gave chase, first overtaking Deffendorf (who had stumbled and fell during his flight); he stabbed Deffendorf in the back before running down Wicks and plunging his knife into Wicks as well.

Deffendorf tried to stumble his way home but made it only as far as Richard Canfield's fence where a policeman stopped him and brought him to the hospital. Wicks made it only as far as the doorway of a saloon at the corner of Congress Street and Searing's Alley where he collapsed and died. [28]

Sadly, Wicks was just two months shy of his eighteenth birthday when he was killed. He is buried in Greenridge Cemetery. [29] Mecora pled guilty to killing Wicks and was sentenced to life in the Dannemora Prison. [30]

The murder of young Wicks was not the end of the violence in Searing's Alley. The very next year a man named William Curtis nearly beat a reverend and his wife to death in Mechanicville. He fled the scene and made his way to Searing's Alley where he had a lover, although he usually lived with his wife near Mechanicville. The motive for the unprovoked beating was said to be robbery or revenge, but no matter the motive, a cry of "murder!" was made and a posse was formed. [31]

The reverend and his wife were white while Curtis was a black man and, had the posse managed to get a hold of him, a lynching was sure to follow as several guns and at least two ropes were reportedly in possession of some of the members of the posse, which numbered about one thousand men. Even though the entire village of Mechanicville seemed to be on his heels, Curtis managed to outpace his pursuers during the night and made it to Searing's Alley. [32]

Word came to the police department around 11:00 AM the following day that Curtis had been spotted in Searing's Alley and Detectives Hennessey and Sullivan were sent to locate him. They knew where his girlfriend lived and burst into the home to make the arrest.

Curtis desired to continue his flight and ran down Searing's Alley with Detective Sullivan in pursuit. A warning shot was fired and then, according to the accounts in the newspapers, Curtis reached toward his waist and Sullivan fired again, the bullet entering Curtis' back and hitting his heart. Sullivan claimed that he tried to shoot Curtis in the legs but to no avail. [33]

Curtis ran another twenty feet or so after being shot and stumbled to the ground right at the entrance to Searing's Alley at Congress Street, in almost the exact same spot that William Wicks had fallen eighteen months prior. Sullivan and Hennessey commandeered a passing wagon to bring Curtis to the hospital, all the while fending off a growing and belligerent crowd while loading Curtis onto the wagon. The near riot was quelled by reinforcements before things got too far out of hand. [34]

Officer Proper was not so lucky two years later in Searing's Alley when he tried to arrest a black man named Lawrence Wallace from Boston for fighting with another fellow. It was a summer night in July and many of the area residents rushed to the defense of Wallace and began accosting Officer Proper. This time a race riot was not avoided as the crowd grew more belligerent and police reinforcements were summoned. [35]

Fighting their way into the crowd, about a dozen police officers came to rescue Officer Proper from the angry mob. Making matters worse, some white residents of the neighborhood joined in the disturbance on the side of the police. After a few minutes of fighting, the officers were able to extract themselves from the confines of Searing's Alley and, under a hail storm of projectiles, managed to get Wallace transported to police headquarters. [36]

By now several hundred African-Americans had gathered, with many doing battle with the local police and white residents. Dr. Richard McCarty was in the area on a house call and joined Officer Proper to offer what services he could, thinking he would probably be needed. He was rewarded by being hit in the face by a rock thrown by one of the crowd. An officer saw the culprit who threw the rock and fired a shot at the person. The officer's aim was off and the suspect disappeared into the crowd. The riot eventually dissipated with cuts and bruises all around. Wallace was sentenced to three months in jail for his part in the affair. [37]

The ladies of Searing's Alley did not refrain from engaging in the general lawlessness there. One woman, Pauline Myers, resisted her eviction by smashing her landlord in the face with a brick. [38] Another time Pauline Hendrickson and Annie Owen got into an argument in

Smaldone's saloon on Congress Street. Pauline left first and concealed herself in Searing's Alley, ambushing Annie as she walked by, clobbering her on the head with a bottle. [39]

This type of behavior continued with regularity through the 1930's. In 1934 City Judge Anthony LaBelle had finally had enough. Declaring, "this court is tired of this Searing's Alley business. I'm going to try to stop that condition there if I possibly can."[40]

Judge Labelle began by imposing jail sentences for minor offenses like disturbing the peace and public intoxication. He gave Martha Robinson and Robert Todd ten days in jail each for being drunk in public. [41] Ninety days in jail was the sentence for Floyd Jackson who got into a fight with a neighbor in the Alley. [42] Martha Robinson apparently did not learn her lesson and received 30 days from Judge Labelle for using vile language in the alley and disturbing the peace. [43] Finally George Freeland came before Judge LaBelle on a charge of public intoxication. Freeland lived at number 4 Searing's Alley and avoided a 30 day sentence by agreeing to, "stay sober, behave himself and stay out of Searing's Alley. "[44] He agreed to move.

It is a shame to think that an alley named for a local war hero became such a den of iniquity. All the fights, killings, riots and every manner of vice and debauchery defamed the memory of a true noble son of Saratoga Springs. Even the local boys of Company L, 105th Infantry Division, when they laid out their quarters at Ft. McLellan in Alabama during the run up to World War II, named the streets of their encampment in homage to their hometown.

Two long streets were named "Broadway" and "Fifth Ave" with a half street blessed with the moniker of "Searing's Alley."[45] One hopes that the naming of the alley in Alabama was in memory of the old Civil War soldier and not an earned descriptor of similar conditions that existed at both the encampment and the real Searing's Alley.

Whether it was Judge LaBelle's harsh sentences or some other factor, after the mid-1930's, Searing's Alley quieted down considerably. The alley itself, along with the nearby road, Cowan Street, and the railroad bridge over Congress Street eventually were erased from the landscape of Saratoga Springs during the Urban Renewal era of the city. Today the entrance to the Embassy Suites Hotel is where Searing's Alley once stood.

Endnotes

Chapter 3

1   "Shorts," The Saratogian, May 4, 1871.

2   "In the Oyer," The Saratogian, September 26, 1867.

3   "Shorts," The Daily Saratogian, January 18, 1873.

4   "The County Court and General Sessions," The Saratogian, February 23, 1865.

5   "Shorts," The Daily Saratogian, July 7, 1875.

6   "Brutal Murder in Saratoga," Hudson Evening Register, March 9, 1871.

7   "Death of Samuel Young-Testimony Before the Coroner's Jury," The Saratogian, March 16, 1871.

8   "Brutal Murder..."

9   "Sentences of Huscher and Vandercook," Troy Daily Whig, May 12, 1871.

10 "Saratoga," The Troy Press, August 19, 1869.

11 Ibid.

12 "Our Village Bastille," The Saratogian, April 27, 1871.

13 Ibid.

14 Ibid.

15 "An Outrageous Affair," The Saratogian, April 20, 1871.

16 "Shorts," The Daily Saratogian, November 16, 1871.

17 "Our Village Bastille..."

18 "Shorts," The Daily Saratogian, December 15, 1871.

19 "Congress Street Nightspot Village Jail 100 Years Ago," The Saratogian, February 16, 1935.

20 "Home Matters," The Saratogian, September 1, 1859.

21 "Police Office and Lock-Up," The Saratogian, April 14, 1864.

22 "Local," The Saratogian, January 18, 1872.

23 Durkee. *Reminiscences of Saratoga.*

24 "An Italian Fracas," The Daily Saratogian, November 7, 1887.

25 Ibid.

26 "A Brutal Attack," The Daily Saratogian, December 5, 1887.

27 "WM. A. Wicks Murdered in Searing's Alley," The Daily Saratogian, February 2, 1904.

28 Ibid.

29 Ibid.

30 "Speedy Termination of Mecora Murder Trial," The Daily Saratogian, June 21, 1904.

31 "Negro Assailant Killed by Officer in Searing's Alley," The Daily Saratogian, August 14, 1905.

32 Ibid.

33 Ibid.

34 Ibid.

35 "Race Riot at Night in Searing's Alley," The Daily Saratogian, July 15, 1907.

36 Ibid.

37 Ibid.

38 "Harris Says Pauline Hit Him with a Brick," The Daily Saratogian, April 16, 1906.

39 "Lies in Ambush with Bottle," The Saratogian, November 30, 1915.

40 "Trouble in Alley Irritates Judge," The Saratogian, April 12, 1934.

41 Ibid.

42 "Searing's Alley Battle Ends in 90-Day Sentence," The Saratogian, April 23, 1934.

43 "Searing's Alley Woman Sent to Jail in Ballston," The Saratogian, July 17, 1934.

44 "Cleared on Charge of Striking Wife," The Saratogian, May 17, 1935.

45 O'Brian, George R, Jr. "Co. L 'Moving-Up' Day Sees Men
Prove Adept Haulers in Shift to Better Quarters," The
Saratogian, December 2, 1940.

Chapter 4

The Honorable John Morrissey

The life of John Morrissey, all by itself, is an incredible story. Born into poverty in Templemore, Tipperary County, Ireland, on February 5th 1831, John Morrissey's life was the one-in-a-million kind of story that is the stuff of legend. *Brandy for Heroes* is a biography of John Morrissey written by Jack Kofoed in 1938. Kofoed's narrative is an excellent resource for recounting the lifetime adventures of Morrissey and is relied upon in this account except for the details of Morrissey in Saratoga Springs, which Kofoed does not pay particular attention to. His boxing and political careers were reported on throughout the country.

John was the son of Mary and Tim Morrissey. If not for a burning desire to succeed in life, he would have been just another of the countless Irish immigrants of the early 19th century who escaped the potato famines and never-ending strife in the motherland, only to live lives of continued abject poverty and misery in the new world. Morrissey's parents improved their situation only marginally by immigrating to the United States through New York City before landing in Troy, NY, among some of their Irish brethren.

Twelve-year old John Morrissey was forced to start working at a wallpaper factory to help with the family finances. The rough environment turned the boy into a rough teenager. He developed a reputation around the streets of Troy as a tough young man and was recruited by a brothel owner named Alexander Hamilton (not to be confused with the Revolutionary War hero and father of the American banking system) to keep the peace at his place.

Hamilton's brothel was the scene of constant brawls. No bouncer lasted long battling the rough and tumble dock workers who frequented the place until Morrissey was hired at a rate of twenty dollars per week. Morrissey was worth every penny Hamilton paid him, as it took him only six months to end the violence at Hamilton's dive.

The salary he was earning in Hamilton's house of ill-repute was a significant step up financially for him. John's parents though, would forever remain one dollar ahead of complete destitution. This was not because of a lack of effort or because they did not deserve better, but because despite all of the hope that America promised, the facts were that life in Troy, New York was not much different than life back in Ireland. Like every other urban center of America in the early 1800's, life for innumerable immigrants was destined to be a life of back-breaking work both physically and spiritually with hardly a penny left after expenses to show for all the toil. John Morrissey knew that his burning ambition for wealth and fame could never be satisfied on the banks of the Hudson River in upstate New York. He knew New York City was where he had to go and took a job on a river boat to secure passage to the metropolis.

So, 17- year- old Morrissey, experienced beyond his years, took his first job in New York City as an immigrant runner. Immigrant runners were paid to herd the newly arrived masses to particular boarding houses, saloons, and brothels where the unscrupulous owners of those places were only too willing to take what little the poor souls had managed to retain after the transatlantic journey. The immigrant runners were also tasked with getting the new arrivals registered with the correct political party, which is how Morrissey began his association with the men who would become the future leaders of the Tammany Hall political machine.

Immigrant running paid good money but it was dangerous. Rival runners were always looking to elbow each other off the docks and violence was not infrequent. Morrissey was ambitious, but was not without a heart. He knew that he was the muscle end of a great corrupt political machine sucking the life and dreams, not to mention any residual wealth, out of the masses then streaming into the ports of entry to the great United States of America.

He soon tired of the business and planned to give it up until a rival group of runners threatened him and dared to come onto a boat he was working. Although he was outnumbered several-to-one, Morrissey gave the intruders a thorough whipping and threw them off the boat, furthering his reputation as a tough man that began in Hamilton's brothel back in Troy.

A rival immigrant runner named Tom McCann decided to hurl a few insults Morrissey's way. Morrissey delayed his retirement from immigrant running in the face of the insults from McCann and decided to stay on the docks for just a while longer, at least until the business with McCann was finished. McCann's anger was not entirely motivated by Morrissey's dominance on the docks. Young John had also begun an intimate relationship with McCann's girlfriend and didn't seem too concerned with what McCann thought about it.

It didn't take long for the two ruffians to lock horns at the shooting gallery in the basement of the St. James Hotel in New York City. Morrissey had been waiting for McCann to show and he swung first, striking McCann in the mouth. The desperate struggle began and soon the two men were grappling wildly around the room as the crowd looked on. The fighters knocked over the stove and McCann managed to land on top of Morrissey, holding him down onto the red-hot coals that had spread across the floor. Morrissey's back was burning as McCann went for his throat. Water was tossed on the coals, surely not to save the opponents from lasting injury, but more to keep the building from burning to the ground around the action. The steam rising from the coals, and Morrissey's back, earned him the life-long moniker of "Old Smoke."

Enraged, Morrissey managed to gain his feet and soon was pummeling McCann unmercifully. The fight ended with both men a bloody mess, Morrissey's back still smoldering, and McCann lying unconscious on the floor. Morrissey walked away from his vanquished foe and from the business of immigrant running for good.

Soon after his fight with McCann, Morrissey went to work for a gambler named John Petrie who ran a small house near the hospital in New York City. Petrie told Morrissey that, "the percentage is with the house, so much so that if a man keeps playing you are bound to get all his money in the end." Honesty is the best policy but gamblers frequently forget this old adage. Petrie taught Morrissey that crookedness in the gambling world was not worth the risk to his reputation, nor of an angry customer's bullet. [1]

Morrissey realized that there was fabulous wealth to be had in the gambling business but had not yet developed the patience of John Petrie. He was after fame and fortune more quickly than the steady shared profits of a small gambling house, even if it was in New York City, and soon he was off to California in search of an easy fortune in gold.

Morrissey and a friend discovered upon arriving in San Francisco that they were too late for the gold rush. All of the prime claims had been staked, and the friends soon found their funds were dwindling rapidly. Then one night Morrissey saw two thugs going through the pockets of an unconscious man in the gutter. Despite his rough and tumble ways, Morrissey did have a kind heart and he quickly dispatched the two would-be robbers and helped the victim home.

The man saved by Morrissey that night was a wealthy Englishman who returned the favor by setting up Morrissey with his own gambling house.[2] The miners of San Francisco were only too happy to spend their money in Morrissey's house and soon Morrissey was raking in the profits. He was also gaining a reputation as a bare-knuckle fighter around the saloons of San Francisco, and an opportunity for a little fame and a paycheck presented itself when friends of his started to talk up the possibility that Morrissey could beat the visiting English fighting champion, George Thompson.

A match was arranged in August 1852 during which Morrissey would make his debut as a prize fighter. George Thompson was a more experienced and scientific fighter, but Morrissey was tough. The two fought at Mare Island in California and the fight went a grueling, bloody, eleven rounds. The fight ended with a foul called on Thompson which gave Morrissey a victory along with a little fame and a little prize money. It was not the overwhelming win that Morrissey had sought, but with his gambling profits, his prize-fighting win, and the bit of fame that came with it, Morrissey headed back to New York at the tender age of just 21.

Morrissey returned to New York with his reputation and fame expanding rapidly. John Petrie took him on again as a partner in his gambling house. Morrissey's reputation kept the house peaceful and his fame increased customer traffic. The success they experienced enabled Morrissey to expand his gambling holdings and he eventually owned his own place on West 24th

Street that turned a profit of $2,000 per week for eight straight years. [3]

While his gambling interests grew, "Old Smoke" continued to fight. Despite the pleas of his wife and the fact that both street brawls and bare-knuckled prize fighting were illegal, Morrissey continued both. He was in a number of alcohol-fueled dust ups over gutter insults between various rivals in the tenement areas of New York City and he eventually took on Yankee Sullivan for the heavyweight championship.

The two men squared off in Boston Corners, Massachusetts, in 1853 in an epic 37 round bloody exchange that left both men exhausted and practically unrecognizable. But Yankee Sullivan was unable to answer the call at the start of the thirty-eighth round and Morrissey became heavyweight champ.

Several years later Morrissey made his one and only title defense, winning a twenty-one minute slugfest against John C. Heenan in a much anticipated fight. The victory was complete but the 28- year- old Morrissey had promised his worried wife that he would fight no more. True to his word, Morrissey relinquished the title to Heenan in 1859 without ever fighting again.

With a heavyweight title, a legendary reputation as a street tough, and his gambling interests secured, Morrissey was invited to join forces with a man named Fernando Wood. Wood, a rising Tammany Hall associated New York City politician, asked Morrissey to secure a few polling places for him. As Wood told Morrissey, "elections are not won by voters, but by the gentlemen who count the votes."[4]

Wood needed his precincts protected from enemies who sought to invade polling places and destroy opposing ballots. Morrissey's toughness and connections would serve Wood well in his rise through the ranks of Tammany Hall and through his three terms as mayor of Gotham. Morrissey's connection to Wood served Morrissey well in his own political career as a United States Congressman and New York State Senator. [5]

Morrissey's connection to Tammany Hall politicians paid off. First, when he and his gang, the Dead Rabbits, were permitted to open up gambling joints in the Five Points area of New York City free from police interference. Later, his connections enabled Morrissey to three times win election to the United States House of Representatives from New York's 5th Congressional District. He served there from 1867-1871 and while his Congressional record could never match his record as a prize fighter, Morrissey soon tired of the corruption of Tammany Hall and eventually became one of its most fearsome enemies.

By 1870 Morrissey had teamed up with Horace Greeley in an all-out fight with Tammany Hall. They travelled together to Albany to fight Boss Tweed and by 1876 Morrissey was serving in the New York State Senate. Representing the 4th District in the State Senate, Morrissey had become decidedly anti-Tammany and his greatest political victory came when he defeated Tammany-backed John Fox in the 1875 election to be the State Senator representing the 4th District of New York. [6]

"Old Smoke" lived a lifetime of adventure. Although his legend lives on in the annals of the original gangsters of New York, in the history of the boxing profession, and in the official records of the United States House of Representatives and the New York State Senate, of greater interest to this narrative are Morrissey's adventures at Saratoga Springs.

John Morrissey, like many of the other gamblers before and after him at Saratoga had established himself in the gambling profession in other places prior to his arrival at the Spa. And like most of the other gamblers mentioned in these pages, he first came to Saratoga as a visitor, rather than an entrepreneur. Almost all of the gamblers of Saratoga, Morrissey, Canfield, and Rothstein, among others, vacationed in Saratoga before investing in the all-but-sure thing that was a Saratoga gambling house.

Morrissey himself was visiting the Spa, probably by the late 1850's, if not before. In 1860, a report in a Troy, NY, newspaper recorded that Morrissey had lost $10,000 at a faro table at Saratoga. Despite the fact that his hometown paper apparently stood by the facts of the story, reporters friendly to Morrissey quickly added some context to the loss by adding to the report that Morrissey had also won $8500 during the next three nights. Furthermore, so as to make sure that it was understood that Morrissey could withstand such a loss, it was pointed out that Morrissey had his own faro bank in Saratoga that summer and he owned all or a part of a handful of New York City gambling joints as well.[7]

During the years between his retirement from prize fighting (1859) and his election to Congress (1867), Morrissey set about associating himself with the top

gamblers and businessmen of the age. As a member
of the business class, he was friends with the likes of
Cornelius Vanderbilt. As a member of the political
class, he was chummy with Tammany Hall politicians
like the Honorable Ben Wood. As a member of the
gambling class, he was associated with Albert Spencer
and Charlie Reed. His fame and wealth enabled him
to rub elbows with the class of American high society;
he even visited with a former president at Saratoga
(probably Franklin Pierce) in Saratoga in 1865.[8]

It will be recalled that Morrissey learned the
gambling business from John Petrie at Petrie's small
operation in New York City. By the mid-to-late 1860's
Morrissey's partners were the true heavyweights in the
gambling world. Albert Spencer, Charles Reed, and
Benjamin Scribner were all his partners in the gambling
game while Morrissey was busy building the racetrack
at Saratoga.

It is hard for the modern resident or visitor to
Saratoga today to envision what the place looked like
in the 1860's. Two of the largest hotels in the world
fronted Broadway. The United States Hotel and the
Grand Union dwarfed any building in pure size that
exist today. The railroad that brought thousands of
visitors to the spa every summer arrived smack in the
middle of the village on Railroad Place. The hustle and
bustle of Saratoga in the few blocks around the railroad
depot during the summer months would have rivaled
any of the teeming urban centers of the day.

Morrissey's first gambling venture in Saratoga was
in the old "Pavilion Hotel" run by Robert Gridley in
earlier decades. The back of the place faced the railroad

tracks at the depot. The roulette wheels of the old Gridley place turned in full view of passing pedestrians and one can imagine arriving on a train and being able to see clearly the spinning wheels before even alighting from the cars of the giant machine.

Morrissey was successful and rich. He was also well known for having an abundance of common sense. He realized that the location of his gambling house was ideal for capturing foot traffic and trapping freshly arrived marks with the allure of the spinning ball and turning cards. But Morrissey also realized that the clientele he sought was not the type to be attracted to sawdust floors and swarthy looking faro dealers. He learned from Petrie that the odds were always in the house's favor and he ran clean games. Morrissey took Petrie's philosophy on gambling as his own, once telling a reporter, "Now I'll tell you something that your Wall Street broker perhaps dare not tell you; the odds of all these games are in favor of the bank. You sit down and play with me a game or two and you might win; but you play with me every night for a month and I'll burst you."[9]

Not only did Morrissey run clean games, he ran a respectable house. Disorder and cheating were suppressed at his houses by his reputation alone. Nevertheless, Morrissey needed to upgrade his gambling house in Saratoga if he wanted to attract a higher class of clientele.

Renovations could have done the trick. Certainly Morrissey could afford the best carpenters to install the finest furnishings to make the decades-old "Pavilion" a fashionable place all on its own. He also must have realized, however, that the authorities would eventually take an interest in seeing that gambling should be suppressed and the most open and obvious places were sure to be targeted first. His place, just steps from the railroad depot and mere yards from one of the world's most impressive hotels, was sure to be high on the list, whenever the mood struck the reformers to address the Saratoga situation.

Morrissey needed a quiet place, not too far out of the way, but just far enough off the beaten path to bring in his wealthy clientele without too much trouble. Morrissey's attention was drawn to a swampy plot of land at the corner of Putnam and East Congress Streets, across the street from the then boundary of Congress Park. He drained the land and began construction of what would be the most elegant of gambling halls ever to be built in the United States of America.

By the time Morrissey's grand offering to the gambling gods was complete in 1870, he had already spent $90,000 to build the building. Descriptions of the elegant hall abound in newspaper accounts at the time of its opening. These include massive mirrors, plush wall-to-wall carpeting, cornices and mantels made of French cheval, ornate carvings in the furniture including elaborate tiger heads on the mirrors, silk curtains, golden chandeliers, and hundreds of lights. The "J.M." monogram was observed prominently throughout the place.

Correspondents seemed barely be able to find the words to describe the elegance of the place and spoke of it in the most glowing of terms. It was no exaggeration that the building that Morrissey built to entertain his guests (and to take their money) was the largest and most extravagant of all gambling halls in America and rivaled the world famous gambling resort of Baden-Baden in the Black Forest of southern Germany.

Before opening for business, Morrissey held an open house for the public to come and admire the extravagance of the place. Eight hundred visitors passed through the doors to marvel at the furnishings and explore the new addition to the gambling dens that had existed in Saratoga for some half century by then.[10] It was during this open house that an encounter occurred between the manager of the club and a little old lady that was recounted in newspapers throughout the country. One newspaper from Indiana carried the story this way,

"Everybody knows "Bolly" Lewis of Cincinnati – the accomplished 'sporting' man and genial gentleman. He is now connected with Morrissey's splendid club-room at Saratoga. Here is an account of Lewis' interview with a pious lady:

Ladies are visiting John Morrissey's new gambling house at Saratoga. A very religious lady was shown through it the other day. After everything had been explained to her satisfaction, and just as she gained the threshold, she turned to Mr. Lewis, one of the attaches, and in a most solemn manner said:

'You are Mr. Morrissey, I presume?'

'No, madam, my name is Lewis; I am one of the attaches of the establishment.'

'Well, then sir,' continued the lady, with her right hand pointed to the ceiling, 'I would like to ask you one questions. What good will it do you to gain all the money in the world in this house and then lose your soul?'

'We don't play for souls, madam,' replied Lewis, 'we only play for money.'

The pious lady was amazed at this answer. She quickly turned on her heel and quit the house, doubtless regarding the handsome Lewis as a heathen sure to be lost."[11]

Morrissey had planned to call his mecca of gambling the "Casino." After all, that is exactly what it was. The local clergy thought the name was perhaps a bit too much, though, so they paid Morrissey a visit and asked him if he would consider calling it something else. Morrissey asked for suggestions and one minister offered that he should call it the "Saratoga Club House" in order that, "People would not think then it was wholly a gambling house."[12]

Morrissey adopted the name and until his death the elegant gambling hall was known as the Saratoga Club House. Apparently, the fact that a sitting United States Congressman was running a world-class gambling den openly, and without fear of the law, was not all that concerning to the men of the cloth, but it would have been too much for their sensitive moral compasses should the place be known as a "casino." Heaven forbid the people should get the wrong idea of what was going on inside!

Naming the place "Club House" and not "Casino" was not the only concession that Morrissey made to the more pious element of the town. He also agreed to close his doors on Sundays. This was no small gesture on the part of Morrissey, as Richard Canfield later pointed out; closing on Sundays meant losing one out of every seven days of business during the racing meet when the crowds were the largest. Canfield also mentioned that, at Monte Carlo at least, Sunday was always the busiest day at the gaming tables and therefore closing on Sunday, in deference to the clergymen was, in fact, a significant sacrifice of profits. Surely not all of the other gamblers at Saratoga adhered to such honorable precepts.

Staying closed on Sundays was one of three concessions that Morrissey made to the sensitivities of the citizens of Saratoga Springs. The other two were house rules that no residents of Saratoga County could be admitted and that no women would be allowed to play.

Women could enter, dine, and watch the games but their escorts would have to actually play on their behalf, so as to protect their delicate natures. Chivalry of the day required the protection of the fairer sex. That women would be excluded from participating in any form of recreation open to men sounds absurd today, but in 1870 it was generally thought of as a good idea, if only to protect the ladies.

The rule against locals gambling came about as a lesson learned from the experience of the famous gambling resort at Baden-Baden. The casino at Baden Baden was initially open to all, locals and visitors alike. As at Saratoga, high society visited the mineral springs of Baden Baden and gambled at the local casino. Visitors who lost all their money generally found their way home by one means or another. But if their losses at Baden Baden were too severe, they returned home destitute and became the responsibility of the locality from which they had come.

Locals who gambled away their last pennies, however, remained at Baden Baden, becoming a drain on the alms houses and local charities to the extent that they soon generated sympathy for themselves and resentment towards the awful casino operators who preyed upon their addiction to the vice of gambling. Before long, enough local residents had become devastated and local families ruined, that local officials soon were moved to bring legislation prohibiting gambling at Baden Baden. [13] Morrissey would not fall into that trap and was serious enough about it that he even once had his own son banished from the casino when the young man tried to get in on the action.

The story goes that Morrissey's son, also named John, once brought a few friends from New York to the Saratoga Club House and started playing roulette. After a few minutes an attendant tapped young Morrissey on the shoulder and asked him to accompany the attendant to the manager's office. Of course the younger John Morrissey knew the manager for many years and was surprised when the manager addressed him without any hint of recognition,

"You are a Saratogian, are you not?" he asked.

Smiling the sheepish grin of a child who has been embarrassed by a sticky situation he has found himself in, young John asked what on earth the manger could be getting at.

Still feigning a lack of recognition, the manager continued, "A rule of this house is that no Saratogian may play here. (The Morrissey family lived in a cottage behind the United States Hotel during summers at the time.) You have $25 in chips on the roulette table. You have lost $10. Here is the amount of your loss. You will be good enough to cash those chips in and never play here again."

Young Morrissey was shocked at such treatment and the beginnings of a temper tantrum were quickly dealt with by the door man, summoned without further discussion by the manager. John Morrissey Jr. found himself unceremoniously tossed out on the street before he knew it. He was banished from that point on from entering the Club House except on specific business which he was compelled to conduct will all due efficiency. [14]

In Morrissey's time, it seemed all American towns, villages, and cities struggled with controlling vice. That gambling and prostitution were illegal was clear. What was less clear was just how much vice would be allowed in any particular locality. Some suppressed vice unmercifully. Some not at all. Some cities and towns allowed gambling as long as the price of graft was right. In still other corners of the US, especially in resort areas like Saratoga Springs, Long Branch on Long Island, Newport, Rhode Island, and Hot Springs, Arkansas, open gambling was tolerated, until it wasn't.

Saratoga Springs in the late 1870's developed an unofficial model of "winking" at gambling, allowing the games to carry on, provided that it did not become too offensive. As long as the citizens benefited and local officials were not too corrupt, the games could be played without interference. As long as the gamblers paid their graft in the form of donations to local charities and churches, the stench of gambling would never get too pungent to be noticed enough to move local opinion to action. It seemed that vice would be allowed in Saratoga Springs up to the imaginary line that the citizens themselves drew and as long as the gamblers kept on the right side of that line, their operations were secure.

Realizing this, Morrissey supported popular initiatives and contributed significantly to various worthy causes in Saratoga Springs. He was a notable supporter of the popular collegiate rowing races that made an annual pilgrimage to Saratoga Springs for competition on Saratoga Lake. Naturally, money started to be wagered on the outcome of the races. The local line was crossed when the gambling started to get out of hand and by 1874, when popular opinion objected to the unseemly gambling on the amateur races, it was John Morrissey who set about suppressing gambling on the races, not the local officials who actually were obligated by law to do so. [15]

In 1871 Morrissey found out that a local woman had fallen behind in her mortgage payments. Facing foreclosure, the poor woman appealed to Morrissey, explaining that she only needed a couple of weeks to make good on the payments she was then in arrears on. Morrissey called the attorney for the holder of the mortgage and threatened to buy the mortgage at sale if the owner would not consider a grace period for the down-on-her-luck mortgagee. The owner thought twice about continuing the foreclosure sale and Morrissey secured the grace period needed for the woman to get back into financial shape and avoid being tossed out on the street. [16]

It was said that Morrissey enjoyed performing the public service of directing traffic in front of his Club House. Standing in the middle of East Congress Street at Putnam Street, Morrissey was a sight to behold as he directed the throngs of people, horses, and carriages to and fro.

Morrissey knew the value of keeping peace. His credentials as a former heavyweight champion were enough to ensure that everyone kept their cool. His days as a bouncer for Alexander Hamilton in the Troy brothel and his career as a bare knuckle fighter were almost always enough to keep local toughs in check. But enough alcohol clouds the judgement of all men and occasionally Morrissey would be called upon to keep the peace.

One day in 1875, long after his career as a fighter was over, there was Morrissey escorting a drunk, unruly patron from the grounds of the Race Course. [17] No accounts of disorder at the Club House under Morrissey are known to exist.

Morrissey knew that his efforts at civic service would buy him the good will of the local citizenry. He knew that in Saratoga, as the old adage goes, he could catch more bees with honey than with vinegar. But Morrissey was not above using his powerful position to get his way when he felt it necessary. Displaying the same ferocity that marked him inside the boxing ring, "Old Smoke" let it be known that despite his generosity to the Saratoga populace, if his interests were interfered with too much he was willing to play hard ball.

In 1870 when the members of the YMCA were agitating for reform Morrissey was reported to have told them, "You have the power to close my doors, but if you do I shall remove the race course, and then what will become of your town?"[18] The threat was enough to keep the reformers away from the doors of the Club House for as long as Morrissey remained the principal owner.

Morrissey led a charmed life for sure. At Saratoga his race track and Club House were doing well and his other business ventures were doing likewise. In 1877 he was re-elected once again to the New York State Senate, this time from the 7th District and again defeating a Tammany Hall backed candidate, Augustus Schell.[19]

During Morrissey's final political campaign he developed a case of bronchitis. He became so ill that he spent the day of his election on his sickbed, rising only to address the crowds celebrating his victory. With the stress of an election passed, Morrissey's health failed to improve and on his doctor's orders he travelled to Savannah and then Jacksonville in an attempt to recover.[20] When the southern climate proved no match for what ailed the Senator, he travelled back north, eventually taking a room in the Adelphi Hotel on Broadway in Saratoga Springs.

Morrissey stayed in the Adelphi with his wife for about a month trying to regain his health to no avail. On the afternoon of May 1, 1878, Morrissey took a sudden and unexpected turn for the worse. Surrounded by his wife, a few friends, and his long time trainer, Lawrence, Morrissey was fading quickly despite the efforts of one Dr. Grant to prolong the life of the great champion.[21]

The news of "Old Smoke's" imminent death spread rapidly through the village and soon a crowd had gathered along Broadway quietly awaiting any news, all hoping they would hear the great man inside room number 5 had regained his strength. But the Honorable John Morrissey would not recover and he drew his last breath at 7:15 PM. The announcement was made to the sorrowful crowd by the manager of the Adelphi Hotel, a man named McCaffrey, who stood in the door and simply proclaimed, "He is gone."[22]

It seemed that Morrissey's death did not follow the narrative of his life. Surely the cause of John Morrissey's demise should have been something more exciting or adventurous than a lingering bout of bronchitis and pneumonia. But alas, the human condition teaches that life is precious and precarious; it cares not for our wealth or worldly accomplishments.

That Morrissey spent his last days in Saratoga Springs is fitting as to this day, nearly 130 years after his death, his racetrack remains the signature attraction of Saratoga Springs and his magnificent Club House remains the signature building of the city that owes much of its present day existence to these two meccas of gambling.

Endnotes

Chapter 4

1   Kofoed, J. *Brandy for Heroes: A Biography of the Honorable John Morrissey, Champion Heavyweight of America and State Senator.* E.P. Dutton and Company. 1938.

2   Ibid.

3   Ibid.

4   Ibid.

5   Ibid.

6   "Death of John Morrissey: A Checkered Career Finished," New York Times May 2, 1878.

7   New York Weekly News, September 1, 1860.

8   The Kansas Chief, August 31, 1865.

9   "Campaign Notes," The Somerset Herald, August 30, 1872.

10 "Notes," New York Daily Tribune, July 13, 1870.

11 "We Don't Play for Souls," The Jasper Weekly Courier, August 5, 1870.

12 Britten, Evelyn. "Canfield Casino marks its 101st Birthday this Year," The Saratogian, February 16, 1968.

13 Schwartz, David G. *Roll the Bones: The History of Gambling.* Gotham Books, NY. 2006.

14 "Gambling at Saratoga," The Sun, July 21, 1901.

15 "News and Notes," The Brooklyn Daily Union, July 21, 1874.

16 "Mr. Morrissey Performs a Kind Act," The Daily Saratogian, August 9, 1871.

17 "Saratoga," New York Evening Express, August 21, 1875.

18 "Saratoga: Preparations for the Season: The Gambling Question," New York Times, June 15, 1871.

19 "Death of John Morrissey," New York Times, May 2, 1878.

20   Ibid.

21   "Senator Morrissey's Death," Daily Saratogian, May 2,
      1878.

22   Ibid.

Chapter 5

Captain Mahedy and the Formation of the Saratoga Springs Police Department

In the years after the Civil War, the village of Saratoga Springs grew rapidly. Much like today, the population of the town doubled or tripled during the summer season. Not only did the constables and night watch officers have to deal with difficult areas of town like Willow Walk and Searing's Alley, they also gradually began to provide the village with some of the more general police services that are common today, like preventative patrols, responding to calls for service, traffic, and crowd control, all with twenty-four hour per day coverage.

In 1874 several of the banks and hotels along Broadway were successful in persuading the village of the necessity of having a general patrol force to keep the peace, prevent crime and capture offenders during the summer season. Five men were chosen to form what was called a "special police" force to patrol the area of Broadway where the banks and hotels were clustered. Fred Johnson was named Captain and was appointed leader of the officers who were: James Howden, George Gorman, Peter Kemp, and William F. Mahedy. [1]

The Special Police Force eventually became known as the "Broadway Squad." The officers maintained a regular patrol during the summer months, commencing in June and ending once the throng of visitors departed for home, usually in the first couple weeks of September. The year after it was initially formed, only four officers were appointed to the Broadway Squad, and they patrolled from the Clarendon Hotel to the Marvin House on Broadway with one officer assigned to patrol Lake Avenue. [2]

In 1876, Officer Mahedy had been appointed as Captain of the squad and he, along with three other men, patrolled Broadway from Caroline Street to William Street. Three men were on duty during the night time hours and one patrolled during the day. [3]

William Mahedy served with the Broadway Squad from its beginning through 1886, when the village was considering the formation of a modern police force. Mahedy was involved in several events of note while he was a member of the Broadway Squad and was generally praised for the performance of his duties.

During the first year of the Broadway Squad, Mahedy was walking his beat when he came upon a man lurking behind a house on Circular Street in the middle of the night. He challenged the would-be burglar who was attempting to enter the home of a Mr. Wescott. The burglar took off with Mahedy in pursuit. When they got to Henry Street, Mahedy was threatening to overtake the man when he suddenly turned, revolver in hand, and fired two shots at Mahedy.[4]

Mahedy fell to the ground after being struck by one of the bullets in his chest. He quickly regained his feet and the sound of the shots drew the attention of the two other officers patrolling in the area. When his fellow lawmen arrived, it was discovered that the bullet had struck Mahedy's shield, denting it and breaking the pin that held it to his coat and keeping the bullet from entering his body.[5]

On another occasion, Mahedy was patrolling on Phila Street and discovered a burglar had broken into Peter Thompson's harness store. A couple of expensive buffalo robes had been removed from the store and placed outside the store when Mahedy interrupted the criminal, who made his escape through the darkened streets.[6]

After working for about ten years as the head of the Broadway Squad and for several years as a Deputy Sheriff, Captain Mahedy would have been the logical choice to head up a new, modern police force for the village. He probably should have, except he managed to get himself into a bit of trouble in 1886, the year before the police force was officially formed. The Daily Saratogian of September 28, 1886, provides an account of the saga.

Mahedy, like many people in Saratoga Springs, rented an extra room in his home to summer visitors. The hotels of the village were often overbooked in the summertime and local residents, as they do today, would often provide rooms for those who could not find other lodging in the town. In 1884

Mahedy took in a young man from New York City named Albert Laridon.

Young Laridon was the son of a silk merchant and was friendly with a rather suspect character named Charles O'Donnell. The two met in a billiard hall and spent the early part of the summer visiting various resorts in the metro New York area, including at least one of the downstate racetracks. O'Donnell and Laridon won enough money playing the races that they felt a vacation was in order and made their way to Saratoga Springs, eventually taking the room at the Mahedy residence.

It didn't take long for their money to run out, as O'Donnell had apparently no limit to his spending habits and no manner of replenishing his bank account other than through gambling. Each had his own ideas on how to raise enough money to secure passage back to New York and Laridon figured they should find work to earn enough money to make their way home. O'Donnell suggested that they cash a check drawn on his uncle in Troy, who, O'Donnell assured Laridon, would honor the paper.

O'Donnell then wrote a check for the relatively modest sum of 35 dollars and brought it to the First National Bank of Saratoga. Not knowing the two lads, the teller asked them to prove who they were and the young men left, returning with Captain Mahedy, who verified the identities of Laridon and O'Donnell. Not satisfied with that, the bank requested that Mahedy endorse the check as well, which he did.

Mahedy would quickly regret the decision as Laridon and O'Donnell soon afterward disappeared from Saratoga without paying Mahedy the balance of what they owed for their lodging. Mahedy was faced with another problem related to the young men as the bank called for him and demanded he make good on the check he endorsed which had been returned from the bank in Troy with the words, "This check is forged" written in red ink across its face. Mahedy was stuck and paid the bank the 35 dollars it was owed. He promptly obtained a warrant for the arrest of O'Donnell.

This all happened in the summer of 1884. The matter apparently was not a priority for Captain Mahedy, as the warrant for O'Donnell sat idle for two years until he went on vacation to New York City in September of 1886. Looking forward to his vacation in New York City, Mahedy recalled that he had a warrant for O'Donnell and brought it with him to New York and had Constable J. M. Fryer meet him there.

Mahedy and Fryer quickly located O'Donnell and arrested him. Fryer brought O'Donnell back to the Ballston Jail. On the way, O'Donnell apparently told Fryer that Laridon was behind the whole plot to forge the check and gave a statement that he was totally innocent in the affair.

With this additional information, a representative of the bank swore out a warrant for Laridon as well, two years after the check cashing took place. In the meantime, aware that O'Donnell would be cooperating with Fryer, Mahedy stopped by the Laridon home and inquired after Albert. The elder Laridon, Gustave, told Mahedy he knew all about the check business as he remembered his son had to walk home to New York City that summer as O'Donnell had taken off with all the money.

According to Gustave, he called for his son and agreed to meet with Mahedy at the Gilsey House, a well know New York Hotel where Mahedy was staying. When the Laridons arrived along with their attorney, Mahedy offered to settle the matter quietly and said that the sum of $3,000 should allow him to forget the matter.

When Laridon hesitated at such a large sum, Mahedy said he could drop the amount to $2500 but that he would have to give the District Attorney and the Judge $1,000 apiece and could go no lower than that. Telling Mahedy that he wished to think over the offer, Gustave Laridon instead went to a judge and obtained a warrant for Mahedy, charging him with extortion.

The following day, Gustave Laridon returned to the Gilsey House, this time accompanied by a court officer who placed Mahedy under arrest. Indignant, Mahedy pulled a paper from his pocket, declared that he had a warrant for Albert Laridon and demanded the local authorities make the arrest. The local officer was having none of it and took Captain Mahedy into custody, locking him up at the Ninth Precinct Station House.

The next morning Mahedy was brought to the Jefferson Street Market Court and appeared before the judge. In attendance were Constable Fryer and a Mr. Breslin who provided the bail for Mahedy. Both Gustave and Albert Laridon were also in attendance along with their lawyer to provide their evidence against Mahedy but no examination was conducted as Mahedy's request for a two-week adjournment was granted by the judge.[7]

Mahedy immediately produced the warrant for Albert Laridon and again demanded that New York authorities do their duty and take Albert into custody to answer the charges he faced in Saratoga. The judge, seeing that the warrant was indeed issued by a Saratoga Springs justice allowed Constable Fryer to take the younger Laridon into custody despite the spirited objections of the Laridon family and their attorney.[8]

The train to Saratoga would not be leaving New York until later that afternoon and the Laridons' attorney set to work obtaining an order for the release of Albert, hoping it could be obtained before the Saratogians left with their charge.

Mahedy and Fryer took Laridon to the central train station and, realizing they were being followed by friends of the Laridons,' unexpectedly boarded a train bound for Harlem and just before the train departed, they hopped off, leaving their pursuers to jump off the moving train when they realized that Mahedy and Fryer were headed for the street with Albert in tow. The pursuers lost their targets on the streets of New York and a few moments later, when the Laridons' attorney arrived at the train bound for Saratoga with the documents securing Albert's release, all he found was a smug Captain Mahedy loitering in the lobby of the depot. Fryer and Albert were nowhere to be seen. [9]

Mahedy would soon have larger problems than just how to get Albert Laridon secretly back to Saratoga Springs. It was reported in the New York City newspapers that the court officer who arrested Mahedy was claiming that Mahedy offered him $100.00 to let him go. [10] Of course, Mahedy denied the accusation like he denied trying to extort Gustave Laridon. In addition, back in Saratoga, the District Attorney and the Police Justice who issued the original warrant for O'Donnell were both claiming to have no knowledge of the warrant for Laridon at all. [11] If Mahedy had planned to extort money from the Laridons, the scheme was not going as planned.

It was not long before other reports of questionable activity by Mahedy were making the newspapers. His per-diem bills to the village and the county for his service as a constable and deputy sheriff respectively came into question. Apparently Mahedy had submitted bills to the village for work he performed on days that there were no records of court having been in session. In fact, Mahedy was accused of submitting over 100 items for which no corroborating court documents could be found and for transporting a single prisoner to two different prisons on the same day. [12]

Nothing was going Mahedy's way. He skipped bail on the New York City charges of attempting to blackmail Gustave Laridon. He was indicted for perjury and two misdemeanors related to his Saratoga accounts and the warrant for Laridon. [13] At first, he fled to Canada, but within a few months he returned to the United States and faced the criminal charges against him.

The two felony perjury charges in Saratoga were dismissed on a technicality and Mahedy pled guilty to two misdemeanors. He was fined $250 on each count and paid restitution to the town and Saratoga National Bank in order to avoid jail time. [14]

As for the resolution of the blackmail charge in New York City, much less public attention was paid to that. It seems likely that restitution was paid, along with a small fine to settle the matter entirely.

Mahedy had been the officer in charge of the Broadway Squad for nearly ten years, but his arrest and conduct prior to the official formation of the police department disqualified him for the post of Chief of Police. Instead, the city fathers chose George Blodget as the first Chief of Police. Blodget had served for many years as a Deputy Sheriff, village constable, and had operated his own detective agency for about five years prior to the formation of the department.

On June 1, 1887, Chief Blodget and eight other men began full time police patrol duties in Saratoga Springs. Michael Carroll was appointed as Assistant Chief while John Van Rensselaer, Patrick Deegan, Joseph Hennessey, Jerry Costello, Walter Mann, Michael Finn, and Charles Allen filled out the roster. It is generally considered that these nine men were the original members of the police department but as a matter of historical accuracy it should be noted that an examination of the city archives reveals that Charles Allen actually joined the force one month after the others.

While the members of the new police force set about patrolling the streets and carrying out their various duties, Captain Mahedy did not fade entirely into obscurity. In 1891 Mahedy was arrested in Syracuse for scamming an associate. He allegedly obtained a loan from the man, Charles E. Crouse, by representing that he owned an expensive horse that Crouse relied upon for collateral on a loan. The only problem was that there was no horse and Mahedy disappeared with the money.

The Syracuse authorities tracked him down after a warrant was issued, but Mahedy escaped from that city's jail. He used an alias to secure lodging in a Rochester hotel before the police of that city caught up with him when the Rochester Chief of Police recognized Mahedy from his days on the Broadway Squad. [15]

By 1895 Mahedy was employed by two horse tracks in Virginia. The owners of the tracks were not pleased with the Pinkerton Detectives that were in charge of security and replaced them with the former Saratoga law man, unaware or unconcerned with his past. [16]

In 1909, the Saratogian reported on Mahedy's visit to Saratoga Springs. He was then living in Chicago. Nowhere in the news accounts of Mahedy's arrest in Rochester, his employment at the Virginia tracks, or of his visit to Saratoga Springs roughly 30 years after his fall from grace, was there any mention of the resolution of the New York City charges that he tried to extort Albert Laridon's father back in 1886.

And so the Saratoga Springs Police Department was born, in the shadow of scandal. The men (they were all men at that time) of the department were not all corrupt or incompetent, but over the years there would be many an instance of nefarious and unscrupulous conduct by the men sworn to uphold the law in Saratoga Springs.

Endnotes

Chapter 5

[1] "Special Police Force," The Saratoga Sentinel, June 11, 1874.

[2] "Locals in Brief," The Saratoga Sentinel, June 10, 1875.

[3] "Shorts," The Daily Saratogian, June 5, 1876.

[4] "Daring Attempt at Burglary and Murder," The Saratoga Sentinel, August 20, 1874.

[5] Ibid.

[6] "Attempted Burglary Frustrated," The Daily Saratogian, February 16, 1884.

[7] "Officer Mahedy Returns," The Daily Saratogian, September 28, 1886.

[8] Ibid.

[9] Ibid.

[10] "Officer Mahedy Arrested," The Daily Saratogian, September 28, 1886.

[11] Ibid.

[12] "Astounding Developments," The Daily Saratogian, December 3, 1886.

[13] "County Court and Sessions," The Daily Saratogian, December 7, 1887.

[14] "Getting Out of the Toils," The Daily Saratogian, December 8, 1887.

[15] "Mr. Mahedy's Meanderings," The Syracuse Weekly Express, July 30, 1891.

[16] "Turf and Track Notes," The New York Herald, July 21, 1895.

Chapter 6

Anthony Comstock and Spencer Trask Take Up the Fight

While the opposition to gambling was always present, though never very vigorous, in Saratoga Springs, the fifteen years after Morrissey's death would see the gamblers of the town come under increasing pressure from the law and anti-vice crusaders.

Before Morrissey's death, the local Young Men's Christian Association took an interest in seeing that open gambling was stopped. In August of 1870 they were even successful in closing down one local establishment known as the Ford and Allen place, and stopping Morrissey's operation for a short time.[1] Morrissey held the stronger hand, however, and donated considerable sums to local charities and religious organizations to curry favor with the locals.

He also held the trump card - ownership of the racetrack. The racetrack was universally accepted as an economic juggernaut for the village and owning it gave Morrissey the ability to threaten closing both the track and the Club House should either experience too much legal interference or moral heat. And while the YMCA officers may have been successful in their requests at stopping gambling in the town for a short time on a voluntary basis, more serious efforts would be just around the corner for the anti-gambling set.

In the mid 1880's the New York Society for the Suppression of Vice in New York City was surprisingly successful in carrying out raids and hauling into court many offenders of the vice laws of New York State. Doing the job that the police were unwilling or unable to do, society members often went undercover to gather evidence. While they could bribe the New York City police at that time, gamblers, prostitutes, and obscenity peddlers found they could not do the same with the Society's agents. None of the agents for the Society was better at obtaining evidence against the vice offenders than Anthony Comstock.

In 1886, the Society decided that Saratoga Springs was as good a target as any for their efforts. Indeed, an attorney for the Society, George I. Nichols, sent an open letter to local newspapers declaring, "The open and flagrant violation of the laws of this State against gambling has long been a public scandal, not only in Saratoga itself, but throughout the state, and in fact everywhere wherever the name of Saratoga is known."[2] Anthony Comstock was secretly dispatched to the Spa.

The local anti-gambling forces joined with the agents of the Society and threw their open support behind the efforts to bring the gamblers to justice. In the summer of 1886 they felt strength enough in numbers to hold a law and order meeting.

On August 3 they held a meeting at the First Baptist Church on Washington Street. Leading the standing-room only meeting was Dr. Herrick Johnson of Chicago with Reverend W.R. Terrett, Anthony Comstock, Joseph Cook of Boston, and Reverend J.L Withrow, each delivering an address to the assembled crowd. [3] While declaring the meeting was not an attack on the horse racing that was being carried on in the village, the supporters of the law and order meeting nevertheless resoundingly passed a resolution declaring all forms of gambling to be "...injurious in the highest degree to the financial, moral, and religious interests of our community..." and resolving to fully support the suppression of gambling and the efforts of the agents of the New York Society for the Suppression of Vice in their work in Saratoga Springs. [4] The resolution was passed with the support of many of the local clergy as well as local citizens, including Spencer Trask.

It was a busy summer in 1886 for local law enforcement authorities. Even though the permanent police force would not be authorized until the following April, the local constables and summer beat officers had their hands full, even before Anthony Comstock and his fellow agents arrived in town.

The son of the former mayor of Troy was arrested in August for creating a drunken disturbance and pulling a pistol at one of the lakeside resorts. [5] The court docket on Wednesday August 18, 1886, included ten public drunkenness cases, two illegal freight train jumpers, and two arrests for operating a vile disorderly (prostitution) house at 30 Railroad Place. [6] A notorious "bunco steerer" named "Doc" Minchin was taken into custody by Officer Tracey in early August. [7]

Bunco steerers were considered undesirable as they would venture out into the crowds, whether at the racetrack, along Broadway, near the train station or the prominent hotels, and, with silver tongue, entice unsuspecting marks to crooked gambling games. Indeed, the local newspaper opined, "…Saratoga has no use for people of the Minchin stripe and it is about time they understood it."[8]

Into this situation Anthony Comstock would arrive. As secretary and agent for the New York Society for the Suppression of Vice, he was well known in New York City for his prominent and recognizable moustache, which he shaved off for his Saratoga adventure. Gathering evidence during the initial stages of the summer racing meet, Comstock made his first official move in early August. He obtained a warrant to search the most prominent of all the gambling houses, the fashionable Saratoga Club House.

While the owners, Albert Spencer and Charles Reed, were at the racetrack on the afternoon of August 6, 1886, Comstock, his associates, and Chief of Police George Blodget entered the building and carried away evidence of the goings-on inside. The raiders secured three double roulette tables and a faro layout.[9] Spencer and Reed rushed to the Club House, but not in time to stop the raid or prevent the arrest of four of their employees.[10]

Under the threat that he would be driven from town in a pine box, Comstock continued his crusade in the coming days, raiding 403 Broadway and arresting six more gamblers. Thirteen more arrests were made during the course of the summer of 1886, including Christian Schaffer (the same long time gambler at the Spa mentioned in the first chapter), G. Bowman, and Henry Davies.[11] Five additional warrants were issued for professional gamblers who, getting word of their pending arrests, skipped town as fast as they could. The local police were unable to track them down.[12]

Caleb Mitchell, once and future President of the village, was arrested during the raids along with several of his employees. Mitchell's chalkboard, used for posting race results in his poolroom on Broadway, was tossed from the window of the building before the raiders could secure it.[13]

While the efforts of the New York Society for the Suppression of Vice and Anthony Comstock were certainly noble, it would be up to the local officials to see that justice ultimately would be done. All of the men arrested during the raids of 1886 were released on bail after appearing before Village Justice Barbour. Their cases were scheduled to be heard at the October term of the Grand Jury when Comstock and his friends would be back in New York City.

Most of the places raided and the men arrested by Comstock went right back to business as usual within days, in some cases less than twenty-four hours after being raided. This prompted one western New York newspaper to make the entirely accurate statement that, "Comstock keeps on arresting the Saratoga gamblers and the Saratoga gamblers keep on not caring that he does."[14]

Once Comstock was known to be in town, it became decidedly more difficult for him to obtain evidence and many of the local townsfolk made it abundantly clear that he and his crusaders were not welcome. Authorities were lukewarm to the idea of pursuing criminal charges against the gamblers, Mr. Comstock was jostled on the streets, and an associate was unable to engage a carriage in town once he was identified as an ally of Mr. Comstock.[15] Such excitement was generated by the raids and arrests that a riot was nearly started on Broadway after news of the warrants and arrests became known.[16]

Local sentiment appeared to favor the gamblers. A reporter asked several Saratogians their opinion of the matter and some of the responses reveal the mood of the village. [17] A tobacconist declared flatly, "It is an outrage." A local printer had the opinion that the closing of the gambling dens "will hurt Saratoga to the extent of $100,000." A jaded ex-judge advised that "the oldest inhabitant will outlive the movement." And a hotel keeper added, "I don't like to see people, comparative strangers, come here and tell us what we shall do. They had better mind their own business and look after their own localities."

A local village official expressed the opinion, "I don't know what the Saratoga People are thinking of by permitting this thing to go on. Some of them will be eating snow balls before spring." Like many townsfolk, this official had no problem turning a blind eye to rampant gambling in the village as long as enough money was brought in to justify it.

There was some support for Comstock's raiders, however. A dry goods seller and insurance agent expressed their support even if the whole town opposed them. And of course the religious element of the village was in favor of the persecution of vice offenders.

Comstock himself summed up his work thus, "...I don't know what will be the result. I wouldn't be surprised if they keep right on selling (referring to the pool sellers at the track and in poolrooms) and gambling. All I can do is to get them before the grand jury; it is the regular course of law. The matter now rests with your officers of the law and your citizens. I have demonstrated in a judicial manner that these things exist, and the work must now be followed by those whom you elect to enforce your laws."[18]

Mr. Nichols, the Society's lawyer, had it correct when he said, "It is openly boasted that this movement has had no permanent effect, and that gambling places at once resumed their operations. But whether it be true or not, that this flagrant insult was offered to the law, and to every law abiding citizen in Saratoga, the work so far done by the society, even if not carried out, has shown that law can be enforced in Saratoga, even if it be only for twenty-four hours." The agents of the New York Society for the Suppression of Vice have "….caused men to be apprehended by due process of law, and has clearly placed the responsibility for indictment and conviction upon the legal authorities of this county."[19]

Sadly for the members of the Society and those in favor of law and order in Saratoga, the local authorities would think better of indicting and convicting the very people upon which the village relied to draw such large numbers of free spending, wealthy visitors. When the grand jury convened in the fall of 1886 no indictments were found for any of the pool sellers or gamblers arrested through the efforts of Comstock and his men. [20]

Just three years after the Comstock raids, the anti-gambling supporters were agitating again. In August of 1889, Ernest R. Bevins of Philadelphia made a complaint in the village court against three gambling dens: the

Club House on East Congress Street, Caleb Mitchell's poolroom on Broadway, and a place operated by one John Frost. [21]

Assistant Police Chief Carroll led a raid on Spencer's Club House on August 29, 1889, while at the same time a squad led by Detective Allen raided Mitchell's place on Broadway directly across from the United States Hotel. After a thorough search was made, no gambling instruments were found at either place, although a sleeve of dusty poker chips was found in a desk drawer in an upstairs room at Mitchell's. Perhaps word had reached the gamblers in time to remove any incriminating paraphernalia. While Comstock was able to surprise the gamblers back in 1886 and secure at least some physical evidence of gambling, this time word of the impending raids travelled faster than the law. [22]

Spencer, Mitchell, Frost, and two others were all arrested for keeping gambling houses that summer of 1889 and posted $300 bail each. Their cases were referred to the October term of the Grand Jury which, of course, failed to find enough evidence to bring indictments against any of the three gamblers. [23]

One of the most interesting and amusing stories related to this series of raids in 1889 was the little trick pulled by one of the gamblers to get a monopoly on the play for a single night. As usual, once the raids were made and bail posted, business would resume just as if nothing at all had happened. Once play got going again after the raids, one enterprising gambler spread the convincing rumor that another series of raids was planned for a particular evening. While all the other places closed their doors for the night, anticipating a visit by authorities, the cunning gambler stayed open and got all the money wagered in Saratoga Springs that night. [24]

The principal accuser in the raids of 1889 was one Mr. Bevins, who was identified as an agent of Spencer Trask. As one of the law and order men of 1886 who invited Comstock and his agents to the village, Trask would engage in a decades-long running battle against the gamblers at the Spa. He would be behind several attempts to stop the open gambling occurring in the village between 1886 and into the twentieth century.

Spencer Trask was not blind to the fact that the population of Saratoga was decidedly pro-gambling. He said, "The community, I admit, is strongly in favor of the gambling interest. This shows what an extent it has exercised its pernicious power in corrupting public sentiment." Trask argued against gambling on a number of points, first that "…the Penal Code of this State pronounces gambling a felony and forbids it under heavy penalties…" and the fact that gambling is illegal should "…be enough for law abiding citizens to resolve to put a stop to the practice…."[25]

Beyond the legal argument, Trask held the opinion that open gambling was morally detrimental to the town, claiming that open gambling "disgraces and demoralizes the community." By allowing the Club House and gambling at the racetrack, shelter was given to "a dozen dives of lower order…"

Furthermore, those most vulnerable to the addiction of gambling were put at risk. He declared that by having wide open gambling in the village, "the youth of the town are thus brought into contact with thieves, toughs and blacklegs from all over the country."[26]

Spencer Trask may have been right in regard to the sort of persons that local youth would have come in contact with in the late 1880's and early 1890's. In 1891, two New Hampshire men, claiming to be in town peddling soap, were arrested for assaulting a Mrs. Cook and her daughter choking the elder woman until she was unconscious and chasing her daughter into nearby woods where she was fortunate enough to escape her pursuers. [27]

Summer burglaries were somewhat common with banker George Bliss and his wife having a large collection of diamonds stolen from their Saratoga summer home in 1890. The reward for the return of the diamonds, with no questions asked, reached $5,000.[28] The theft was high profile enough to be referred to in papers across the country as the "Bliss Diamond Robbery."

Swindlers and scammers of all types visited Saratoga Springs at this time with one unlucky summer visitor conned out of $12,000,[29] while pool sellers at the track often short-changed winning ticket holders by small amounts that would go unnoticed by individual winners but would add up very nicely for the pool seller in the aggregate. [30] It was not unheard of for telegraph operators to tap into the Western Union wires carrying race results in an effort to swindle the bookmakers and poolroom operators, an offense for which one man served a sentence of 60 days in the County Jail. [31]

Despite the power held by the gambling fraternity in town and the acquiescence of the local authorities and populace, Trask made a public vow to fight the gamblers at the Spa saying, "I propose to keep hammering away at this until the community awakes to a sense of self-respect and throws off the thrall of the gamblers once and forever." Trask even started an anti-gambling newspaper and was forced to hire several uniformed boys to hawk the paper on street corners when the newsstands refused to sell it. [32]

For his part, Albert Spencer responded to the assault on his business interests by Mr. Trask by comparing the gambling at the track and the Club House to be no greater a danger to the general welfare of society that the unscrupulous stock brokers of the day who operated the so-called bucket shops. Clearly Spencer seemed to indicate that Mr. Trask's stock brokerage office on Broadway was no less a risk to the financial or moral well-being of the community as the elegant Club House he ran. It was a common opinion held by many people at that time.

While acknowledging that his Club House operation was clearly not within legal bounds, Spencer echoed the sentiment of the town when he declared that, "People here had no idea how wicked they were until Mr. Trask found it out and informed them."[33]

After the gambling raids of 1886 and 1889 failed to result in indictments of the accused, smaller scale raids would be conducted in 1890 and 1891. The end result this time, however, would be different, as in 1892 blatant corruption would be exposed by none other than Albert Spencer himself, but the story of the raids comes first.

During the evening of Tuesday, August 26, 1890, Officer Costello, along with Officers Van Rensselear and Galligan, went up to the Chicago Club on Woodlawn Avenue armed with a warrant for George E. Mann, a native of England who had been accused by Rudolphus E. Whittlesey of playing a gambling game in the club about one week earlier. Mann was arrested on the spot and the officers observed a faro game in progress inside. As the officers made entry into the building, the dealer took notice and snatched up the money, fleeing out the back of the place before he could be caught. About fifty other players in the club at the time of the raid also beat a hasty retreat at the appearance of the officers. [34]

Although not fast enough to capture any other gamblers, the officers did manage to secure some of the gambling paraphernalia. A deck of cards, a gaming table, and roughly 1800 chips were seized and brought to the police station. Mr. Mann, whose bail of $500 was paid for by strangers in town, was brought before Police Justice Charles Allen, who features prominently in the next part of this on-going saga. [35]

The whole affair in 1890 seemed more a personal attack against Mr. Mann than any concerted movement to close down the gambling at any of the places then operating. Perhaps the officers, upon making the arrest outside the Chicago Club and observing the activity inside, were deemed as being a little too vigilant in their duties - as no other raids were carried out that summer.

In the summer of 1891, as in three of the previous five summers, an effort was made by anti-gambling forces to bring some justice to the village. Applications for warrants were made by a lawyer named W.J. Miner. He brought the warrants, based upon the affidavit of a man named Riker, to Village Police Justice Charles Allen who refused to sign them.

Justice Allen explained that convictions could not be made upon the uncorroborated testimony of a paid informant (Riker) and since neither the lawyer Miner, nor the informant Riker, could provide any additional evidence, Justice Allen decided that he could not sign the warrants. [36] It is interesting that Justice Allen declined to sign the warrants based upon his opinion that a conviction was not possible based on the uncorroborated testimony of a paid informant when his duty was to decide if there was probable cause to issue the warrants, not if there was enough evidence provided in the application for a warrant to gain a conviction. Justice Allen's legal gymnastics shows the reluctance of local judicial officials to take action against the gamblers even when warranted.

In 1886 and 1889 the grand jury failed to find indictments against the gamblers despite what appeared to be significant evidence secured by authorities. In 1890 police officers were unable, first to catch the gamblers at the Chicago Club as they slithered away, and then to make any additional arrests once gambling paraphernalia was recovered. By the time Justice Allen was declining to sign warrants in 1891, the anti-gambling crusaders would certainly have thought that perhaps all was lost. The following year would prove otherwise and perhaps give them hope that law and order might finally make a stand in Saratoga Springs.

Endnotes

Chapter 6

1 "Y.M.C.A. and the Saratoga Gamblers," The Daily Evening Telegraph, Philadelphia, August 19, 1870.

2 "Saratoga Sinfulness," Evening Journal, August 1886.

3 The Daily Saratogian, Saratoga Springs, Wednesday August 4, 1886.

4 "Law and Order Meeting," The Daily Saratogian, August 4, 1886.

5 "Troublesome Flagg- A Pistol in his Pocket," Saratoga Evening Journal, August 14, 1886.

6 "Police Court Items," The Daily Saratogian, August 20, 1886.

7 "Shorts," The Daily Saratogian, August 6, 1886.

8 Ibid.

9 "Comstock's Raid," The New York Times August 7, 1886.

10 Ibid.

11 "More Gamblers Arrested," The New York Times, August 6, 1886.

12 "Saratoga Sinfulness," The Saratoga Evening Journal, August 12, 1886.

13 "Gamesters in Court," The Saratoga Evening Journal, August 5, 1886.

14 "The Modern Sisyphus," The Auburn Bulletin, August 7, 1886.

15 "The Saratoga Gamblers," The New York Times, August 5, 1886.

16 Ibid.

17 "Gamesters in Court," The Saratoga Evening Journal, August 5, 1886.

18 "Gamesters in Court," The Saratoga Evening Journal, August 5, 1886.

19 "Saratoga Sinfulness," The Saratoga Evening Journal, August 12, 1886.

20 "Court Notes," The Saratoga Evening Journal, October 9, 1886.

21 "Chips were Dusty," The Daily Saratogian, August 29, 1889.

22 Ibid.

23 "Saratoga Gamblers Go Free," Buffalo Sunday Morning News, October 13, 1889.

24 Gardiner, Alexander. *Canfield: The True Story of the Greatest Gambler*. Doubleday, Doran and Co. Garden City, 1939.

25 "The Tiger in His Lair," The New York Press, August 11, 1889.

26 Ibid.

27 "Three Brutes Caged," Elmira Gazette, August 13, 1891.

28 "The Bliss Diamond Robbery," The New York Times, July 21, 1890.

29 "Arrested on the Charge of Swindling," The New York Times, January 30, 1894.

30 "Cash in the French Pools," The New York Times, July 29, 1878.

31 "He Tapped the Telegraph Wires," Buffalo Evening News, May 27, 1892.

32 "Saratoga Full of Gayety," The New York Times, July 28, 1889

33 "The Tiger in his Lair..."

[34] "Caught in the Act," The Daily Saratogian, August 27, 1890.

[35] Ibid.

[36] "Can't Break it Up," Buffalo Courrier, August 16, 1891.

Chapter 7

The Police Commissioners' Scandal of 1892

Perhaps the anti-gambling forces recognized the strength of the gamblers and so decided to re-direct their enforcement efforts toward corrupt local officials. Police Commissioner John Webb, a law and order man, in March of 1892, made a statement in the Saratoga Daily Union that he had evidence to prove fellow Police Commissioners Robert F. Knapp and William H. Gailor had extorted protection money from the operators of several gambling houses and the madams of several houses of prostitution in Saratoga. The allegations were immediately denied by Commissioners Knapp and Gailor and they sued both Commissioner Webb and the Daily Union for libel. They demanded an investigation into the outrageous accusations that Commissioner Webb had publicly made about them. [1]

The allegations were serious. Albert Spencer of the Club House and Kirk "Curt" Gunn of the Chicago Club were supposed to have paid $3000 and $1500 respectively for protection. Madame Hattie Adams and Madame Landry both of New York City and Madame St. Clair of Washington DC were said to have paid hundreds for immunity from arrest for managing their brothels within the village limits.

Madame St. Clair operated on Walworth Street in the summer months using the name of M. E. Sharp. Madame Landry (real name Anna Logue) operated what was called "The East Farm" while Madame Adams maintained the resort known as "The North Farm."[2] The names, not too cleverly, referred to the general orientation of the brothels to the center of the village.

The public allegations would have to be investigated and the burden would be on Commissioner Webb to bring forth his evidence. To the great surprise of many, his informant in the matter was none other than the owner and operator of the famous Saratoga Club House, Albert Spencer. Webb had visited Spencer at the gambler's residence in New York City in the spring of 1892 and it was during this visit that Commissioner Webb learned the following from Mr. Spencer:

In June, 1891, Police Justice Charles Allen paid a visit to Albert Spencer at his summer residence in Saratoga Springs at the corner of Phila and Circular Streets in the village. Justice Allen asked Mr. Spencer to accompany him on a carriage ride, during which the jurist called the gambler's attention to the closing of the gambling dens in the village. Spencer asked, "Well, Mr. Allen, you are Police Justice are you not? You issue warrants for the arrest of parties, do you not?" When Justice Allen responded in the affirmative, Mr. Spencer asked, "Well, I suppose you get your share?" to which Allen replied, "I had ought to get some of it."

A day or two later the village justice called again on Mr. Spencer, and this time, brought him to the Burbridge House at the corner of South Street (now Lincoln Avenue) and Broadway. Justice Allen dropped him off and drove away.

Upon entering the residence, Spencer found Police Commissioners Knapp and Gailor. It was near dark at the time and in the unlit residence the commissioners explained to Spencer that there was much anti-gambling talk in the village during that spring and summer and that they felt it was necessary for them to be compensated for the burden of being on the police board of a village where uninterrupted gambling was permitted. Spencer flatly asked what the price would be and was told by the commissioners that it would be $3,000. For those with a keen memory the amount would have reminded them that $3,000 was the exact same sum that Captain Mahedy tried to extort from Gustave Laridon. After securing the promise of the commissioners that the amount to be paid absolutely protected him from arrest, Spencer asked for a day to consider the offer.

Upon discussing the matter with a prominent local citizen, Spencer decided to pay the money for protection. During the last week of June he withdrew the required amount from his account at the First National Bank and paid Commissioner Knapp the cash directly. The transaction took place in Knapp's office in the Arcade building on Broadway.

Curt Gunn, then managing the game at the Chicago Club on Woodlawn Avenue, visited Spencer after he too was told to close until he paid up. Spencer advised him to pay the bribe and inquired how much the commissioners required of Mr. Gunn to allow the game on Woodlawn Avenue to remain open. Fifteen hundred dollars was the price for Gunn.

Madame Hattie Adams was interviewed by a newspaper reporter in New York City when the story broke and claimed to have never paid any money for protection in Saratoga. She did, however, move her operation just outside of the village limits at the suggestion of Justice Allen in 1891, despite her offer of one thousand dollars to retain her privileges in town. She claimed to be surprised, however, when two other brothels were allowed to operate within the village and was suspicious of the "pull" that the other two seemed to have with local authorities.[3]

Because it was a given that gambling houses were necessary for the economic vitality of the village, and because the open gambling conditions appeared to have widespread public support, protection money was not thought to be as necessary in Saratoga Springs as it was in other localities.

In New York City, police officers blatantly extorted gamblers and prostitutes. Men like "Clubber" Williams and Lieutenant Charles Becker would become notorious grafters, and gambling houses would be required to pay a percentage of their weekly profits for protection.[4] Lt. Becker would eventually become the first American police officer executed for his part in the gangland murder of Herman Rosenthal.

Albert Spencer paid New York City authorities like Lt. Becker, as did Richard Canfield. Certainly, Chicago men operating in Saratoga like Kurt Gunn and Joe Ullman would be familiar with bribe paying practices. But in Saratoga Springs the corruption of public officials was always believed to be less of an issue, with donations to local charities and religious groups being the most popular method for a gambler to remain in the good graces of village officials.

The charges made by Commissioner Webb revealed that perhaps Saratoga was not as immune from the evil of corruption as many believed. The charges would have to be addressed. Village President Deyoe Lohnas (who had appointed both Commissioners Knapp and

Gailor) called for an investigation by the Village Board of Trustees.

Things began to move quickly now for the growing scandal. The public allegations were first printed in the local papers during the first week of March, 1892. The Board of Trustees was scheduled to begin their investigation of the police commissioners on March 16th. [5] According to the Village Charter, members of the police board could only be removed by a vote of the Village Trustees and only for misconduct in office.

Village Attorney John Henning prepared to show that several people paid protection money to Commissioners Knapp and Gailor, including Albert Spencer of the Clubhouse, Richard Croker of New York City who had a place in the Duell building on Broadway, Caleb Mitchel and an associate named "Marshall" who were forced to pay for their Broadway location, McCormack and Walsh of Saratoga and John Mitchell of Albany who conducted a gaming joint on Broadway's west side, and Kirk (Curt) Gunn of Chicago then running the Chicago Club on Woodlawn Avenue. Madams Hattie Adams and Landry were running disreputable houses in the village, and they too were forced to pay for protection. [6]

Despite their initial declarations of innocence, Commissioners Knapp and Gailor thought better of standing trial before the Village Trustees and resigned their positions on the eve of the local investigation. By law, the village trustees only had the right to remove the disgraced commissioners from office; they could do nothing more and the investigation was closed. The resignations of the commissioners were clearly indications that they were afraid to face the accusations drawn up by Village Attorney Henning and, even though the gamblers were thought to be all powerful, District Attorney T. F. Hamilton announced that he would move forward with bringing the matter before the grand jury.

The Grand Jury convened on April 18, 1892, in Ballston Spa and heard testimony from both Albert Spencer and Hattie Adams regarding the protection payments to local officials.[7] Madame Adams, clearly not recalling her public statement that she had never paid for protection at the Spa, testified to her part in the payoffs of the local officials.

In less than two weeks the grand jury would find enough evidence to indict thirteen people on charges related to the scandal. Ex-Commissioners Knapp and Gailor, along with Police Justice Allen, were indicted for bribery and extortion.

Indicted for keeping gambling houses were: Albert Spencer, Charles F. Mahon, Michael McCormack, James Walsh, John Scidmore, Alexander Trimble, John T. Sweeney, and Michael Dwyer. All of the defendants pled not guilty with the gamblers posting $500 bail each and the ex-commissioners and Justice Allen posting $1000 bail per man.[8]

Astonishingly, Caleb Mitchell, indicted with the others for keeping a gambling house on Broadway and paying, like the others, for immunity from arrest, was elected Village President just three weeks before the date of his indictment. [9] Even more incredibly, he would be re-elected in 1894, within two years of the whole fiasco!

The entire scandal and wholesale indictments created considerable excitement around the village in 1892. Widespread press attention was bringing the name of Saratoga Springs much unwanted negative attention. On July 20 the police board, consisting of Commissioners Webb and Wakefield, along with the replacements of the ex-commissioners indicted by the grand jury, H.L. Waterbury and J.A. Smith, ordered all gambling dens to close their doors. [10] It would be a quiet summer that was considerably less profitable for everyone in 1892.

As District Attorney Hamilton prepared for the upcoming trials, he was successful in defeating defense motions for dismissal of the indictments. Most of the gamblers were allowed to plead guilty to minor offenses and pay small fines. Only one gambler declined to plea bargain, Village President Caleb Mitchell.

It was likely that the agreements included provisions that the gamblers would be required to testify truthfully against the public officials involved in the scandal. On May 24, 1892, ex-Commissioners Knapp and Gailor made one final motion before their trials were to begin and when they were unsuccessful, they were allowed to plead guilty to receiving gratuities related to their official duties. They were fined $500 dollars each, which was the stiffest penalty that could be imposed by law. [11]

Caleb Mitchell, gambler and recently elected village president, took his case to trial, his defense being that he did not actually own the building in which the gambling was taking place. He perhaps forgot that the name "Mitchell" was built into the stonework of the three story building. The jury didn't buy the argument and Mitchell was found guilty after the trial concluded on May 25.[12] He escaped any jail time and was fined like the others. There was no political fallout from his arrest and conviction.

Of all those involved in the bribery scandal of 1892, only one defendant managed to escape unscathed. Police Justice Charles Allen managed to avoid trial and conviction although his resignation from office on June 1 seemed an admission of his guilt.[13] It appeared that by resigning from office on the eve of his trial that Justice Allen was about to accept a plea deal as had all the others involved in the scandal. But, one of the material witnesses for the prosecution against Allen was to be ex-Commissioner Knapp. Conveniently, Knapp claimed illness on the day of the trial and the case was postponed until a new jury could be selected, probably in the fall.

As soon as the news broke that Justice Allen was to avoid trial it became apparent that he was unlikely to ever be held legally accountable for his part in the extortion of the Saratoga gamblers. Even newspaper accounts of his resignation speculated that he would never see the defendant's chair in the courtroom.[14]

Popular opinion would prove correct as the next sitting of the County Court in the fall of 1892 failed to see a trial for Justice Allen and the indictment was quietly disposed of.

Commissioner Knapp should not be remembered only as a corrupt ex-police commissioner. A Civil War Veteran who saw action in the battles of Antietam, Fredericksburg, and Vicksburg while serving in Company B. 108th Regiment, New York Volunteers, he was sent into action with only two months of drill and no rifle practice. He came to Saratoga Springs after the war and spent many years in real estate with offices in the Arcade Building and later in City Hall. Knapp lived at 55 Walton Street, was appointed a trustee of the Grant Cottage on Mount McGregor, and was active in veteran's affairs serving as Commander of the local Luther M. Wheeler Post, Grand Army of the Republic, for many terms. Upon his death in 1938, he was the oldest living Civil War Veteran in the city. His obituary, respectfully made no mention of the corruption scandal of 1892.[15]

Charles Allen would go on to practice law in Glens Falls for many years after resigning from his Village Police Justice post. Commissioner Gailor, who ran a livery stable in the village, quietly faded from public notice after resigning from the Police Board.

All of the gamblers indicted during the commissioner scandal of 1892 eventually pled guilty and paid fines to resolve their criminal cases. Most of them were not heard from again and managed to avoid notoriety of the kind they found for themselves in the spring of 1892. Others however, did not.

Albert Spencer, perhaps tiring of the battles with Spencer Trask and the anti-gambling folks, decided that he would be better off selling his interests in the racetrack and Club House. He sold the Club House to Richard Canfield in 1893. Thinking it best to have a gradual ownership transition, Spencer sold a fifty-per cent stake in the Club House to Richard Canfield,[16] who would make the full purchase a year later and open as sole proprietor in 1894. Spencer would divest himself of his interest in the race track as well.

Albert Spencer eventually would become disillusioned with the United States and moved to London, England, in the last years of his life. He died in London on December 3, 1907, and left sizable fortunes to his wife and nephew. In death his distaste for the country that made his fortune possible lived on; his will declared, "When I am dead let my body be burned: the ashes under no circumstances do I want ever taken to America." [17]

Kirk Gunn was a Chicago man who operated gambling joints all over the United States and was quite a card player in his own right. In addition to the Chicago Club in Saratoga, Gunn operated three prominent places in Chicago. [18] He once won $82,500 on a single hand of poker at the Ocean Club at Long Branch, NY,[19] and $15,000 at the Canfield Club House in Saratoga during the summer of 1901.[20] On the other side of the table, Gunn lost $40,000 to a gambler named Robert

Tucker at the Chicago Club in Saratoga in 1894.[21] Gunn was a good business man, however, and he managed to keep enough money to avoid the types of financial problems many professional gamblers suffer through during their lives, retiring from the gambler's life with a respectable nest egg.

Although he was caught up in the 1892 scandal, Saratogian Alexander Trimble managed to avoid too many legal entanglements as he operated his place at number 6 Railroad Place for many years after the scandal. Prior to his 1892 arrest, Trimble found himself on the wrong side of the law only once.

In 1887 he was arrested by Assistant Chief of Police Carroll when a warrant was secured by a local attorney, James Arnold of Nelson Avenue. [22] It seems that an employee of a Broadway grocer had swindled the business out of some cash, around $900 worth, and spent the money at two local gambling dens, Trimble's being one of them.

When the theft was discovered and the money tracked to the gambling halls, the suspected thief claimed that since it was well known that he had an uncontrollable gambling problem, he should not have been allowed to gamble by the owners of the establishments and that they, the gamblers, should make appropriate restitution to the grocery from which the money was originally stolen.

Trimble disagreed, believing that the attempt to regain the money was akin to blackmail and the whole affair wound up before the village justice, who issued warrants for Trimble and his son. They eventually would plead guilty and pay a small fine. However, they never did make restitution for the stolen money that had been gambled away in their establishment.[23]

Charles F. Mahon was keeper of a liquor business at 19 Phila Street when he was arrested in 1892 with the others. He continued in his gambling endeavors for many years after the Commissioner scandal. He was arrested, but never indicted, for keeping a slot machine at his place in 1909.[24] Unfortunately, like many gamblers, he would experience financial difficulties and file for bankruptcy in 1911.[25] His friends would remember him upon his death in 1917 as a lifelong Saratoga Springs resident (born in the village in 1866) and a member of the Ancient Order of Hibernians, Saratoga Court, Foresters of America, and Saratoga Aerie of Eagles.[26]

One other local resident John T. Sweeney, was a well- known Saratogian. He owned the Sweeney Hotel and restaurant at 18 Railroad Place for 37 years.[27] An Excise Commissioner for the village and member of the water board, Sweeney had 8 children, one of whom went on to practice law. He was once robbed of thirty nine dollars in 1876 by John Dunham, who would spend some time in jail for his crime.[28]

John Sweeney would lose his hotel to the great fire that burned the train depot in 1899. This came just after he added twenty new rooms to his hotel. The fire would tragically also claim the life of the night baggage-man, 72 year old James V. Snyder.[29]

Rebuilding his establishment, Sweeney would be arrested in 1904[30] for "maintaining a place for gambling purposes" and was fined for violating the liquor law by keeping his bar room open on Sunday and permitting gambling on his premises in 1908.[31]

The bribery scandal of 1892 was a victory for the anti-gambling forces. At the least, the Grand Jury found indictments against those brazenly flouting the law. At the least, this investigation resulted in guilty pleas and fines for most of those indicted. At the least, public officials profiting from graft were forced to resign their offices. And at the least, law and order were upheld for one spring and summer in 1892. Indeed, for perhaps the first time, a jury in Saratoga County found a gambler guilty at trial. Of course that gambler also happened to be the sitting Village President and that conviction would set up perhaps one of the most tragic events in the history of Saratoga Springs.

Endnotes

Chapter 7

1   "Shared Gambling Profits," The World, March 8, 1892.

2   Ibid.

3   Ibid.

4   Dash, Mike. *Satan's Circus: Murder, Vice, Police Corruption and New York's Trial of the Century.* Crown Publishers, New York, 2007.

5   "The Saratoga Police Scandal," The World, March 16, 1892

6   Ibid.

7   "Testified Against the Officers," Buffalo Evening News, April 21, 1892.

8   "Saratoga Springs Officials Indicted," The Schuylerville Standard, April 27, 1892.

9   "Indicted by the Grand Jury," The Buffalo Evening News, April 22, 1892.

10 "Closing Order," The Brooklyn Daily Eagle, July 20, 1892.

11 "Bribery and Extortion," The Syracuse Courier, May 25, 1892

12 "The Saratoga County Cases," The Buffalo Express, May 26, 1892

13 "A Strange Unpleasantness," The Watertown Times, June 2, 1892

14 "Tacitly Confessed His Guilt," The Daily Leader, June 3, 1892.

15 "Robert F. Knapp Dead; City's Last Civil War Veteran was 97," The Saratogian, December 19, 1938.

16   "An Interest in a Club House," The Troy Daily Times, May 19, 1893.

17   "Didn't want his Ashes Taken to America," The Daily Standard Union, July 22, 1908.

18   "Chicago Gamblers," The Evening Telegram, July 17, 1886.

19   The New York Press, July 19, 1903.

20   "Gamblers Make Great Fortunes," The San Francisco Call, September 1, 1901.

21   "How late Turfman Ran $5 up to $40,000," The New York Herald, March 27, 1910.

22   "The Arnold Gambling Case," The Daily Saratogian, October 1, 1887.

23   Ibid.

24   "Local Gossip," The Daily Saratogian, September 13, 1907.

25   "Saloon Man Bankrupt," The Semi-Weekly Times, September 26, 1911.

26   "Charles F. Mahon is Dead," The Saratogian, March 28, 1917.

27   "Hotelkeeper Dies," Schenectady Gazette, June 10, 1912.

28   "Local Notes," The Daily Saratogian, August 19, 1876.

29   "Saratoga's Depot Burned!" The Schuylerville Standard, February 15, 1899.

30   "Saratoga Gambler's War," Mechanicville Saturday Mercury, September 10, 1904.

31   "Dangerous Business," Stillwater Hudson Valley Times, 1908

Chapter 8

The Suicide of Caleb Mitchell

IF one travels north of Saratoga Springs on State Route 9, about a mile north of the city line, the middle school for the Saratoga Springs City School District is located. In front of the school is an historical marker indicating the spot where an old fashionable resort was kept called "Glen Mitchell."

The Glen Mitchell Trotting Tack was established where now stand soccer and football fields. Trotting races were run for several years with a seating area for 800 spectators built in 1871 for a four day meet. The trotters ran for high purses with many excellent horses present for the meeting held January 17-20.[1] The Fair Grounds of the Saratoga County Agriculture Society were also located at Glen Mitchell with the attendant buildings required for the operation.

The Glen Mitchell hotel was elegant, with 80 feet of road frontage and a plaza of 125 feet for guests to enjoy. Three fresh water trout and bass ponds were nearby, ensuring a supply of fresh fish for the kitchen. Later, a long snow slide was added for the winter entertainment of locals and guests.[2] The owner of Glen Mitchell was Caleb W. "Cale" Mitchell, a nationally known restaurateur and poolroom operator who would three times be elected village president of Saratoga Springs by popular vote.

Born in Troy, NY, in February of 1837, Caleb Mitchell would begin his career as a newsboy but soon became a successful businessman and poolroom operator in New York and Washington, D.C. He and his brother would amass a fortune, mostly from the operation of poolrooms at various locations throughout the country, including one at 402 Broadway in Saratoga Springs.[3]

As the operator of the Glen Mitchell resort and with some natural political skill, Caleb Mitchell would be elected village president in Saratoga Springs for the first time in 1871. He was known throughout the country in gambling circles and locally as somewhat of an entrepreneur with his Glen Mitchell resort, poolroom on Broadway, and grocery of fine imported goods, all located in or near the village.

By the late 1880's Mitchell's poolroom was becoming well known for all the wrong reasons. His place was referred to by a metro New York newspaper as "Caleb Mitchell's Dive" and was described by the author of the article:

"Passing through the bar and behind a screen on the first floor, one entered a long, low-ceilinged wooden addition. Four games of roulette are usually in progress at two tables along the right-hand side. On the left two games of stud poker are dealt and one table is devoted to hazard. The floor is uncarpeted and dirty, the air polluted by the fumes of tobacco, beer and bad whiskey. Chips are as low as five cents. Dealers and croupiers in the shirt sleeves, and with hats tipped over their eyes and cigars stubs in their mouths, yell competitively, "Room for more players here! Chips only a dollar a stack and he may be a-bluffin'!"[4]

Patrons were described as beardless boys, dusty-coated workmen, poor clerks, and down-on-their luck sporting men.

More games could be found upstairs at the Mitchell place. Here, a half-hearted attempt at a more respectable atmosphere was made. The floor was at least carpeted, the tables of a bit better workmanship, the chips a bit more expensive, and the patrons a little less rough around the edges.[5]

Despite the quality of the upstairs accommodations the place was still a stain on the village and ladies, in particular, wanted to avoid Mitchell's place. It was said to be so rough and notorious that they would cross Broadway in order to avoid walking in front of number 402 and exposing themselves to the kind of language being spoken by the ruffians hanging about the front of the place.

The trouble with Caleb Mitchell's place, in the eyes of the local powers-that-be, was that it was not a first-class club house like the Saratoga, Manhattan, or Chicago Club houses, made worse by its location on Broadway. Indeed, the difference between club houses and poolrooms is at the heart of why Saratoga's decision makers and political power brokers historically struggled with enforcement of the gambling laws.

The prevailing feeling was that the club houses were all right, as they attracted a clientele that could afford to lose, but poolrooms attracted the lower socioeconomic classes and led to all sorts of ills that the Saratoga populace did not want to be associated with. Club houses were viewed as harmless resorts that were economically valuable to the community while poolrooms were not viewed in the same positive light and considered as attracting the worst kind of patron. Yet if gambling was all right at Canfield's luxurious casino, why then was it not all right at Caleb Mitchell's joint? After all, illegal is illegal.

In his book, *For Gold and Glory*, Charles B. Parmer provides a description of the poolrooms of the time: "A poolroom was an evil of the day, not to be confused with "parlors" where billiards was played. It was a room connected with the racetracks by telegraph, where one made pools or bets on the races. In the early days of this century many American cities were splotched by them, fungi which operated like speakeasies of a later era. Race track operators fought them, for they enticed patronage from the gate. Now and then one would be raided, but it was a time of laxity in morals among certain municipal officials. Itching palms would be soothed with greenbacks, and the poolrooms opened again."[6]

A dozen poolrooms were scattered around the streets of Saratoga Springs, mostly near the railroad depot, by the turn of the century. Two of them catered exclusively to African-American patrons. One of the two African-American places was located on Federal Street where a player could obtain two chips for five cents and was called a "dirty, vile-smelling hole."[7] Attracted to the poolrooms of Saratoga were gamblers from all levels of the social strata. Men, women, black, white, young and old, they all played at these dives.

In stark contrast to the poolrooms were the club houses. Most notable among these was, of course, the Saratoga Club House built by John Morrissey and dubbed the "Monte Carlo of America" when Richard Canfield operated the place.

The Manhattan Club at 6 Spring Street, across from Congress Hall, was second in luxurious appointments only to Canfield's place. For many years the Manhattan Club played second fiddle to the Saratoga Club House but was nevertheless a spectacle in its own right. Conducted at various time by gamblers "Deacon" James

Wescott, Tom Jolly and James "Big Jim" Kennedy, the club was outfitted with fine tables for roulette and faro. Two small balconies overlooked the gaming floor where the ladies could watch the action from a respectable distance. [8]

The Chicago Club and United States Club were counted among the club houses, although they were smaller and less opulent. They did do a brisk business and, like the Saratoga Club House and Manhattan Club, the patrons were expected to be able to lose the amount wagered without too much difficulty.

Where poolrooms allowed anyone with currency to place a bet, the club houses generally had higher standards. Most of the club houses did not allow women to actually play the games. The poolrooms had no such desire for self-imposed limits like the club houses.

Morrissey, Spencer and Reed, and Richard Canfield all barred local residents from playing as well, to avoid any lingering problems during the off season. The poolroom operators, who fancied themselves as more democratic that their clubhouse competitors, allowed anyone with a dollar to wager it with them.

But perhaps the biggest difference between a poolroom and a club house was the class of the clientele. Whereas Canfield's Club House would host any number of the fabulously wealthy including Vanderbilts and Whitneys, along with judges, politicians, and other respected public officials, Mitchell's poolroom hosted men like Jere Dunn.

Jere Dunn was a notorious Chicago based gambler whose obituary noted four remarkable things about the man The first three were the stories of the three men that he killed during the course of his life. The fourth remarkable event in Jere Dunn's life was the $12,000 he won at a single sitting at Caleb Mitchell's poolroom in Saratoga in 1891.[9] A man like Jere Dunn would not likely have been granted entry to any of the classier places in Saratoga but Mitchell's place welcomed him with open arms.

The election for village president in 1892 provided voters with a choice of Mitchells. Caleb Mitchell ran on the Democratic ticket while a grocer named Albert F. Mitchell was the Republican offering. The election was reported to be one of the most contentious in the village in a long time with the clergymen of the community solidly backing Albert Mitchell. Caleb Mitchell was known as the owner of a gambling den as his two arrests prior to this election proved to any who cared to know. The election campaign was based on the moral question of whether or not gambling should be permitted in Saratoga Springs or not. Despite his undeniable ownership of the gambling dive at 402 Broadway, Caleb Mitchell won the election by 383 votes.[10]

The election of a gambler as village president was just too much. Certainly this would bring unwanted negative attention to the village. While it was one thing to look the other way as visitors chased lady luck in the gaming joints around town, it was quite another to have the village president operating a gaming joint of his own, and on the main street of the town!

Clearly something would need to be done. What was decided upon was one of the most blatantly obvious political power plays that has ever occurred in Saratoga Springs. Caleb Mitchell would be legislated out of office, with the support of the most powerful Republican in Saratoga County, Edgar T. Brackett.

Edgar Truman Brackett was born on July 30, 1853, in Wilton, New York. His family moved to Iowa when he was a child and he remained in that state for fifteen years. He returned to the county of his birth, making the village of Saratoga Springs his home for the remainder of his life. After graduating from Cornell College in Mount Vernon, Iowa, Brackett was admitted to the bar in 1875.

Edgar T. Brackett was the undisputed Republican power in Saratoga County for many years and a large part of the civic, political, and business life in Saratoga Springs. He was elected to the New York State Senate for the district encompassing the village, serving from 1896-1906 and then again in 1908-1912.

While in the State Senate, Brackett would be instrumental in rooting out corruption in the insurance industry and was responsible for the passage of several reform measures that ended the blatant graft and corruption practiced by insurance companies at that time. In 1909 he sponsored the bill that protected the mineral springs of the area from overuse and certain destruction at the hands of private owners. The bill established what is now the Saratoga Spa State Park and is probably the greatest legislative triumph of his career. Saratogians commemorated the man and his work to preserve the springs with a plaque that can be found today at the entrance to Congress Park.

An excellent lawyer who worked both locally and in New York City during his professional career, Brackett was a founding member of the Adirondack Trust Company in 1902 and the MacGregor Country Club in Wilton.

Yet for all of Senator Brackett's civic achievements, he was party to a naked political maneuvering shortly after Caleb Mitchell was elected village president for the third time in 1894. As noted previously, the election of an active poolroom operator as village president was just too much, even for Saratoga.

Brackett and his friends deemed that some control must be placed on the gambling situation lest Saratoga truly lose all semblance of morality, law, and order. What they came up with was a plan to introduce a bill into the state legislature that would require the president of the village of Saratoga Springs to be appointed by the board of trustees and not popularly elected by village voters.

The McNaughton village charter amendment in the State Legislature in 1895 codified in the law that the Saratoga Springs Village President was to be elected by the village board of trustees and not by popular vote of the citizens of the village.[11] The bill applied to Saratoga Springs and no other municipality in the state and the year of 1895 just happened to coincide with the election of Edgar T. Brackett to the State Senate for the district encompassing Saratoga Springs.

The result of the McNaughton legislation requiring the village president to be appointed by the village board of trustees was that a special election was held in the spring during which the Republican candidates for the village board of trustees scored an overwhelming victory. The trustees promptly elected Charles H. Sturges village president. Poor Caleb Mitchell, a Democrat, was thus removed from office one year before the end of his duly elected term was to expire.

President Sturges, being swept to power during the movement to remove the embarrassment of the village president also being the operator of a notorious poolroom, had little choice but to take the position that all gambling was to be halted in the village. He gave direct and positive orders to the police board that all gambling laws were to be enforced vigorously. Police Chief Blodget declared, "There will be no gambling here this summer."[12]

Indeed the summer of 1895 was perhaps the first time in Saratoga Springs history that a concerted effort by local officials to suppress gambling actually worked. Very little open gambling was conducted in 1895 at any of the usual places, including at the famous Saratoga Club House where Richard Canfield was anticipating his second full season as sole proprietor of that particular gold-mine.[13]

A full ban on gambling was probably not what the residents wanted but President Sturges was true to his word. An honorable man, his tenure was marked by increasing pressure to ease the restrictions on gambling and the awkward situation every year of having Caleb Mitchell appointing police commissioners and making other political appointments that his lawyer advised him to continue doing as he filed appeals of his being ousted from power in 1895.

For two years Mitchell would go through the motions of appointing people to various positions and Sturges would then hold the legal meeting and appoint his people to the same jobs. Mitchell decided to bring his case to the courts and he was defeated each time, eventually losing all hope of reinstatement when his appeals were finally exhausted.

This embarrassment of being legislated out of office was probably the beginning of a long descent into depression and perhaps mental illness for Caleb Mitchell. No longer able to operate his poolroom on Broadway and no longer able to hold onto political power, he looked around for those responsible for his downfall and found Senator Brackett and Richard Canfield.

Brackett controlled all political power on the Republican side of the political world in Saratoga County at this time and all important political posts and candidates would be vetted through him before any action was taken. Mitchell blamed Brackett for his troubles and not without just cause.

It seemed that what Brackett did was side with the anti-gambling forces in ousting Mitchell from office when in reality Brackett was working for the one and only Richard Canfield as his attorney! Imagine Caleb Mitchell being raided and legislated out of office through the workings of the very man on the payroll of another gambler- and a sitting State Senator to boot!

What Brackett's position was, and it was shared with many people in Saratoga Springs, was that poolrooms were not good for the village while the club houses were a necessary evil. Club houses were acceptable, so the theory went, on the basis of the self-imposed restrictions they placed on their clientele, the absence of troubling incidents at these places and the ability of those who played there to suffer the negative economic consequences of being a loser without resorting to criminal activity or the public dole.

The poolroom operators insisted that gambling at their places was no different than the gambling happening at the club houses. But their cries went unheeded as the general opinion was that poolrooms were low class and dangerous while the club houses were no detriment to the moral and ethical environment of the town. The character of the poolroom patron was decidedly less polished than the visitors to the club houses. Thefts, fights and arguments were more common than at the club houses and there were no self-imposed restrictions on who could play in the poolroom hells in the village.

Brackett and the powers-that-be favored an open town, so long as the clubs were regulated and the gambling was discreet. Caleb Mitchell's poolroom across from the United States Hotel, on the main thoroughfare of the village, was in no way discreet and in no way regulated by the owner, or the authorities.

In 1895 President Sturges made sure that there was no gambling in the village. For probably the only time in Saratoga Springs history the lid was closed down exceptionally tight. Players couldn't find a game and frequent inspections by police of the popular places kept things that way. Brackett and company had gotten what they wanted with the closing of the poolrooms, particularly on Broadway. But what they did not want was for all gambling to stop. They soon found that there was an economic detriment to the village by closing all gambling joints. So the following year, they allowed a few of the more well-run establishments to open.

The opening of the club houses would become an economic necessity for the village in 1896 as the Saratoga Race Course failed to hold a summer meeting that year. The race track had been sold to Gottfried Walbaum and associates who proceeded to manage the track in such a corrupt and incompetent manner that in 1896 no horsemen would bring their animals to run at the Spa.

No horse racing was not an option for the village! The good old days of the 1870's and early 1880's would have to be brought back and that meant racing during the day and casino gambling at night. Without the racing card during the days, the economic importance of the gambling houses became apparent, essential even, during the summer of 1896. This would of course mean a more permissive atmosphere for the gamblers and Caleb Mitchell had a glimmer of hope that he could re-open. But alas, he was prevented from doing so as his old enemy, Senator Brackett, continued to put the pressure on the poolrooms.

By 1901 Caleb Mitchell had grown to despise Senator Brackett and the high class gamblers who had been muscling him out for the past several years. He was checked at every turn and repeatedly closed down before he even had a chance to operate. The final straw came after Caleb Mitchell forced a warrant to be served on Canfield who was arrested by the authorities that summer.

Of course, just like when Mitchell himself was arrested in 1886 during the Comstock raids, Canfield was able to post bail and continue right on gambling upon his release. The fall Grand Jury failed to indict Canfield, or anyone else for that matter, as could probably have been predicted.

Canfield getting off scot free was not enough for Brackett however and he would use his political position in an effort to ensure that the right gamblers remained protected in the village.

Criminal procedure law allows judges in towns and villages to issue warrants that are legally executable in other towns and villages within the same county. This is a reasonable method of ensuring the law is enforced, as a neighboring judge would be able to stand in for a vacationing (or otherwise absent) judge of another town or village in the same county.

Clearly if a sitting judge in Clifton Park was taken ill for example, a judge from Halfmoon or even Saratoga Springs could sign a warrant if needed. This happened to be the case in Saratoga Springs during the summer of 1901 when Mitchell's allies went looking for a Saratoga Springs village justice and were unable to locate one. They travelled to a town in the southern part of Saratoga County and obtained their warrant for Canfield's place there.

In the mind of Senator Brackett this was simply unacceptable, so he introduced a bill in the State Senate that required any warrant intended to be executed in Saratoga Springs to have the signature of a Saratoga Springs Village Justice. While Brackett claimed that his bill was simply a matter of "home rule" (after all he was merely protecting the rights of village justices) most people viewed his proposal as ensuring that the gamblers were protected as the local justices were all Brackett allies. And wasn't Brackett Canfield's attorney anyway?

Indeed, years later another senator openly accused Senator Brackett of practicing law on behalf of Richard Canfield on the floor of the New York State Senate. [14] Surely this was what Caleb Mitchell must have been thinking in the summer and fall of 1901. He was powerless to stop the Brackett machine. Canfield was about to have a secure monopoly on the gambling trade at Saratoga and Brackett's political force was too great to be overcome. Senator Brackett's power was enough for the measure to pass in the Senate and in early January 1902 the bill was sent to the Assembly for consideration. [15]

In late January, 1902, the "Saratoga Gambler's Bill," as it was called, was to be debated in the New York State Assembly in Albany. On the same morning the bill was to be debated, in Saratoga Springs, Caleb Mitchell awoke for the last time in his life.

Ex-VillagePresident Mitchell had decided that something needed to be done. It was generally known around town that he had threatened to get even with Senator Brackett for all of the trouble the politician had caused him. Most people believed that his threats were of a political nature. He had been trying repeatedly since being removed from office to re-open a gambling joint but was checked on every move he made. People had noticed that he was declining in his mental faculties and physical appearance.

On the morning of January 28, 1902, between seven and eight o'clock, Caleb Mitchell walked to Towne's hardware store on Broadway and met with clerk George H. Wentworth. He explained to the clerk that he was being kept awake at night by cats outside his window and to put a stop to the misery of the wailing felines he would like to purchase a handgun. A Johnson Arms, .32 caliber hammerless self-cocking revolver with a chamber capacity of five bullets was finally decided upon. Mitchell asked Wentworth if he would load the gun for him. The clerk declined but did sell Mitchell a box of bullets. The troubled man loaded the revolver's cylinder fully, leaving the remainder of the box of bullets on the counter after completing his purchase.

As Caleb Mitchell made his way from the hardware store to the town hall, he spoke with several people, some of whom realized later that his physical appearance had deteriorated considerably in recent days. His destination was Senator Brackett's office in town hall. He was spotted by a janitor inside the building, pacing back and forth in front of the senator's office with his hands shoved in his pockets.

At just about 8:00 AM a shot rang out from inside town hall. One of Brackett's young clerks, James Leary, opened the office door to find Caleb Mitchell's lifeless body slumped on the floor, a single, fatal, self-inflicted gunshot wound to his right temple. People nearby rushed to the scene, many unable to recognize the formerly well-known and well-liked village president and poolroom operator due to his disheveled appearance and the massive trauma and blood now covering poor Caleb Mitchell's face.

Police would arrive in short order and soon Coroner McCarty was called to remove the body. He would recover a diamond scarf pin, a pair of gold eyeglasses, and $1.04 from the body.

Speculation was rampant that Senator Brackett was the intended target of Caleb Mitchell's bullet. Brackett himself would later say, "Mitchell had never threatened me personally but I understand he had said that he would someday shoot me or kill himself."[16]

Mitchell never did get the chance to confront Brackett over his long simmering complaints. Brackett had left his office just a few minutes before Mitchell arrived at his office door to catch the 8:10 train for Albany where his Saratoga gambler's protection bill was scheduled to be debated on the Assembly floor that morning.

When word of Mitchell's suicide reached the assembly, it seemed that the mood of the gathered politicians changed. Although the bill passed without controversy in Senator Brackett's home chamber, the suicide of Caleb Mitchell drew attention to the bill in the Assembly. Many politicians, with public scrutiny now on the bill, hesitated to simply go through the motions on this bill being sold by Brackett and friends as a mere matter of home rule. The issue of home rule each politician could understand. But wasn't it true that this bill only applied to the village of Saratoga Springs, not all the other villages, towns, and cities of the state? Wasn't Brackett in the employ of the greatest gambler in the world and wouldn't passage of the law create a virtual monopoly for that gambler on the riches to be had in the notorious gambling town of Saratoga Springs? Why would someone commit suicide over something as benign as a police justice bill now before the State Assembly? All of these questions must have been on the minds of the members of the Assembly when they failed to pass the bill and place the gamblers of Saratoga, for all practical purposes, beyond the reach of the law. [17]

Caleb Mitchell's descent into despair that eventually led him to take his own life, logically followed as he lost power and was thwarted in every attempt to regain it. Once a powerful and well-liked politician, he was legislated out of office after being elected by a majority of Saratoga citizens. A once successful business man, owning a fashionable resort on the outskirts of town, a store of fine imports, and his own poolroom on Broadway, he was all but destitute in the winter of 1902 after years of battling with the Brackett forces. Unable to defeat Canfield on the legal battleground, and unable to best Bracket on the political battleground, Mitchell fell victim to the darkest forces inside of himself.

Sadly, Mitchell's family was not inexperienced with the issue of suicide. His mother killed herself in Troy about 40 years before Caleb's death. His brother William hung himself in a bar he owned on Spring Street in New York City, and another brother George also killed himself at Glen Mitchell, reportedly over money troubles. [18]

The tragic suicide of Caleb Mitchell stands in stark contrast to the Saratoga experience of the "Prince of the Gamblers," Richard Canfield.

Endnotes

Chapter 8

1   The New York Sun, January 14, 1871.

2   "Glen Mitchell and the New Fair Grounds," The Daily Saratogian, May 18, 1871.

3   "Caleb W. Mitchell A Suicide," The New York Times, January 30, 1902.

4   Pronger, Paul. "The Tiger in His Lair," The Press, New York, August 11, 1889.

5   Ibid.

6   Parmer, Charles B. *For Gold and Glory*. Carrick and Evans, Inc. New York, 1939.

7   Ibid.

8   "How Fortunes are Won and Lost at Saratoga, Gambler's Paradise," The World, August 28, 1901.

9   "The Strange Adventures of Jere Dunn, Picturesque American," The Morning Telegraph, March 4, 1906.

10   "The Democrats Won," The Johnstown Daily Republican, March 30, 1892.

11   "Local Lines," Mechanicville Saturday Mercury, April 11, 1896.

12   The Troy Daily Times, May 7, 1895.

13   Waller. *Saga of an Imperious Era*.

14   "Savage Attack Made on Senator Raines," Geneva Daily Times, March 23, 1904.

15   "Gambler's Bill for Saratoga," The New York Times, January 23, 1902.

16   The Daily Saratogian. January 29, 1902.

17   "Brackett Saratoga Bill," The Sun, October 27, 1902.

18   "Caleb W. Mitchell a Suicide," The New York
      Times, January 30, 1902.

Chapter 9

Richard Canfield:
The Prince of the Gamblers

Perhaps no single gambler had a greater impact, or had a more successful career at Saratoga, than Richard Canfield.[1] Although John Morrissey built the red brick building that still stands in Congress Park, it is widely known today as the Canfield Casino. It was during Canfield's ownership that the Club House enjoyed its highest play, wealthiest clientele, and greatest reputation. Indeed it was during Canfield's reign that

Saratoga would solidify an international reputation and come to be known as the "American Monte Carlo."

Born on June 17, 1855, in New Bedford, Massachusetts, Richard Canfield was the fifth child born to William and Julia Canfield. The Canfield family would struggle somewhat financially due to injuries William suffered in his twenties working as a sailor on a whaling ship.

The Canfields would lose two daughters in infancy and Richard's older brother Charles would be lost at sea while working on a whaling boat. William and his wife would move about the New Bedford and Boston areas for several years, finding employment in printing and publishing, keeping a saloon, and opening a general store. After the patriarch of the family died when Richard was just ten years old, his mother brought Richard and his younger brother to her hometown of Providence, Rhode Island, where she took on boarders to earn money.

When he was thirteen years old, Richard was sent to his grandmother's farm back near New Bedford. His attempts to find a job in New Bedford proved fruitless. Farm work and employment on a whaling ship were both available to young Canfield but he decided that working on a farm was too hard, and whaling ships held the memories of a father's crippling injury and a brother's death at sea. Neither career seemed a particularly attractive option for young Richard Canfield.

Realizing that employment of the sort he sought (office work perhaps) would require an education,

Richard returned to grammar school and finally graduated in 1869. Employment soon followed as a clerk in a shipping firm. Unfortunately, he did not last long in the corporate world of 1870 Boston. He quarreled with his boss and soon found himself back in Providence at age 15 without a job and not too motivated to get one.

No job did not necessarily mean no money for teenage Richard Canfield. By the time he was eighteen, he had established himself in a small stakes poker game in Providence. The local policeman, whose beat covered Canfield's place, soon discovered the game and warned Canfield and his partner that they would have to stop.

He would spend the next couple of years refining his gambling skills on the customer side of the table, learning all he could about the sporting life. It was during this time in his life that Canfield would meet his best friend, who would manage his various gambling houses for his entire career, David Bucklin.

When Canfield was twenty-one years old he won a large sum of money gambling. He travelled to Europe and spent all of his winnings gambling, sightseeing, and studying the great gambling resorts of the continent. He returned to the United States six months later, penniless.

A relative of his mother managed the Union Square Hotel in New York City and offered to take on Canfield as a night clerk. Richard Canfield now had his first legitimate employment since he was 15 years old and he made the most of the encounters he would have with the young moneyed set returning to their hotel rooms late at night. His easy going manner allowed Canfield to converse with anyone, and he made fast friends with the local gamblers who were soon inviting him on their late night adventures. He could not keep up with his newfound companions on his night clerk salary and smart as he was, Canfield realized that fortune lay on the other side of the gaming table anyway.

Talented and full of potential, Canfield also caught the eye of his employer. Soon he was managing summer resorts on the Jersey Shore and it was assumed that he would make a terrific hotel owner or perhaps a lawyer. But the lure of the gambling tables was too strong, and the riches to be had were too attractive, for Canfield to resist.

By the early 1880's Canfield had returned to New England, married, and established his own gambling place in Pawtucket, Rhode Island. His Pawtucket poker room only ever made enough money to support himself and his family in Providence. There, Canfield established his own, more up-scale operation with a partner, Thomas Sprague.

The Providence operation was running well and, unlike police protection in New York City, where a gambler who paid the customary graft could operate freely without interference from the police, the most that Providence law men could offer was a promise that they would not conduct a raid themselves without first giving warning. This arrangement worked well enough for Canfield until April 26, 1884, when he and

Sprague, along with a clerk named Clark, were all arrested in a surprise raid. It was reported that on this night, Canfield was the look out as Sprague dealt the cards.

The raid itself was unusual as the three men arrested at the Canfield-Sprague house were three of only five gambling arrests made in Providence in the year of 1884. The following year, the Providence Police were unable to ferret out any gamblers in their fine city.

In addition, Canfield and Sprague were sentenced on July 17, 1885, to the surprisingly stiff sentence of six months in jail on the charge of being a common gambler. Whispers around Providence society at the time were that the raid and sentence were the result of an indiscretion on Canfield's part with the wife of a prominent local businessman.

The severity of the sentence was a blessing in disguise; however, as it was during his time in the Providence County Jail in Cranston, RI, that Canfield claimed to develop his lifelong habit of voraciously reading books on every topic that he could get his hands on. Art, history, and fiction were all topics that Canfield read in the county lock-up, thus enabling him to be conversant on any number of topics that his future high class guests cared to discuss. He later claimed his time in jail was the happiest time of his life, devoted to reading and free of the troubles and worry of running an illegal gambling enterprise.

Upon his release from jail in 1886, Canfield ventured back to New York City with Sprague tagging along. His vision of opening his own gambling place was not realized for almost a year.

He originally tried to get hired on as a dealer at Dave Johnson's place at 818 Broadway, which was commonly known simply (although not too creatively) as "818." Dave Johnson was a major gambling figure in the middle 1880's with places in a number of locations on the east coast, including New York City and Saratoga Springs.

While seeking employment at one of the well-known gambling places, Canfield began to meet many of the high-end gamblers around the city, including "Honest John" Kelly and "Dink" Daly, along with Albert Spencer and Charles Reed. These connections would later pay dividends for Canfield, but he would be required to start small. He took a partner named William Glover and established a small stakes poker room on Broadway between 18th and 19th Streets.

Within a year Canfield borrowed money from relatives and cash from a mortgage taken on Sprague's Providence home to establish the Madison Square Club at 22 West 26th Street near the St. James Hotel. His partner in the venture was David Duff, who was a dealer in one of Charles Reed's gambling houses. In order to open a gambling club in New York City at that time, a $200 down payment was required to be made to the local police precinct. The sum was considered a part of doing business and Canfield paid without a second thought.

Success came quickly to Canfield and Duff, along with the unfortunate consequence of increasing protection payments being required by New York City police officials. At first the payments were doubled and then, as with all the most successful gambling joints, payoffs would eventually become a percentage of the house take.

Another side effect of the early success was that Duff was unable to handle it. He became a heavy drinker and a heavy gambler. At first Canfield could stomach paying off Duff's gambling debts with house profits but eventually Canfield's patience wore thin and he muscled Duff out of the partnership.

The whole unpleasant affair was made public, being chronicled in the metro newspapers at the time (1890). Duff's behavior was having a negative effect on the reputation of the place and draining profits, something Canfield simply would not stand for.

With Duff out of the way, Canfield's gambling business would soon make him a millionaire. His connections included two prominent gamblers of the era, Albert Spencer and Charles Reed, who also happened to be the successors to Morrissey's Saratoga Club House. Canfield soon was interested in expanding to the summer resort, and by 1893, had taken a half-interest in the Saratoga Club from Albert Spencer who had bought out his partner Reed back in 1887.[2]

Canfield and Spencer agreed on the fifty-fifty arrangement for the summer of 1893, believing that a gradual change of ownership would be better for the psyche of the regular customers. In 1894 the sale of the Saratoga Club was complete and Canfield became sole owner of the property for $250,000. [3]

Canfield's Saratoga business model was really quite simple. It was all about customer service. He believed that wealthy patrons would not hesitate to be seen in a club that provided excellent food and drink at expensive prices. The atmosphere had to be elegant, the grounds well-manicured, and the conversation delightful. This would draw the wealthiest patrons to the club. The brilliance of Canfield's business model led to his staggering success as a gambler and he became unique in the sense that he was able to stand alone and did not require partners to operate his multiple gambling houses, unlike almost all other gamblers of the day. [4]

His love of art, culture, and his never-ending reading would take care of the conversation. Canfield would spare no expense in improving the grounds and the interior accoutrements of the house. No expense was too high for the kitchen and dining room, which would eventually become an attraction in its own right.

Canfield's instincts in creating the right conditions to attract wealthy patrons would be displayed by his purchase of nearby land. For many years a group of Native Americans would travel down from Canada in the summer and establish a camp on property adjoining the Saratoga Club House. The location is now part of Congress Park adjacent to Circular Street.

The encampment was a source of distress for local townspeople who considered the inhabitants with their trinkets for sale, shooting exhibitions, and a perceived tendency to drink too much, as a blight upon the village. Canfield purchased the property, evicted the Native Americans and established his famous Italian Gardens on the spot, thus improving the property a great deal in the eyes of local residents and his wealthy visitors.

He would import a famous French chef, Jean Columbin, to run the kitchen in the summer for the handsome salary of $5000.[5] The lavish dining room for his wealthy patrons lost him vast sums of money every summer. The dining room alone cost Canfield $70,000 in just the first year of its existence, but the gaming profit was so great that he was able to make back almost his entire purchase price of $250,000 in his first Saratoga summer.[6]

The attraction of the dining room, as a central meeting place for high society in Saratoga, brought in enough high rollers that the cost of the dining room was worth it as they would inevitably be attracted to the roulette tables and faro layouts calling to them between the floor-to-ceiling doors that separated the gaming and dining rooms.

A humorous story about Canfield's French chef is recounted in George Waller's excellent Saratoga history resource, *Saga of an Imperious Era*. It seems that as an added attraction to the grounds, Canfield had installed a trout pond near the building and one of the highlights of a visit to Canfield's would be that patrons could choose which trout they wanted for dinner from the pond. Attendants would snatch the desired fish and walk it back to the kitchen where Columbin, who found the whole affair completely ridiculous, would toss the chosen fish into a pipe that ran from the kitchen back to the pond and prepare a portion of pre-selected trout that was more appropriate to his culinary talents. The diner remained unaware of the reprieve granted to the poor fish.

A visit to Canfield's was an adventure in itself. High society enjoyed the elegance, even without the gambling. The entire experience was of the highest quality, with Canfield holding court nightly. Even the ladies, who were prohibited from playing the actual games of chance, enjoyed the entertainment and there certainly was no prohibition against their suggesting a particular wager for a husband or suitor and then enjoying the outcome as if they had actually placed the bet themselves.

But Canfield was a businessman. The gambler's money was what he was after. He recognized that wealthy patrons required certain courtesies. He was one of the few gamblers who would allow extensive credit to those who could afford it. A man named John B. Northrop was employed by Canfield each summer at the Club House to determine which players were extended credit and how much each should be allowed when their cash ran out. His judgement was never questioned and his word was final.

Canfield believed that, like him, the extremely wealthy did not care to carry large amounts of money on their person as it ruined the tailoring of their evening attire.[7] Checks would leave a paper trail and a good gambling house was always ready to pay in cash to a lucky winner, if only to ensure its reputation. Canfield's reputation was that he would immediately pay any sum in cash, in full, if a patron was able to beat the house on any particular night and he therefore kept one million dollars in cash on the premises in a safe with three doors and five combinations.[8]

Richard Canfield's fortune, obtained from his various gambling operations, was once estimated at be $4.9 million dollars, of which $2.5 million was secured through his Saratoga operation. The profit made by Canfield at Saratoga is astonishing when it is considered that the longest he ever stayed open in Saratoga Springs was two months; usually he was only open for four weeks. And during three of his thirteen summers, the Saratoga authorities had shut down gambling altogether. His New York City operations ran year round and were still unable to account for more of the Canfield gambling fortune than Saratoga.[9]

Canfield got off to a rocky start in Saratoga. His first full year, 1894, was a success but the following year the pro-gambling mayor, Caleb Mitchell, was ousted as village president and new president Charles Sturges's closing order was faithfully enforced. No open gambling was conducted in the village during 1895.

The following year, the reformers were pushed back a bit and Canfield was allowed to open along with a few other clubs, notably the Manhattan and Chicago Clubs on Phila Street and Woodlawn Avenue, respectively. The pro-gambling element was no doubt helped by the closing of the racetrack that had been so poorly run by Gottfried Walbaum that honest trainers and owners refused to bring their stock to Saratoga.

Without the racetrack to bring in the gambling dollars, concessions were made to the off-track gambling establishments and President Sturges, despite encouragement from many people around the country, was forced to accept limited off-track gambling for the economic vitality of the village.

In the late 1890's Caleb Mitchell had returned to the gambling fraternity along with Dan Stuart, a Texas gambler who fancied himself a rival to Canfield. They established a poolroom across the street from the entrance to the racetrack that attracted some of the most undesirable clientele.

The Mitchell-Stuart poolroom was not a concern to Canfield as the patrons of the Mitchell-Stuart place were unlikely to make it through the front doors of the magnificent Club House. The fact that the poolroom was located just outside the gates of the famous race course apparently did not bother Walbaum too much either, as there is no record of any attempt to stop the operation until William C. Whitney took ownership of the track in 1901.

Where Walbaum ran the track poorly, William C. Whitney was much more concerned about the Sport of Kings as an institution. His vision was to bring elegance and class back to the track. He certainly was not about to tolerate a low-class poolroom outside the gates of the famous racetrack. Whitney demanded that the local police shut down the poolroom and, knowing how important Whitney was to the village, the local authorities obliged and closed the Mitchell-Stuart place before the summer season had a chance to get started.

This infuriated both Dan Stuart and Caleb Mitchell. Mitchell knew well the futility of fighting the powerful Brackett-Canfield partnership and his mental deterioration resulting in his suicide the following winter is told previously in this book. Dan Stuart, however, was a millionaire turf man and fight promoter from Texas who was probably not used to being denied the opportunities he sought.

Stuart backed a plan, in partnership with Mitchell and the Mayer brothers out of New York City, to strike back at Canfield and his protector, Brackett. Believing that their rights to operate a gambling joint were at least as worthy of respect as Canfield's, Stuart paid the prominent New York City law firm of Howe and Hummell to assist him in his battle with Canfield.

A public war of words developed between Stuart and Canfield, with Canfield enjoying the public support of native Saratogians. He threatened to throw

Dan Stuart into Saratoga Lake if Stuart interfered with the operations of his elegant Club House. [10]   Stuart countered that he planned to fight Canfield to the death in the name of defeating the hypocrisy of Saratoga authorities who dared to close down other gamblers while Canfield remained unmolested. [11]

Even Senator Brackett commented publicly that neither he nor the citizens of the village appreciated the "…spectacle of a New York lawyer coming up here to teach us our duty in either law or morals…"[12]

Stuart then publicly accused Brackett and the Republican State Committeeman from Saratoga, William Worden, of accepting graft from the gamblers. [13]

The New York lawyer referred to by Brackett was Benjamin Steinhardt who was employed by the Stuart syndicate through the Howe and Hummell firm. Steinhardt had the unenviable job of gathering evidence and presenting warrant applications to local authorities in an effort to close down Canfield's place. Steinhardt turned to a private detective agency out of New York City for assistance and one of their top detectives, John M. Boland, was assigned to the case.

John M. Boland was the son of John Boland who was a partner in the Mooney and Boland detective agency in New York City, and in 1901 was an experienced detective having worked on a number of high profile cases in the 1890's, many of them expensive divorce cases in the metro New York area.

Unfortunately, after Boland's appearance in Saratoga Springs during the summer of 1901, his reputation gradually declined when he was indicted for perjury in a divorce case, skipped bail, and disappeared. [14] He was later found beaten and near death in a café in Seattle. He had apparently attempted to avoid responsibility for the indictment by taking refuge in that northwestern city. [15]

Finally, toward the end of his career, Boland was indicted in a murder-for-hire plot in Maryland where he and two other private detectives agreed to kill the husband of a bank secretary along with the wife of the bank's president so that the two remaining spouses could be together. [16]

But Boland's troubles would all be in the future. In 1901, he investigated Canfield's famous Club House and gave the information that Steinhardt would use to obtain warrants against Canfield.

Steinhardt wasted no time in drawing up the search and arrest warrants for Richard Canfield and his Club House. He brought the papers to Village Justice Charles Andrus who signed the warrants, even though he typically did not handle criminal matters. The warrants that Justice Andrus signed charged Richard Canfield with being a common gambler and directed the sheriff to seize two faro tables and seven roulette wheels. [17]

Steinhardt and his associates believed, correctly, that they would get no cooperation from village officials and brought the warrant to Ballston Spa, looking for Sheriff Carpenter. When they arrived at the Sheriff's office, they found only the Under Sheriff. It quickly became apparent that the Under Sheriff was none-too-pleased at being handed warrants for Richard Canfield and his place, but after a short delay, he handed the paperwork to the only deputy sheriff in the office.

Upon examining the warrants, the deputy remembered that he had recently been kicked by a horse and expressed the belief that his health would most certainly not endure the trip to Saratoga Springs by either train or carriage.[18] Efforts to find other deputies in the immediate area were not successful until Deputy Sheriff Freyer finally arrived after a long delay.

Deputy Freyer called Sheriff Carpenter, who soon arrived and advised Steinhardt that he would obey the law, but would do so on his own time. He told Steinhardt that he would execute the warrants, but indicated that he would do so on Monday, apparently desiring to hold the matter off as it was Saturday evening and Canfield's was closed on Sundays.

Steinhardt was becoming understandably furious. He offered to bring the Sheriff to Canfield's place and show him the gambling that was going on right then and there. Sheriff Carpenter casually declined.[19]

While Steinhardt was unsuccessfully endeavoring to get Sheriff Carpenter to execute his warrants, Senator Brackett heard what had happened and hastened to Justice Andrus's office. Brackett was angry. Did Andrus sign warrants against Richard Canfield?

The justice answered that he had, explaining that he felt obligated to do his duty and sign warrants presented to him in the proper legal manner. When Brackett learned that Justice Andrus could not stop the execution of the warrants, he became enraged and stormed out of the office. According to the August 4, 1901, edition of the New York Herald, Brackett threatened Andrus on his way out of the building, telling him, in reference to the warrant, "you had no business to issue it, and you'll be sorry for it!"

Upon leaving, Brackett was met in front of Andrus' office by Deputy Freyer with warrant in hand. The two discussed the matter and Freyer later told an associate of Steinhardt's that Brackett had told him to do nothing with the warrant until Sheriff Carpenter had had time to consult with his attorney on the matter. [20] And that is just what Deputy Freyer did - nothing.

With a valid warrant, but a Sheriff unwilling to execute it, Steinhardt would have to apply for another warrant addressed to a law enforcement officer not associated with the Sheriff's Office. Unable to locate a justice in Saratoga Springs, Andrus was not available this time; he found it necessary to travel all the way to Mechanicville in order to find a judge willing to sign a warrant against Richard Canfield. That judge was Mechanicville Justice of the Peace Robert Baxter [21] and the warrant he signed was placed in the hands of a Stillwater Town Constable named John Welsh,[22] not a Sheriff's Deputy or a Saratoga Springs Village Policeman.

Of the five warrants that Steinhardt was able to secure against Canfield during the summer of 1901, the warrant signed by Justice Baxter was the only warrant served on Canfield. And that was probably only because Justice Baxter accompanied Constable Welsh to the Club House to ensure the warrant was executed properly.[23] The warrants presented to Sheriff Carpenter were, simply, never executed. The roulette wheels and faro tables described in the warrants went untouched by authorities.

Upon arrival at the Club House, Constable Welsh was met by the always courteous Richard Canfield himself. Canfield assured the Constable that he would appear voluntarily before the court with his attorney Willard J. Miner, a prominent Saratoga Springs area lawyer to answer the charges contained in the warrant. There would be no need, the constable was assured, to use the handcuffs or accompany Mr. Canfield to the court.

Canfield and his attorney promptly presented themselves to the court that very night and, after a brief hearing, Canfield was released into the custody of his attorney until Monday morning when he was scheduled to appear before Village Justice Andrus.

The issuing of the warrants, the Sheriff's refusal to execute them, the constable arriving at the Club House, and Canfield's arrest and appearance before the judge all occurred on Saturday evening August 3, 1901. That very evening a reporter for the New York Herald declared that the largest crowd of the season played right on through Canfield's arrest. His arrest was of such little concern that the players hardly noticed and his friends that were aware of what was happening dropped into Canfield's private office on the second floor to offer their condolences for the situation.

On Monday morning, Canfield appeared before Justice Andrus, who refused to throw out the warrants and ordered Canfield's case to be held for the fall term of the Grand Jury. His bail was set at $1,000 which was promptly secured by two of Canfield's associates. During the proceedings Andrus made it clear that he would issue no more warrants for Canfield as he believed the warrants thus far executed would settle all of the legal questions at issue and that he had no intention of allowing the village court to be used by the Mitchell-Stuart cabal for partisan purposes. [24]

Steinhardt and company realized that they would get no further in attacking the Canfield place and they quickly tried another tactic. First, they brought forward a warrant to Village Police Justice Delaney for the arrest of Police Commissioner Carleton H. Lewis for Neglect of Duty under section 344 the Penal Law. [25] Steinhardt's claim was that he had offered to bring Commissioner Lewis to Canfield's in order to show him the wide-open gambling that was happening there but that Commissioner Lewis refused to go with him. Justice Delaney refused to sign the warrant until the district attorney had a chance to review it. This, of course, threw Steinhardt into a rage. [26]

Second, the anti-Canfield coalition brought charges against Sheriff Carpenter for neglect of duty to Governor Benjamin O'Dell. A Steinhardt associate, Edwin Weed, a former Saratogian who assisted with the agitation in the summer of 1901 sent a letter to the governor asking for an investigation of the Sheriff and his removal from office. His charges were simple and they were published in the March 31, 1902 edition of the New York Sun:

"To Gov. Benjamin Odell, Governor of New York:

I hereby charge against Sheriff Carpenter of Saratoga County, New York, neglect of duty, that on the 3rd day of August, 1901, he refused to serve a warrant issued by Justice Andruss (sic) of Saratoga Springs for the arrest of Richard Canfield, proprietor of a gambling resort in Saratoga County, known as the Saratoga Club, and with permitting gambling to be continued in Saratoga County in open violation of the law thereafter. I am prepared to prove the charges I make. Yours respectfully,

Edwin A. Weed. 65 East 123rd Street, New York City."

Although his arrest was a minor inconvenience, and he certainly did not go seeking out Dan Stuart in order the throw him into the lake as he had threatened, Canfield felt that he needed to at least send a message to his enemies that he would not sit idly by while attempts were made to shut down his operation.

Dan Stuart and Caleb Mitchell had been shut down by village authorities at the suggestion of William C. Whitney. The other Club House operators were not involved with Stuart and Mitchell and so they were not counted as enemies.

But someone had to suffer retaliation and Canfield decided on Mechanicville Justice of the Peace Baxter. After Baxter signed the warrant against Canfield and went the extra step of accompanying the constable to the Club House, Canfield sent his lawyers to the task of getting even with the jurist. Canfield's lawyers drew up an arrest warrant for Justice Baxter for malicious trespass. They accused Baxter of knowingly issuing a defective warrant and making entry into private property based on that warrant.

Justice Delaney was the lucky magistrate to hear the case against Baxter. He heard from Canfield's lawyers as well as Canfield manager Patrick MacDonald. Charges and countercharges were made and the evidence taken was of great interest to locals and gamblers alike. In the end, Justice Delaney reserved his decision on the matter, leaving everyone wondering what the outcome of all this legal wrangling would be.

Perhaps Justice Delaney recognized that the whole affair was destined to come to nothing. Time and again reform movements swept through Saratoga Springs and time and again it all amounted to little more than entertainment for the masses and something to write about for the journalists.

The squabbling during the summer of 1901 would prove to be no different. Canfield's case against Baxter was forgotten. The Stuart-Mitchell offensive died a slow death when the grand jury failed to indict Canfield that fall. Mitchell eventually killed himself during the following winter and Stuart moved on to other enterprises. All in all, the events of the summer amounted to very little. What was not little, however, were the profits that Richard Canfield pulled out of Saratoga Springs that summer of his arrest, reportedly $500,000.[27]

The following summer may have been the best on record for the venerable Club House and with a profit $100,000 more than the previous summer, Canfield set about to improve his Saratoga holding. He began construction on what would become the famous restaurant adjacent to the rear of the old brick building that Morrissey had built. He also purchased a plot of unimproved land adjacent to his Club House property that ran along Circular and Spring Streets. On this property, known as the Kilmer Estate, an annual gathering of Native Americans was located.

Every summer Native Americans from Canada came to the Kilmer property to sell trinkets and offer small carnival type games to the tourists at the Spa. They built small temporary huts and tents in which they lived and peddled what items they had to offer. The gathering was not to the liking of the locals who considered the yearly invaders somewhat of a black spot on the world famous resort. Too many of them caused too much trouble after drinking too much liquor, according to the locals. For many years the owners of the Kilmer estate had expressed little interest in either removing the encampment or selling the property. It was a relief to the locals when Canfield finally prevailed upon the holders of the Kilmer property to sell it to him during the winter of 1902.[28]

The improvements to the property at first glance might have seemed a simple business decision designed to enhance the stature of the Club House. However, the truth was a little more complex and in reality the improvements were Canfield's attempt to secure his position in Saratoga as the winds of change and reform began to threaten his valuable holdings in New York City.

At this time the District Attorney in New York City was William Travers Jerome. He was an anti-gambling crusader who recognized that the tools available to honest law enforcement were simply not enough to combat the evil of the gambling dens. To boil it down, Jerome recognized that it was just too difficult, time consuming, and costly for police to introduce an operative into the prestigious gambling houses in order to obtain evidence. Most of the high end gambling operators did not allow unknown persons to play anyway and police were more likely to take payoffs from the gamblers than they were to make a legitimate investigation of their own. With accounts of massive winning and losing in the gambling establishments throughout the country reported on in the newspapers, it was clear that cooperation from someone on the inside was necessary.

Cooperators, however, were few and far between since patrons of the gambling establishments were breaking the law themselves. Should a player testify that they lost (or won) money while gambling, they could just as easily be arrested for violating the gambling laws as the manager of the house. If there was a way to compel testimony from players against the owners of the gambling houses, real reform could take place.

There was no way for this to happen as all Americans have a right, protected by the Fifth Amendment of the United States Constitution, against self-incrimination. Jerome and his allies sought a remedy for this situation and they introduced a bill in the New York Legislature called the "Dowling Bill" that would allow District Attorneys to subpoena players of gambling establishments into secret grand jury proceedings in order to give evidence in gambling cases. Persons required to appear before the grand jury under the Dowling proposal would be protected from arrest and prosecution for their part of the gambling exchange provided that they told the truth.

The Dowling Bill essentially gave District Attorneys the power to compel testimony from players, even if they did not want to. If they refused to attend the grand jury proceedings or answer any of the District Attorney's questions, they could be arrested for contempt of court or obstruction of justice. If they gave testimony that was false, they could be arrested for perjury.

That the Dowling bill was controversial was an understatement. The bitter fight over the bill on the floor of the Senate was among the most dramatic scenes that could be conceived of in that stately body. Brackett was vigorously opposed to the bill and District Attorney

Jerome fanned the flames of the obvious by alleging that Brackett was practicing law on the floor of the legislature for the benefit of his client, Richard Canfield. Even more dramatically, he reminded the public that Brackett had been advocating for the so-called "Saratoga Gambler's Bill" at the very moment that "Caleb Mitchell's blood was staining his (Brackett's) doorstep."[29]

Senator John Raines, an advocate for the bill and leader of the Senate, showed his frustration with Brackett by thundering, "There ought to be inscribed on Mitchell's tombstone: 'I made a terrible mistake, I shot the wrong man.'"[30]

Not to be outdone in the mudslinging fray, Brackett publicly alleged that Jerome allowed liquor sales to take place on Sundays and that he committed crimes to obtain evidence. He referred to the District Attorney as, "half child and all wild." So as not to leave out Senator Raines, Brackett described Raines on the floor of the Senate as "furtive and shifty," and bluntly accused him of taking bribes.

Brackett fought the Dowling Law with all his political might. [31] The opponents of the bill used whatever means they could, including tampering with the Dowling Law's companion bill in the Assembly called the Wainwright Bill. The Wainwright Bill was essentially the Dowling Bill, only it originated in the Assembly where the Dowling Bill was introduced and had been passed in the Senate. It was discovered, however, that when the Wainwright Bill reached the committee considering both bills, the Wainwright Bill had had language added to it that made the bill effective only after the Saratoga racing season had concluded. [32]

The bill's author confirmed that his original bill had included no such language to protect the Saratoga gamblers and the committee soon disposed of the Wainwright Bill and passed the Dowling option on to the full Assembly, which ultimately passed the bill.

With the passage of the Dowling Law and reform winds blowing across the state, it was obvious that the freedom of operation that the old-time kings of the gambling world enjoyed was coming to an end. Even Brackett's support of Canfield was beginning to show signs of weakness. It was about this time when Brackett made this public statement, "They say here – that is my enemies do – that because I defended Canfield I was getting a rake-off. The fact is I never defended Canfield. Once in my life I acted for him in a legal matter, but it meant only a short visit to New York and had no connection whatever with his profession. I defended Canfield because I thought if we were bound to have gambling, in spite of the law, it was my duty to have it of the very best type and among those people who could afford to give up their money without value received. Canfield had shown that he catered only to the rich, and I stood for Canfield as against the men who would put the temptation before those who could not afford the expense. That was my position, and I maintain that it was right, and is still right. Of the two evils, I chose the one that does the less harm; and I chose Canfield.

At the same time, I stand for the supremacy of the law, and as between Canfield and the law I say the law."[33]

There was no doubt that Edgar T. Brackett, political power for many years in Saratoga, had once been considered a friend to the gamblers. It was he who gave the go-ahead for each gambling house and controlled the police, sheriff, and district attorney. His principled stand for "home rule" in the case of his so-called "Saratoga Gamblers Bill," his defense of the constitutional rights of the individual in the Dowling Bill debates, and his furious outburst at Judge Andrus for signing the warrant against Canfield, along with his interference with the Sheriff's Deputy sent to enforce it, could not hide the fact that his maneuvering was indeed beneficial to the gambling fraternity in Saratoga Springs in general and for Richard Canfield in particular.

Brackett was very powerful in state politics for many years. He was considered by many to be a potential candidate for governor and it was the opinion of political observers that his connection to Canfield had cost him that post. [34] An able attorney, he was also considered for the position of Supreme Court Justice, but again his connection to Canfield was thought to have cost him that job as well. One newspaper described him as being "devoid of any sense of decency"[35] yet by 1905, ex-Senator Brackett was solidly in the anti-gambling camp and would become a leader of the fight against gambling locally for many years to come.

But before Brackett would convert to an anti-gambling crusader, the summers of 1903 and 1904 would be trying times for Canfield. He had invested in the purchase of the unseemly Indian encampment and installed the most beautiful Italian Garden in its place. And 1903 was also the year that his magnificent restaurant was added to the building.

While these improvements were universally approved by the press and public alike, the mood of the village officials was less enthusiastic. The business and political leaders of the day were of the feeling that gambling, if allowed at all, should be much more discreet than it had been in the past and allowed only a handful of places to even open up that summer.

The powers that be insisted that the gambling be behind closed doors and even insisted that the doors between Canfield's wonderful new dining room and the gambling floor remain closed. Previous owners of the Club House (Morrissey, Spencer, and Reed) always had the trump card of ownership of the famous racetrack in addition to the gaming house. They were always able to deflect any anti-gambling sentiment with threats to shut down the thoroughbred racing. Canfield could play no such hand and his improvements to the grounds were not enough to sway the village authorities. What other choice did he have except to close the doors and make the best of the situation?

Saratoga was considered immune from too serious an attempt to close all the gambling houses. The owners of the Manhattan Club, (Deacon James Wescott, Thomas Jolly, and James Welsh) like Canfield, had invested heavily in their Saratoga holdings prior to the 1903 season and had to endure the indignity of operating with shades drawn. But they did, and they all had a profitable year despite the offensive conditions they were forced to operate under.

By 1904 it seemed that Canfield was being assailed from all sides. The Dowling Bill was passed into law. Jerome's crusade was in full swing in New York City and it was only a matter of time before Canfield would have to face a court of law. He had been arrested in New York City the previous winter but the case was dismissed when the detective responsible for obtaining the evidence against him was himself arrested for perjury in the case. [36]

His Saratoga protector, Brackett, was losing his will to fight and the requirements of the Saratoga officials that play be kept behind closed doors were distasteful to Canfield, who saw his profession as no more corrupt or evil that that of a stock broker.

That summer, the Manhattan, United States, and Chicago Clubs were all operating under the restrictions imposed by the village authorities but Canfield, chafing under the perceived oppression by the village powers, refused to open. Not even the restaurant, which always lost money, was permitted to be opened.

The closing of Canfield's place in 1904 was detrimental to the economy of the town. William C. Whitney and the other owners of the race course recognized that the "Saratoga Experience" was incomplete for their wealthiest patrons without the Club House. They desired to play at the American Monte

Carlo, not the second rate clubs, no offense intended to the Manhattan, United States, and Chicago Clubs, of course. They needed the Club House to complete their days. The exclusivity of the grounds, the dining room, and the gambling floor were sought after as the perfect ending to a day at the race course for America's wealthiest citizens.

Whitney and a few associates approached Canfield and asked if he would reconsider his position, for the good of all, but Canfield refused. He would operate with doors wide open or he would not operate at all. Growing desperate, they tried to rent the property from Canfield, offering to pay whatever sum Canfield could fathom. He refused. They asked if he would consider opening only the restaurant. Again, Canfield refused.

Without Canfield's place as a compliment to the race course, the summer season was a dull one in 1904. Local police kept busy by busting small craps games near the track. On August 5 police arrested twenty four men and boys for throwing dice outside the fence of the track, considering them (according to one reporter) as "an unwashed and unkempt nuisance."[37]

A few poolrooms were winked at by police as and the club houses operated under the prescribed restrictions. Trouble did bubble up later in the season when one of the poolroom operators, Robert Massey, threatened to reopen the old "White House" poolroom across the street from the track.

The former Mitchell-Stuart place, at the heart of the whole affair in 1901, had been refused permission to operate as a poolroom in successive years. Mitchell's son, also named Caleb, owned the property and in Massey, found a willing partner to attempt a re-opening of the place under the same theory of equal treatment for all gamblers that Mitchell and Stuart had tried previously.

Massey did re-open the White House in early September, not content with his poolroom on the road to Ballston Spa. He was quickly raided and several employees were arrested, the police being content to let alone the twenty or so patrons who were there when the raid took place. [38] Detective Costello, along with Officers Morrison and James Sullivan, arrested Massey, Robert Fitzmorris, Michael Holleran, Joseph Quinn, and James Mitchell on gambling charges and Caleb Mitchell Jr. for obstructing an officer. All were quickly released on bail as was the custom of the day.

Like his father however, young Caleb Mitchell could not sit idly by in the face of hypocrisy and the next day he lodged complaints against other gamblers who had also operated small games during the racing season. Police obliged Mitchell and arrested John T. Sweeney, Eugene Sullivan, and Thomas Fennel on charges of keeping a gambling house. They too were released on bail. [39]

The budding gambler's war never reached the same ferocity as the 1901 fight. There were no threats between the gamblers of either throwing people into the lake or fighting to the death. There was no state senator taking sides in the dispute and no ex-mayor committing suicide over the whole affair.

Cooler heads would prevail and agreements would be reached for the conditions that would be allowed in 1905. By now Brackett was firmly against gambling of all forms but the Whitney syndicate had recognized the need for Canfield and he and a few others were permitted to operate openly as he had in the past.

With the doors between the dining room and roulette tables open once again, the experience at Canfield's was complete and enjoyed by all who visited. But the play was among the slowest that Canfield had ever experienced at Saratoga. Although he and seven other places were allowed to operate, there was no doubt that the Dowling Law was having an effect on the enthusiasm of wealthy patrons who preferred to avoid having their names associated with gambling through a grand jury subpoena, which was exactly what was happening in New York City as Jerome continued his crusade there.

Canfield's legal bills were mounting as well, with one lawyer taking Canfield for $30,000 - which was said at the time to be the highest legal fee ever paid for a gambling case. [40] Another in the long line of public political fights involving his one-time ally (ex-Senator Brackett) was bringing unwanted attention to the village from officials in Albany, yet again. And finally, a couple of bombings brought violence to the doorstep of the magnificent Club House for the first time in its storied history.

During the third week of the racing meet a loud explosion was heard outside the Club House. Some minor damage to the building was the effect and it caused some temporary excitement but that was about it. Canfield and his manager claimed that the explosion was simply caused by a gas build up.

The following night two more explosions occurred, once again outside Canfield's and another, almost simultaneous blast, outside the United States Club on Railroad Place. The dual bombings did no damage but did draw a crowd estimated at 5,000 to the Club House.

There had been a series of bombings in New York City that summer and a note was found outside the Canfield place after the bombing that read, "Twenty pounds of dynamite found outside Canfield's ready to go off. Canfield and Ullman to be dynamited, beware! Canfield says gas, I say dynamite."

The reference to Ullman in the note was ominous. Joe Ullman was a long time bookmaker and gambler who was operating a club on Phila Street called the Bridge Whist Club for the first time in 1905. The concern was not so much Joe Ullman himself, as the only real violence in his past seemed to be a fist-fight with fellow gambler Leo Mayer in front of the Grand Union Hotel in 1902.[41] The concern was that Ullman was from Chicago and it was well known that Chicago area gangsters were more apt to use bombs during their disputes than their New York City based cohorts. The initial fear was that mid-western underworld interests had followed Ullman to Saratoga Springs that summer.

Another theory, initially considered by police, was that the explosives were the work of so-called yeggmen. Yeggmen were members of criminal gangs who would throw diversionary devices while their confederates would steal valuables during the ensuing commotion. The tactic had been tried at a Chicago area race track the previous year when thieves had targeted the money rolls being moved about the grounds. A yeggman had been thrown out of Saratoga three years earlier and reportedly had admitted that he was employed to blow up one of the gambling houses in town. New York City Police detectives, hired for temporary service during Saratoga summers, pursued this theory of the bombings but were unable to unearth any supporting evidence. [42]

Ullman had bragged that he had assurances he would be allowed a free hand in his operation. Canfield was running with open doors again as well. The poolroom operators, specifically Caleb Mitchell Jr., were not. Another theory of the bombings was that rival local gamblers were upset with Ullman, Canfield, and Brackett for their being unable to open that summer and the bombings were an effort to coerce the town into opening up for all of the gamblers. [43]

The police were never able to find the culprit in the bombing scare. Most people, the police included, eventually settled on the explanation that the whole thing was the work of a jokester. About the only the thing that the bombings accomplished was that they helped convince the local authorities that a return to the restrictive policy of only a few gambling joints being allowed to operate under cover was desirable. And so it was that 1906 opened with the same restrictions as 1904.

Canfield, of course, was not happy with the conditions although the Club House, the Manhattan Club and the venerable United States Club were on the short list of authorized establishments. Ullman was confident that he would be allowed to open as well but the green light was not forthcoming for him.

Like ex-village president Mitchell, Ullman insisted upon his right to operate the same as Canfield and threatened to go to the governor if he was denied that right. He made a public statement that he would open his doors as long as other places were allowed to operate and that police were free to raid him if they liked, but he made it clear he would not go down without a fight.

On the morning of August 5, 1906, the daily edition of the New York Sun arrived in Saratoga and brought the news that all gambling would be suppressed in the village that summer except for the three places noted previously. That afternoon, in the lobby of the United States Hotel, Ullman practically dared the police to raid his club.

The Chief of Police, with a squad of officers, took up the dare and raided the Bridge Whist Club shortly after 11:00 PM on the fifth of August, within 24 hours of Ullman opening for the season. [44] Although the club was full of patrons, only employees were arrested. Among them were notorious gamblers Max Blumenthal and William Macklin who, along with Ullman, were arraigned before Justice Delaney and posted $500 bail to secure their appearance before the fall term of the grand jury. [45]

Ullman was indignant that he was raided while others remained free of police interference. Like Mitchell before him, Ullman blamed Richard Canfield for his troubles, telling a reporter after the raid, "We were raided because we interfered with somebody. Mr. Canfield is a rich man; but I have never heard that wealth makes an illegitimate business, immune." Adding that, "Had we run a ten-cent joint nobody, I imagine, would have found any fault, and we would not have been found in the way of anybody's progress to greater wealth." Ullman would end by claiming that he was against all monopolies and would insist on his right to open as long as anyone else enjoyed the privilege. [46]

Whether Ullman carried out his threat to bring the matter to the attention of the governor if he was closed down is open to debate. Ullman denied that he made any formal complaint to the governor yet the day after the raid Sheriff Kavanaugh received the following telegram from Governor Higgins: "It having come to my notice that the statutes prohibiting the keeping of gambling establishments and gambling apparatus and otherwise prohibiting gambling, are or are likely to be systematically violated in the county of Saratoga, I hereby specially call your attention to the same matter, and warn you that you will be held strictly accountable for the due execution of the law in this regard in your county."[47]

It was thought by some commentators that Governor Higgins was simply a shrewd politician who, realizing the Saratoga authorities were making an effort to stamp out the wide open conditions of previous eras, made a public move against the Saratoga gamblers in order to reap the political benefits of having been the Governor to finally put an end to the world- renowned "Monte Carlo of America."[48]

Others thought that Ullman was behind the closing order for sure, as he had been involved with gambling in Minneapolis, Chicago, and Long Branch shortly before those places were shut down by authorities. Saratoga was merely a continuation of Ullman's pattern of predicting the demise of a particular gambling town shortly after his arrival.

Nevertheless the closing order was final. The Sheriff and Saratoga village police ensured that all public gambling was suppressed for the remainder of the summer. Canfield had removed his roulette wheels and faro boxes from the main gambling floor and the Manhattan and United States Clubs followed his example. A few small private faro games were rumored to be available from time to time that summer, but even the smallest of outfits was raided by police as was the case with a small game run in a back room of a saloon near the track.

For many years a small game run by a man named Chandler and the Breen brothers, Thomas and Daniel, was considered too small to bother with, despite its proximity to the race track. When the closing order came in 1906, however, this little game escaped notice for about ten days. When police finally raided the place shortly after the last race had been run on August 17, the departing patrons were treated to the spectacle of an important police operation and Daniel Breen's attempt at resisting the police, injuring an officer in the process. [50] An indication of just how serious the 1906 gambling crackdown was can be seen in the remarks of one reporter covering the situation, "From the present outlook it seems probable that matching pennies for drinks will soon subject the reckless perpetrators to instant arrest."[51]

If 1906 was a sour year for the gambling fraternity at Saratoga, 1907 would be even worse. Open gambling was not allowed. Canfield opened his restaurant as a favor to his friends and some private gambling occurred in the upper floors of his famous building, but all-in-all, it was a poor summer in terms of excitement and profit for Canfield.

Getting nowhere with the authorities, the gamblers tried another tactic. They conceived a plan to boycott the local businesses and asked the hotel managers, who were also largely in favor of open gambling, to join them in closing their doors in an attempt to force the village authorities to take the lid off for the good of all. If that didn't work, the gamblers thought they might try to threaten a move against the race track and the betting ring there. [52] But none of the gamblers, other than Richard Canfield, had the power or public favor to take the lead on the endeavor.

Joe Ullman had left Saratoga and had a nervous breakdown while travelling with an opera show that he was backing in San Francisco, so he never even made it back to Saratoga for the 1907 season. [53] "Big Jim" Kennedy, then running the Chicago Club, had a mixed reputation in Saratoga due to his previous ownership of poolrooms in Saratoga and New York City. Indeed, of the three clubs that were to be permitted to operate in Saratoga during 1906, Kennedy's Chicago Club was noticeably absent from the list. Some people believed he was discriminated against precisely because of his previous ownership of a poolroom in the village.

Only one gambler could unite the fraternity and Richard Canfield was having no part of it. He understood that divisive public machinations would not work and he worked hard to gain a respectable reputation despite the nature of his profession. Without Canfield to lead them, the other gamblers simply gave up under the pressure of the anti-gambling forces.

Police kept the lid closed down tight. They even went so far as to suppress a nickel-in-the-slots machine owned by Charles Mahon at 19 Phila Street. [54]

By the end of 1907 Canfield had tired of the fickleness of the Saratoga situation and when he closed the doors of the magnificent brick building for the final time in 1907, he would never return. A "For Sale" sign was immediately put up and, though he had had many offers over the years for the property, he now was unable to find a suitable buyer. Without the guarantees afforded the owners of the Club House of past generations, no one would take the chance of purchasing the property without being able to spin the roulette wheels inside.

The property sat vacant until 1911 when the village of Saratoga Springs purchased the building and grounds for $150,000. The sum was reported to be $50,000 less than the 1909 asking price when talks began between the village and Canfield's representatives. Between the original purchase price and the money spent on upgrades, the selling price totaled about twenty per cent of Canfield's total investment in the property.

Richard Canfield looms so large over the Saratoga of yesterday that the building is no longer known as the Saratoga Club House. It is not even referred to as the Saratoga Springs History Museum, which it is today. Many people have no idea that Albert Spencer and Charlie Reed even owned the place. Everyone refers to the place as the "Canfield Casino" in Congress Park. The name is deserved. It harkens back to an era when the Saratoga Club House and Richard Canfield hosted the highest of high society. The true stories are of vast sums of money won and lost and Canfield's incredible profits. Visitors with names like Lillian Russell, "Diamond Jim" Brady, and "Bet-A-Million" Gates remind us that Saratoga was once the summer home of not only millionaire families like the Vanderbilts, Whitneys, and Sanfords, but society's biggest celebrities and fashion leaders.

Canfield's popularity in Saratoga allowed him to escape having to pay the kind of protection money that was a necessary expense for him in his New York City endeavors. Canfield spent lavishly on local charities. Recognizing that the goodwill of the people was essential, he even purchased from Saratoga businesses anything necessary for the operation of the Club House and restaurant that was available locally, thus endearing him to the local merchants at a time when many of the hotels imported what they required. [55]

This is not to say that Canfield was not opposed to paying bribes for protection. In New York City, he often paid the $1,000 monthly retainer and 10-15 per cent of the profit from the house to the local precinct Police Captain himself. His generous contributions to the local populace simply made the payment for protection in Saratoga (and at his Newport, RI club) not as necessary as it was in New York.

Like Morrissey, Canfield continued the tradition of not allowing women to gamble in his house. No locals were allowed to play and the place was closed on Sunday. He ran a tight ship and not a single incident of violence or angry dispute was reported as having occurred inside the walls of the gambling den during his tenure. His manners and cultured conversation gave him an aura of respectability despite the illegality of his business.

His reputation was international, and he was so well respected, that after his retirement from running gambling joints, he was offered the opportunity to open legal gambling houses in locations throughout the world including; Paris, Cannes, San Sebastian, the island of Cofu, Ostend in Belgium, Havana, and Mexico City. [56]

There was never a whisper of his being involved with any other vice activity such as prostitution or drugs. He was not a piker. His games were run honestly. A man was allowed to play to his own limit and was expected to recognize that limit himself. Losses were met with a warning from Canfield that further play would result in additional loss to the player. That was simply the nature of the business. He offered no assurances to a loser that his luck would turn; he simply pointed out the fact that losing was expected as the percentages of the roulette wheel always favored the house and no amount of luck would ever change that.

The historical record has benefited from Canfield's willingness to speak with reporters regarding a variety of issues. It is inconceivable today that a proprietor of an illegal business, however famous or popular it may be, would risk public comment on its activities. But times were different at the turn of the last century and Canfield's articulate and well considered thoughts on a variety of matters were recorded on more than one occasion. It is perhaps best to allow Canfield's own words to be heard:

On the future of gambling, Richard Canfield made this incredibly prophetic statement in 1907, "There will come a day, perhaps not in our lifetime, when gambling will be licensed. The reason why I am convinced that there will eventually be a license is that gambling cannot be stopped. As has been done with liquor, it will be found that the best public policy is to regulate it and to obtain a revenue for the State. The license will be very expensive, and it will involve strict regulations, such as a prohibition by youths or men employed in fiduciary capacities and handling the funds of institutions. The license will necessitate surveillance of some kind, including an examination of all the paraphernalia in use, and will be to a certain extent a certificate of integrity."[57] It is interesting to note that Canfield does not mention women being restricted from gambling in his comments on the future of gambling despite his own long standing policy prohibiting the fairer sex from participation in the games of chance he offered. Even more interesting is just how prescient Canfield was as his description of licensing, regulation, and surveillance mirrors almost exactly the procedures followed by the State of New York when gaming was reintroduced to the state in recent years.

On the limit and the play at the Club House he offered this, "Although the limit that has been announced for Saratoga has been smaller than in Monte Carlo, I have never refused a special limit to a man of means who asked for it. It would be foolish to let a man with nothing to lose bet recklessly. For persons of a certain type the limit has been maintained, but where it has been enforced against some men, whom I might designate as undesirable, I have made a special limit that was far higher than was ever given at Monte Carlo. From the standpoint of the house all the customers are as one player; the house should take no cognizance of individual play, all being exactly the same as one man, and in the long run the game gets its percentage and no more. If the house accumulates bad debts or is under unduly heavy expense it may fail in prosperity and still have won. The percentage does not come in always each night. On the contrary, I have known the seven or eight roulette tables and the two faro tables that were running all to show a deficit on the same night, and one of the most phenomenal evenings I ever knew resulted in the net winning of $1." [58] This statement of Canfield's verifies the fact that only two games were ever played on the public gaming floor at the Club House during his tenure, faro and roulette. Private card games of other varieties were played in private rooms, not open to the public.

Canfield recalled that the single greatest winning night for him at Saratoga resulted in a $150,000 gain for the house. He commented, "It would be impossible for me to estimate the amount that changed hands on a night like that. One man may lose $100,000 and two others at the table with him may win $50,000 each, and as the bank has done nothing there is no reason for any record."

Perhaps lamenting the even greater profits that could have been had, Canfield mentioned the duration of the Saratoga season and the self-imposed restrictions the Club House operated under, "The Saratoga Club House has been the only important pleasure resort casino in the world where no woman has ever played, and, as you may imagine, the importunities have been innumerable. The place has never been opened on Sunday since it was built. Morrissey could have started the games on Sunday, but he relinquished the privilege in deference to the wishes of the townspeople, and those who followed him continued in the same line, though this meant the sacrifice of four days out of a season of four weeks, and the four days when business would certainly have been the greatest. When the gambling houses were open at Long Branch Sunday was always the star day.

"The Saratoga season has always been short. The longest period in which the club was ever open was two months. The experiment has been tried of having racing here in July, but for some reason it has been possible to collect crowds here only in August. Racing has been tried here three days in a week and various other tests have been made. With racing in August the season is confined to four weeks, and then is at top speed for only two weeks, for there is one week that the crowds are coming and a final week when they are disappearing. In Monte Carlo where they have three times as many roulette tables as we use, the season extends over twelve months, and is at top speed for about six weeks, especially if Lent comes early."[59]

His opinion as to why reform efforts were ineffective: "The reformers go at it upside down and after they have used their bludgeon gambling continues, though less openly. When the honest places are kept in seclusion the other kind reap a harvest. If they stop my Club House men ready to perpetrate any fraud will spring up on every corner, ready to do business. What is to prevent one of these men from saying, 'I have been associated with Canfield, and while he cannot do business openly he is dealing for a few private customers' and the would be player is led to some place where he is apt to be fleeced.

"Gambling is a violation of the law. There is a reason why the sentiment against gambling is not strong and why the punishment is usually not severe. Whenever a gambling case comes up in court it is probable that ninety-five per cent of those who are assembled in the courtroom have participated in gambling games, perhaps poker or some mild form of gambling that has not become any more respectable on account of its privacy."

Canfield's considered thoughts, business acumen and long term thinking was probably the reason that his fortune was once estimated at over 12 million dollars. At that time, $2.5 million of his fortune was credited to his Saratoga operations; another $7.5 million was attributed to his investments in Wall Street, with the remainder split between his New York City and Newport gambling facilities.

Canfield exited the New York City gambling market on the last day of 1901. He recognized that District Attorney Jerome had the upper hand and that the law and public sentiment there was moving against the widespread corruption that allowed the gambling halls to exist and by extension the gamblers who were profiting from the conditions.

As was mentioned previously, Jerome's first attempt to bring Canfield before the courts was stymied by the perjury of his own detective. After the Dowling Law went into effect, however, there was no chance Canfield would be able to open again in New York City.

Jerome was successful, finally, in securing an indictment and a plea of guilty for being a common gambler against Canfield in December of 1904. On the same day that he was indicted, Canfield paid a $1,000 fine to avoid jail time in the case. [60]

Canfield continued in Saratoga until 1907, enduring the flip-flopping of local officials. But by then he was already moving away from gambling. He sold the Nautilus Club in Newport in 1905 and was completely out of gambling at the end of the summer season in Saratoga in 1907. In later years he would attribute his move away from gambling to the influence of his young daughter, rather than the legal troubles associated with his profession. [61]

After his retirement from gambling Canfield went into business. He built a factory in West Virginia that was intended to make bottle stoppers, but instead ended up turning out lighting fixtures and other glass products. That company was a success, adding a second factory and at one time employing between five and six hundred people. He then returned to the bottle stopper business and created the Spring Stopper Company in New York City. The patented design that he backed was at one time used by most pharmaceutical companies in the packaging of their various products.

Canfield briefly got back into the gambling business in 1910 when the government of Mexico offered him 15 million dollars to head up the official Mexican Lottery. He worked diligently in planning the system but the Mexican Revolution in 1911 put an end to this endeavor rather quickly.

Perhaps most dear to Canfield himself was his inclusion as an original member of the Walpole Society. Founded in 1911 in New York City, the society was limited to 25 members of high standing in the art and literary worlds. His inclusion in the society is probably the best evidence of his standing in high society circles that forgot his felonious past and appreciated his lifelong devotion and appreciation of the arts. In 1914 he would sell his Whistler collection for $200,000.

On December 11, 1914, Richard Canfield visited a building in New York City that he was considering as a new headquarters for one of his businesses. After looking the place over and deciding it would, indeed, make an excellent location for his business, he made plans to return the following day and purchase the property. On his way home he got off at the wrong subway station. Realizing he was at the wrong terminal,

Canfield quickly turned around on the stairway in the hope of returning to the car before the doors closed again. He slipped and struck his chin on the stairs.

Taken home in a taxi, Canfield appeared fine, although he decided against eating any dinner that night. The following morning an attendant was unable to wake him and a doctor was quickly summoned. It was determined that the blow to his chin had fractured the base of his skull and before an operation could be performed, Canfield died. Just as quickly as so many fortunes had turned at his gaming tables, 59-year-old Richard Canfield passed from this earth.

Two days later services were held before a standing room only crowd at the Congregational Broadway Tabernacle in New York City before the body was cremated and the ashes delivered to the family burial plot in New Bedford.

Only two curious New Bedford residents and a reporter gathered as Richard Canfield, Prince of the Gamblers, was laid to rest in Oak Grove Cemetery on December 15, 1914.[62]

One hundred years later Richard Canfield's name is still remembered in Saratoga Springs, a tribute to the one man more responsible than any of the others before or after him, for the creation of the "Monte Carlo of America."

Endnotes

Chapter 9

1   Gardiner, Alexander. *Canfield. The True Story of the Greatest Gambler*. Doubleday, Doran and Co. Garden City, NY, 1930. **Unless otherwise noted, Gardiner's work is relied upon for much of the information on Canfield**

2   Troy Daily Times, September 20, 1887.

3   Waller, George. *Saga of an Imperious Era*.

4   Schwartz, David C. *Roll the Bones: The History of Gambling*.

5   Waller, George. *Saga of an Imperious Era*.

6   Ibid.

7   Ibid.

8   Ibid.

9   Gardiner. *Canfield...*

10   Gardiner. *Canfield...*

11   "Dan Stuart Admits that He is Behind the Crusade in Saratoga," New York Herald, August 5, 1901.

12   "R. Canfield Held to the Grand Jury," New York Herald, Aug 7, 1901.

13   Gardiner. *Canfield...*

14   "Husband Missing, Money Hers," The Sun, May 13, 1910.

15   "Find Man with Crushed Skull," Elmira Star-Gazette, December 6, 1912.

16   "Indict Wife in Murder Plot," Syracuse Journal, May 23, 1935.

17   "Anti-Gambling Crusade at Saratoga Opens with Sensational Move," The New York Herald, August 4, 1901.

18 Ibid.

19 Ibid.

20 Ibid.

21 "Wants to Close Canfield's," The New York Sun,
    March 31, 1902.

22 "Canfield Retaliates on His Enemies," The Evening
    Telegram, New York. August 23, 1901.

23 "Raided Canfield's and Must Face Grand Jury,"
    The Brooklyn Daily Eagle, September 3, 1901.

24 "R. Canfield Held to the Grand Jury," New York Herald,
    August 7, 1901.

25 The Albany Evening Journal, August 10, 1901. "

26 Ibid.

27 Gardiner. Canfield…

28 Waller, Saga…

29 "The Jerome Bill Signed," The Mechanicville Mercury,
    May 14, 1904.

30 "When Brackett, Brown and Elsberg Rebelled in 1903,"
    The Watertown Daily Times, April 5, 1924.

31 "E.T. Brackett, Republican Warwick, in Bitter Fight for
    Political Life," The New York Herald, March 27, 1916.

32 "Bill Tampered With," The Syracuse Herald,
    March 31, 1904.

33 Watertown Daily Times, February 29, 1924.

34 The Sun, August 9, 1906.

35 "Political Notes," The Sun, June 12, 1904.

36 "Detective Arrested," Oswego Daily Palladium,
    November 23, 1904.

37 "Raid in Saratoga on Crap Shooters," Amsterdam
    Evening Recorder, August 5, 1904.

38 "More Arrests Follow the Poolroom Raid," The
    Daily Saratogian, September 3, 1904.

39   Ibid.

40   "Staunchfield's Big Fee," The Utica Journal,
     January 17, 1904.

41   "Mayer and Ullman Battle in Street," The Morning
     Telegraph, August 22, 1902.

42   "Think Yeggmen Dropped Bombs," The New York
     Herald, August 21, 1905.

43   Ibid.

44   "A Saratoga Club Raided," The Rome Daily Sentinel,
     August 7, 1906.

45   "Saratoga Gambling Fight On," The Sun, August 7, 1906.

46   Ibid.

47   Ibid.

48   "To Keep Higgins on Lid Job," The Sun, August 9, 1906.

49   "Saratoga Gamblers Held for Grand Jury," The
     New York Times, August 16, 1906.

50   "Saratoga Police in Gambling Raid," The Amsterdam
     Evening Recorder, August 18, 1906.

51   Ibid.

52   "Richard Canfield Won't Budge," The Sun,
     August 10, 1907.

53   "Joe Ullman Insane," The New York Times, April 12, 1907

54   "Local Gossip," The Daily Saratogian, September 13, 1907.

55   "Saratoga's Big Season Now Thing of the Past,"
     The Morning Telegraph, August 25, 1905.

56   "Saratoga Club House Looks for New Owner,"
     The New York Herald, September 1, 1907.

57   Ibid.

58   Ibid.

59   Ibid.

60   "How Jerome Made Good," The Evening Post,
     August 3, 1905.

61   "Canfield's Daughter Inherits Big Fortune," The
     Herald Dispatch and Daily Gazette, December
     19, 1916.

62   "No Mourners for Canfield," The New York
     Times, December 16, 1914.

Many of the early gamblers in Saratoga Springs ran their operations near the railroad depot. Robert Gridley's place would have been just outside the view of this photo to the right. It was said that passengers could see through the open windows of the gambling joints before they even stepped foot off of the train platform.

Photo courtesy of the George S. Bolster Collection of the Saratoga Springs History Museum

The first Constable in Saratoga Springs was George Bliven who was appointed when the village was established in 1826. Later, law enforcement was delivered by a system of constables and night watchmen who were appointed annually by the village. A modern police force, providing twenty-four hour coverage to the village, had its first day of service on June 1, 1887. The photo above is the official roster for the first day of the Saratoga Springs Police Department. Chief of Police George Blodget, Assistant Chief Michael Carroll, and Patrolmen John Van-Rensselaer, Patrick Deegan, James Hennessey, Jerry Costello, Walter Mann and Michael Finn.

Photo courtesy of the collection of the Saratoga Springs City Historian.

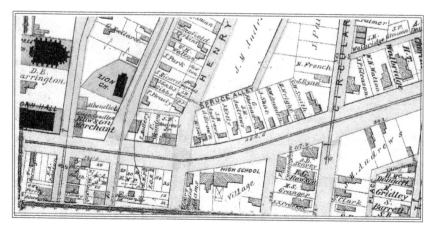

Willow Walk is known today as High Rock Avenue. There are many stories of violence and crime in the Willow Walk area of the village. On this map from 1876 Willow Walk runs between the Zion Church and the building owned by Patrick Brady, who also had a contract with the village to run the local lock-up. On this map the present day Fire Department is located where the High School is shown..

Map Credit: Combination Atlas of Saratoga Springs and Ballston. F.W. Beers and Louis H. Cramer. 1876. Collection of the Saratoga Springs City Historian.

The Honorable John Morrissey. United States Congressman, New York State Senator, Heavyweight Boxing Champion, and builder of the two most iconic structures in the history of Saratoga Springs; The Saratoga Race Course and the Saratoga Clubhouse.

Photo courtesy of the George S. Bolster Collection of the Saratoga Springs History Museum.

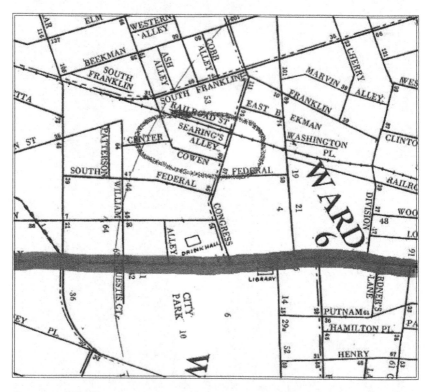

Searing's Alley gave no end of trouble to the authorities in Saratoga Springs. From the late 1800's through the mid 1900's the area was plagued by violence of all sorts. Two murders, a police involved shooting and a race riot were all reported in Searing's Alley over the years. The map above, from the 1956 City Directory, shows the location of Searing's Alley in relation to Congress Street.

Map credit: Collection of the Saratoga Springs City Historian.

The photo above is from the Urban Renewal archives and shows the alley running next to Jack's Restaurant. Today, the area is near where the Embassy Suites Hotel stands on Congress Street.

Photo credit: Collection of the Saratoga Springs City Historian.

When John Morrissey built the Saratoga Club House he established three rules. No women and no local residents were allowed to gamble inside the famous building and there was to be no gambling on Sundays. Subsequent owners Albert Spencer, Charles Reed and Richard Canfield all adhered to Morrissey's regulations.

Photo courtesy of the George S. Bolster Collection of the Saratoga Springs History Museum.

Spencer Trask was one of the first leaders of an anti-gambling
reform wave in Saratoga Springs. In 1886, Trask and his allies
were wildly successful in making raids in Saratoga and having
the proprietors of the gambling dens arrested. Unfortunately
none of the arrests resulted in an indictment by the Saratoga
County Grand Jury and soon the gamblers were back up and
running as they had before.

Photo courtesy of the Collection of the Saratoga Springs City Historian.

Richard Canfield (right) owned the Saratoga Club House from 1893 through 1911, when he sold the building and grounds to the village of Saratoga Springs. It was believed that there was only one photograph of Richard Canfield ever taken, until two photographs were recently discovered by the Director of the Saratoga Springs History Museum, James Parillo. Note the historic Spit and Spat fountain in the background. With Canfield are his longtime manager at Saratoga Patrick MacDonald (left) and John "Bet-A-Million" Gates.

Photo courtesy of the George S. Bolster Collection of the Saratoga Springs History Museum.

Caleb Mitchell (left) was elected three times as President of the Village of Saratoga Springs despite his ownership of a pool room on Broadway across from the United States Hotel. After losing several legal and political battles to keep his gambling interests alive, Mitchell committed suicide at the office door of his longtime nemesis, State Senator Edgar T. Brackett. Seated with Mitchell in this photo is his son, also named Caleb.

Photo courtesy of the George S. Bolster Collection of the Saratoga Springs History Museum.

Arnold Rothstein, known as the "grandfather of organized crime" built the Brook nightclub out Church Street in 1919. Rothstein ran the Brook until 1925 when he pulled out of the Saratoga Springs gambling market for good. Three years later Rothstein was gunned down in New York City.

Photo courtesy of the George S. Bolster Collection of the Saratoga Springs History Museum.

In 1919 police made a successful gambling raid at 210 South Broadway. In this photograph it is the brick building with arched windows behind the white building on the corner. Today 210 South Broadway is a Stewart's Shop at the corner of Circular Street and South Broadway. The white building in the photograph is the Aldine Hotel and today is the Stewart's parking lot.

Photo courtesy of the George S. Bolster Collection of the Saratoga Springs History Museum.

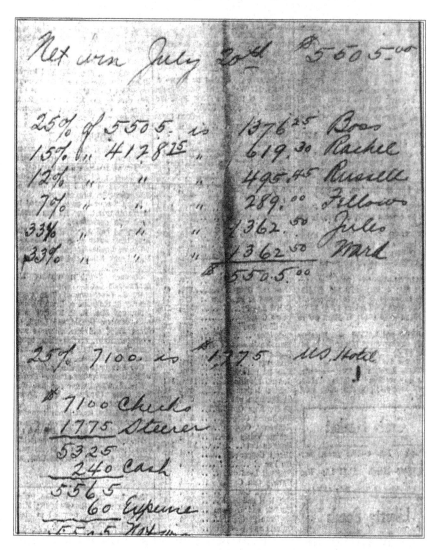

The infamous "divvy sheet" produced by gangster Rachel Brown during the trial of Jules Formel. Brown claimed that the notations indicated the split of the profits from gambling at 210 South Broadway. "The Boss" was allegedly the Saratoga County District Attorney, Charles B. Andrus.

Photo courtesy of The Saratogian.

This photograph of the Saratoga Springs Police Department in early 1919 contains several officers who played significant roles during the turbulent decade of the 1920's. Chief James King is at center in the dark hat. After Chief King's retirement in 1919 Thomas Sullivan (fourth from right) led a raid against the gambling house at 210 South Broadway. Edward Carroll (far right) allowed gangster Rachel Brown to remove gambling evidence from a locked jail cell inside the police station. Hugh Dorsey (fourth from left) resigned from the police force in 1920 and joined the staff of special prosecutor Wyman Bascom in his efforts to clean up Saratoga.

Photo courtesy of the George S. Bolster Collection of the Saratoga Springs History Museum.

State Senator Edgar T. Brackett (above) was a long-time political power in Saratoga Springs. Initially a proponent of open gambling, except on Broadway, Brackett served as attorney for Richard Canfield for a time. Later, Brackett became firmly convinced that open gambling was detrimental to Saratoga's

Brackett photo courtesy of the Collection of the Saratoga Spring City Historian.

future and joined with Wyman Bascom (above) who was appointed as a special prosecutor to root our gambling and corruption in Saratoga Springs in 1920. Brackett and Bascom led many successful raids but were not as effective in obtaining convictions against public officials.

Bascom photo courtesy of the Fort Edward Historical Association.

Wyman Bascom and Edgar T. Brackett were successful in obtaining convictions against many of the gamblers in Saratoga Springs in the early 1920's however they were unable to achieve convictions for any of the public officials indicted for corruption. Two of those officials are pictured here. Commissioner of Public Safety John Gaffney is standing at left and City Court Judge Michael McTygue is seated at left. Both men had all charges against them dropped after the acquittal of District Attorney Charles B. Andrus.

Photo courtesy of the Collection of the Saratoga Springs City Historian.

Chapter 10

Arnold Rothstein and the Rise of the Gangsters

Each year a special train nicknamed the "Cavanaugh Special" arrived in Saratoga Springs in the days before the opening of the racing meet. All of the greatest bookmakers travelled on this train and it was considered a mark of distinction if a bookmaker arrived at the Spa aboard the exclusive coach. In 1904, an up and coming gambler and bookmaker named Arnold Rothstein arrived in Saratoga Springs for the first time in his life aboard the Cavanaugh Special.[1]

Born in 1882 on East 47th Street in New York City, Arnold Rothstein was the second of five children born to a deeply religious and well respected father, Abraham Rothstein.[2] He started his criminal career committing petty crimes around the neighborhood and past-posting with another neighborhood youth, Max Kalish.[3] Young Rothstein was a genius when it came to numbers and he soon developed a knack for developing schemes and scams that netted him a bit of a bankroll so that he could start backing his own gambling operations and investing in other criminal ventures.

Rothstein was an early rum smuggler, a pioneer in the early years of prohibition. He is considered the "Grandfather" of modern organized crime and one of the few gangsters to successfully operate a multi-ethnic and multi-religious criminal organization. He was a mentor to many of the most prolific gangsters who would rise to power during and after prohibition.

He was partners with Max (Big Maxey) Greenberg and Irving (Waxey) Gordon in bootlegging. Dutch Schultz drove a Rothstein truck early in his own fantastic criminal career. Charles "Lucky" Luciano ran drugs for Rothstein and he, along with Meyer Lansky, worked for a time spinning roulette wheels and dealing cards at Rothstein's Saratoga resort "The Brook" in the early 1920's. The "Prime Minister," Frank Costello, was a well-known associate of Rothstein's. Louis (Lepke) Buchalter and Jacob "Gurrah" Shapiro teamed up with Rothstein in labor-busting activities. [4] The Diamond Bothers, "Legs" and "Eddie," were employed for a time as bodyguards when Rothstein received word that some Chicago gangsters were planning to kidnap him. This was a job for which the Diamond siblings were paid the tidy sum of $50,000. [5]

Rothstein was an international criminal mastermind. He was an early bootlegger for sure, but after making millions in the liquor trade, he quickly realized that diamonds and drugs could be smuggled much more easily than alcohol and soon he was importing both while other gangsters fought to the death over the rum trade. He fenced stolen goods, jewels, and bonds. He was a racketeer and prolific bookmaker. Rothstein's criminal mind was relentless in looking for advantage.

Drug dealers who applied to him for a loan were required to purchase life insurance policies with Rothstein named as the beneficiary. The life insurance policies eliminated the argument of delinquents who claimed that if they happened to be killed, Rothstein wouldn't get his money back.[6] His thug associates were employed as strike busters. His criminal capabilities seemed limitless and records found after his death led authorities to several multi-million dollar heroin seizures all across the country.[7]

Despite his international criminal interests, Rothstein still found Saratoga Springs desirable as a summer getaway. He visited every year from 1904-1925. He married his wife Carolyn in Saratoga Springs in 1909 in a small white house at 185 Washington Street, the home of Village Justice Fred B. Bradley, which still stands today just west of Beekman Street. In 1909 he was not yet the multi-millionaire he would become and at the end of the summer of the year of his wedding, he would pawn his wife's jewelry (including her engagement ring) in Saratoga in order to bankroll his gambling adventures. Poor Carolyn would eventually get her jewelry back six months later.[8]

The first few years of Rothstein's visits to Saratoga Springs were not all that friendly to the gambling fraternity. Canfield's had closed down. Local authorities were lukewarm at best to the idea of returning to the old ways of the turn of the century when Canfield was enjoying some of his most lucrative summers. Gone were the days of dozens of poolrooms, some operating openly on Broadway. Betting at the track was severely restricted and even out-right banned for a time. Between 1907 and 1916, few places on or off the track operated with the confidence that that they were free from interference by the law, as Richard Canfield and "Big Jim" Kennedy were able to do just a few years earlier.

The situation was so bad for the gamblers in Saratoga during the summer of 1908 that even the betting at the track came under attack. Anti-gambling men were successful that year in bringing charges against the Sheriff of Saratoga County, John Bradley, Jr., for not taking action to prevent gambling at the racetrack. In a hearing before the governor, a witness testified as to how the betting was taking place during the meet.

Before each race twenty to thirty groups of ten or twelve men would scatter about the grounds and surround a bookmaker who would set the odds and accept the bets. A clerk would record each bet on a piece of paper. Runners would accept the money from the patrons and act as the middle man for the bankers. What got under the skin of the reformers was testimony that money was passed openly between betters and runners, and occasionally the bookmakers themselves, while police officers and sheriff's deputies stood nearby, making no attempt to suppress the wagering on the track grounds. Furthermore, it was brought up in Sheriff Bradley's hearing that after the race card was finished for the day, the bookmakers would return to the grand hotels of the village and accept wagers for the races scheduled for the following day.[9]

The betting described in Sheriff Bradley's hearing was illegal at that time. The pari-mutuel betting system recognizable today as the system for wagering on horse races had not yet been authorized by the State of New York. The fact that a sitting Governor would appoint a hearing officer to investigate allegations of authorities who did not enforce the gambling laws was certain to cause considerable heartburn among other local Saratoga authorities.

From time to time gambling rooms and club houses had been the subject of raids, but the betting at the track had always been off-limits for government officials and reformers alike. Anti-gambling crusaders were always careful to distinguish between the betting at the track and the true evil of the gambling establishments in the village. But if the Sheriff could be held responsible for the gambling at the track, then how much more accountability would be demanded of village authorities whose duty it was to enforce the laws of the land off the racetrack grounds?

The local politicians and police got the message. The lid was closed down tight for several years before 1917. In 1909 Commissioner of Police James H. King and District Attorney Moore investigated gum ball machines that operated in a similar manner to slot machines. The devices were thought to entice young boys to gamble. Although it took some time to determine that the machines were in fact illegal, Commissioner King didn't wait for a legal opinion before ensuring that all of the offending apparatus were removed from the businesses of Saratoga Springs.[10]

No arrests were made for possessing the gum ball machines as the owner had no intent to operate slots machines in the traditional sense, but it was certainly a sign that Saratoga Springs was serious in ferreting out gambling in the village and a reflection of Chief King's longstanding commitment to the betterment of the youth of Saratoga Springs that he was remembered fondly for upon his death in 1932. [11]

In 1913 police raided a village residence after hearing there was a game going on. They made no arrests but declared publicly that they would permit no gambling that summer in the village. Unable to open the lid even a crack, many of the bookmakers and gamblers left the Spa early in the racing meet of 1913, looking for a more favorable locale.[12] The local police even raided a place at 2 Madison Avenue on their own initiative in 1916.

On Thursday, August 10, 1916, a team of six Saratoga Springs Police Officers surrounded Edward L. Taylor's house on Madison Avenue. Inside were several well-known businessmen from New York City playing roulette and poker. When an officer knocked on the door, he was met by Taylor who, recognizing that a raid was in progress, slammed the door shut and alerted the patrons.

The officers quickly broke down the door and swarmed the building. They captured one player coming up from the basement who claimed he was the chef. But his plea was ignored and he was arrested along with five others. The one person who was not taken into custody during the raid was the owner of the house, Edward Taylor. He managed to slip out of the house during the commotion through the basement and was seen by neighbors scampering away through a nearby alley.[13]

The roulette table seized during the raid was discovered to be crooked. Coiled magnets were found underneath the wheel. They were connected by tiny wires and controlled by the operator of the wheel. When subtly activated by the operator, the apparatus allowed for the manipulation of the result. Apparently the odds in favor of the house were not enough for Edward Taylor.

The wood for the tables was of such high quality that when Sheriff William J. Dodge was obliged to destroy the gambling apparatus taken during the raid, the wood was salvaged and made into tables for the jury room in County Court.[14]

Taylor's time on the run from the law would last but one day. Detectives James Sullivan and George Mason returned to the residence and found him there. Detective Mason approached from the front of the house, Sullivan took a post in the rear. The trap was sprung when Mason rang the doorbell and Taylor predictably took flight out the back door, into the waiting arms of Sullivan. "Hold on there Eddie, you're some sprinter," commented Sullivan as he stopped the escape attempt.[15]

Police withheld the names of the five businessmen from New York City who were arrested in the raid. There is no mention of their appearance before a local judge after their arraignment. It is likely the charges against the out-of-towners were quietly dropped, sympathy probably being a factor in the men's case since the crooked tables indicated they were being cheated anyway. Taylor, represented by attorney James A. Leary, was found guilty of being a common gambler in November of 1916 and paid a $500 fine for a penalty. [16]

Something had gone askew in Saratoga after Canfield left the scene for good at the close of the summer of 1907. Authorities were not as open-minded, or forgiving, of the gamblers operating in the village. Perhaps they wanted things kept quiet as the village moved towards incorporation as a city in 1915.

Maybe everyone was pre-occupied with the run-up to America's involvement in World War I. Or just maybe, even most likely, no one had enough money to calm the jittery nerves of local politicians and police officials who worried that the Governor's interest in the goings on at Saratoga would be renewed.

Arnold Rothstein, the so called "grandfather" of modern organized crime, would help to put things back to the way they were in the glory days of Morrissey and Canfield. Known as a political fixer and grafter in metro-New York, Rothstein couldn't resist a sure bet and was a master at arranging things and manipulating situations and people to his benefit. He enjoyed nothing more than a well-played scheme, whether it was pulling a fast one on a sucker for small stakes or paying bribes to escape the legal jeopardy of his black-market operations. Already a millionaire from his various criminal enterprises, Rothstein decided to enter the Saratoga Springs gambling market in 1917.

In that year, Rothstein was approached by a well-known sporting man named Henry Tobin who had a secluded place out by Saratoga Lake that he planned to open as a gambling joint. Tobin was associated with other prominent gamblers of the era, particularly Max Blumenthal, and had been visiting Saratoga Springs at least as long as Rothstein.

Being an old-time sporting man with a good reputation didn't ensure that Tobin had the ready cash to back the game he intended to run for the summer season of 1917, however, and this is where Rothstein would come in handy. "The Brain" (another nickname for Rothstein) loaned Tobin $35,000 to bankroll the venture with the principal and ten percent interest due at the end of the season along with a 50/50 split of the profits.[17]

The Tobin place apparently did not attract the attention of authorities and was wildly successful. The ability to run openly was assuredly helped along by a $40,000 donation to the ruling political party's campaign fund that Rothstein was alleged to have paid to secure protection.[18] In just the few short weeks that the season lasted in the summer of 1917, Tobin was able to pay back the entire $35,000 Rothstein outlay, along with the 10% interest and $50,000 as A.R.'s share of the profits.[19]

In 1918 Rothstein and Tobin were joined by John Shaughnessey. They spent $150,000 building a clubhouse on a parcel of property owned by Ben Riley (at the end of present day Arrowhead Road) and opened their new resort, calling it the Arrowhead Inn.

Shaughnessey was a Long Island gambler and general go-between for gangsters and politicians- which would come in handy for Rothstein.[20] The attention of authorities was sure to come, given the profits of the gambling places popping up by the lake, and Rothstein would be looking for another set of hands to get between him and the local officials as added protection.

The situation would require some more planning and certainly more greasing of palms if it was to continue, and this was Rothstein's specialty, with Shaughnessy playing the role of middle man. A lover of money with a severe competitive streak, Rothstein could not resist the lure of profits available to the one who could pry open the legendary Saratoga market for the gamblers and Rothstein would put his whole effort into establishing his own gold-mine in upstate New York.

Rothstein told his long suffering wife, Carolyn, that he intended to make everyone forget all about Morrissey and Canfield by starting his own exclusive clubhouse.[21] He bought the Bonny Brook Farm from the ex-wife of George Saportas, a great steeplechase horse owner and breeder of the day, with the only stipulation of the purchase being that Rothstein could not retain the name "Bonny Brook."

The farm was not purchased officially by Rothstein, although Rothstein money certainly was used to buy the property. Rothstein's chauffeur, Harry M. Hathaway, made the purchase for $60,000 and sold the entire grounds and all the buildings just a few days later to Rothstein's partner Nathaniel J. (Nat) Evans for $100.[22] Clearly Rothstein was distancing himself from legal ownership of the property even though everyone knew that he had bought it and the property belonged to him.

The farm was located out present day Church Street on fifty rolling acres near the intersection of present day Brook Road. Rothstein spent $100,000 improving the grounds and buildings in preparation of the opening of his soon-to-be world famous resort, "The Brook."

The exclusive club catered to the wealthiest of patrons, much like the famed Club House of earlier days. No prices were listed on the menu, the same as at Canfield's place almost two decades earlier. While Rothstein and his resort never did quite make everyone forget Canfield or Morrissey, it was the sight of some pretty heavy play and interesting stories.

Two future mob legends got their start working for Rothstein at the Brook. Lucky Luciano and Meyer Lansky both dealt cards and spun roulette wheels for A.R. at the Brook in Saratoga before moving on to their own lucrative criminal careers.[23] Locally, Luciano would operate the Chicago Club on Woodlawn Avenue for many years while Lansky would take over the Arrowhead Club and Piping Rock Club out by Saratoga Lake. Lansky would also take the casino-cabaret-resort business model of the Brook and bring it to Las Vegas with Bugsy Siegel. Thus it may be said that the idea of Las Vegas style casino resorts was born at the Brook nightclub in Saratoga Springs.

Charles Stoneham, one of the wealthiest men in America in those days, found himself visiting Saratoga one summer but unable to visit the Brook owing to an ankle injury. He couldn't resist the temptation to gamble though, and called the Brook by phone, eventually getting the owner himself on the line. Rothstein accepted Mr. Stoneham's bets over the phone and as A.R. spun the roulette wheel and called out the winning color and number, poor Charles soon found himself $70,000 in arrears.[24]

One of the leading jockeys of the mid 1920's, Clarence Kummer found the Brook to be as irresistible as Charles Stoneham. Racing officials had given him one warning to stay out of the Brook, it being common knowledge that gambling and bookmaking went on there. Kummer decided that he could ignore the warning but he was mistaken. After a second visit, his license to ride was revoked for one season. [25]

Rothstein's Brook night club was also linked, if only tangentially, to the infamous 1919 "Black Sox" scandal. During the Chicago grand jury investigation of the fixing of the 1919 World Series, former Chicago White Sox owner Charles "Lucky Charlie" Comiskey testified. He told the prosecution that in August 1919 he chanced upon Chicago gangland figure Mont Tennes in Saratoga who told him that the World Series would be fixed.

Mont Tennes, a multi-millionaire who survived multiple attempts on his life, owned and controlled the Trans Continental wire service that delivered the race track results to poolrooms nationwide. Tennes told Comiskey that he knew the Series would be fixed and that several known gamblers, specifically Arnold Rothstein, Nat Evans, and Abe Attell would make the arrangements, with Nicky Arnstein handling the money end of the deal.[26]

Arnold Rothstein was never indicted for participating in the fixing of the 1919 World Series. He did appear before the grand jury investigating the fix, but emerged having convinced the prosecution and the grand jurors that he was uninvolved. Nat Evans was indicted, however, for his part in the affair as were other gamblers, like Rachel Brown, who was arrested that same summer of 1919 at a gambling joint in Saratoga Springs (an event that will be recounted in a later chapter).

Even though most of the men indicted for their involvement in the Black Sox Scandal undoubtedly had connections to Arnold Rothstein, it is most likely that the small time gamblers used the Rothstein name to support their scam and that he probably had very little to do with arranging the dastardly scheme other than giving advice and profiting from knowing who was going to win which game.

During the time that The Brook was in operation (1919-1934) the club was visited by authorities only twice in connection with law enforcement activities. The first time police visited The Brook was in the inaugural season of the club. The second was in 1930 when the place was raided by prohibition agents. Both incidents will be recounted here.

In the summer of 1919, Arnold Rothstein had reportedly paid $30,000 to local officials in order to secure permission to operate The Brook without official interference.[27] Despite his payments and his ability to operate out by Saratoga Lake the previous two summers, Saratoga Springs Police Superintendent Thomas J. Sullivan and Sheriff Austin L. Reynolds found it necessary to visit The Brook during the last week of July.

During the trial of another gambler who had been arrested after local police raided a gambling joint on South Broadway earlier in the summer, Superintendent

Sullivan testified that he had learned of possible gambling at The Brook through reading the local newspapers. He thought it would be appropriate to pay the location a visit and asked Sheriff Reynolds and a deputy Sheriff to accompany him. Sullivan stated under oath that he and Sheriff Reynolds arrived at the club without a warrant and were allowed inside by the only two men present, unidentified staff employees.

Being completely cooperative, the two men were polite and courteous as they escorted the law men throughout the premises. They searched the house thoroughly, Sullivan claimed, and found no evidence of gambling. Sheriff Reynolds backed up the testimony of the head of the local police force. But when pressed if he had inspected EVERY room in the building, Superintendent Sullivan admitted that he did not personally examine one room on the second floor and that he took the word of Deputy Sheriff Hovey that a woman was sleeping in the room and he had seen no gambling apparatus inside.

The men sworn to uphold the law apparently quietly moved on so as not to disturb the sleeping woman, since after all, it was between ten and eleven o'clock at night. The two men found at the home, who were so generous in allowing the officers of the law to search the place without a warrant, remain anonymous - as neither Superintendent Sullivan nor Sheriff Reynolds could recall their names and neither bothered to make a note of who they talked to during their visit. The following morning, residents awoke to the following headline in the local newspaper, "Raid on Church St., Nothing Uncovered..."!

What could have been the reason that Sheriff Reynolds and Superintendent Sullivan failed to find any evidence of gambling at The Brook during their visit, when it seemed the whole world knew what was going on there? It could have been the protection money paid by Rothstein. The workers of the establishment might have been tipped off and the gambling items removed prior to the arrival of the cops. It could have been that both the Sheriff and Superintendent of Police realized that at this particular night club it was in their best interest not to see too much.

Whatever the reason for the lack of success during the "raid," Rothstein had escaped the clutches of the law in Saratoga Springs. He would never again feel as much heat from Saratoga area authorities.

In 1930 The Brook was visited by Prohibition Agents. Rothstein had been murdered in New York City in 1928 at the Park Central Hotel (it was said he refused to pay a gambling debt because the game was crooked) and Nat Evans was sole proprietor of the place.

During August, Prohibition Agents visited the Kit-Kat Club and The Brook in Saratoga Springs. At The Brook the head of the kitchen staff, Charles A. Faissole, and a waiter, T.J. Mara, were arrested for selling liquor to undercover operatives. Faissole was a well-known restaurateur, famous for his European establishments in Paris and Deauville. Both pled not guilty and were released on bail pending their court appearances. Recalling Rothstein's claim that he would make everyone forget about Morrissey and Canfield, locals might have noticed the similarity to Canfield's importation of French culinary assistance and The Brook's employment of a Parisian restaurateur.

It was said that the play at The Brook rivaled that during the heyday of Canfield's run and that the food and entertainment were equal to the glory days of the famous Club House.[28] Regardless of the high play, it is likely that Rothstein never made a greater score at Saratoga than he did while manipulating the 1921 Travers Stakes. David Pietrusza in his book, *Rothstein: The Lifetimes and Murder of the Criminal Genius Who Fixed the 1919 World Series*, gives an excellent account of the story.

Considered the best horse of 1921, Harold Payne Whitney's filly Prudery was one of only two horses entered in the Travers Stakes. The other was Sporting Blood, a good colt in the Rothstein stable. Sporting Blood was a good runner but it was generally acknowledged that he was not in Prudery's class.

Like most excellent gamblers, Rothstein valued information more than anything else, especially when the information could lead to a possible strategic advantage and a considerable pay day. The obvious advantage to a gambler who knew that a particular horse might be suffering through nagging injuries or a particular illness was that the gambler could adjust his play accordingly. Rothstein, like many others, was willing to pay a premium for information and he happened to learn on the morning of the Travers that

Prudery had been "off her feed."

"Off her feed" is a term used by horsemen when a horse does not eat as much as they typically do after a workout. It is usually a sign of some minor illness the horse is suffering from and generally coincides with poor performance by the horse.

There would be no betting for second place but even if Sporting Blood didn't win, Rothstein would still pocket second place purse money for simply running Sporting Blood in the race. But knowing that Prudery was not at the top of her game and that Sporting Blood had been running better than ever recently, Rothstein decided to put some money down on his own horse to win.

Being the master manipulator that he was, however, Rothstein was not content simply to run the race and hope that Sporting Blood came out on top. After all, the race would still be contested by Prudery. Whitney was too much a sporting man himself to scratch Prudery and allow Sporting Blood to win the Travers Stakes unchallenged. There was still a chance that Sporting Blood might lose, even though Prudery might not be at full strength.

Once he decided to bet on his own horse to win, Rothstein had two problems to solve. First, the odds in a two horse race might not make the risk worth it. He would need to bet a considerable sum of money just to win back enough to make the bet worthwhile. He needed Sporting Blood's odds to increase. He got his wish when another great horse named Gray Lag was suddenly entered.

Gray Lag might have been the only horse during that year of 1921 who could challenge Prudery on an even playing field. The horse's entry almost immediately raised the odds for Sporting Blood to win, with most handicappers believing that Sporting Blood would be a distant third in the three-horse race. Rothstein took Gray Lag's entry in stride and put his agents to work placing bets in modest amounts at race tracks and poolrooms all over the country. In this way he avoided placing a large sum of money on his own horse at any one location which would certainly set off alarm bells to veteran gamblers and probably put a stop to the adventure before it began. Getting his money down just before the race would allow Rothstein to get his bets in before the other gamblers realized what was happening and threw their money on Sporting Blood as well, decreasing the odds.

According to the rules of the day, any horse could be scratched up to thirty minutes before post time without any explanation. Whether Rothstein had any hand in it or not, Gray Lag suddenly was scratched from the race without explanation just over one half hour before the race. All seemed in order for Rothstein until one of his agents placed his large bet just a few minutes too early and as a result, the astute gamblers recognized that something was amiss and money started flooding onto Sporting Blood, crashing his odds just before the race.

The race went off with Sporting Blood a respectable 3-1 to win. Prudery would indeed falter during the race and Sporting Blood would take the Travers by a decent margin. Rothstein's payout was $300,000 on his winning bets but a far cry from the millions he would have won had one of his agents not placed his bet just a little too early and the odds remained ever more in his favor.

It was true that many of the wealthiest men of high society in 1920 visited The Brook for entertainment, much as the most fashionable and wealthy gambled their summers away at Canfield's. The titans of industry, Vanderbilts, Whitneys, and Wideners played the games of chance at The Brook, yet it somehow never achieved the status of the legendary Club House.[29]

Rothstein himself eventually tired of pursuing the title of Saratoga's greatest gambler and publicly renounced his gambling operations in 1920. In the October 1, 1920, edition of the Saratogian Rothstein is quoted as making the following statement, "My friends know that I have never been connected with a crooked deal in my life, but I am heartily sick and tired of having my name dragged in on the slightest provocation or without provocation whenever a scandal comes up. I have been victimized more than once and have been forced to bear the burden as best I could, simply because of the business I was in and the peculiar moral code which governs it. But that is all in the past. The unwarranted use of my name in this unfortunate baseball scandal was the last straw. I made up my mind to retire from the gambling business as long ago as last June, as plenty of witnesses will testify, but this has led me to make the announcement publicly, instead of dropping out quietly as was my original plan."

It was an interesting admission from Rothstein, considering that neither the Superintendent of Police nor Sheriff were able to locate any evidence against the publicly self-admitted gambler and his place was never raided or even seriously investigated. Pledging to devote his time to his horse stable and real estate business, Rothstein remained an owner of The Brook on paper only until 1925 when he sold it to his loyal manager, Nat Evans.

Evans operated The Brook for another eight summers before he sold it in June 1934 to another prominent member of the New York City gambling fraternity and a longtime friend, Max "Kid Rags" Kalish,[30] who spent summers in Saratoga renting the Willard A. Braim family home on Caroline Street. "Kid Rags" ran the place for only one summer before Evans bought the property back at the end of the 1934 racing season. Evans promptly insured the building and grounds for $117,000 in November of 1934.[31]

Evans' decision to insure the property was providential. On the morning of December 31, 1934, the Brook burned to the ground. Local resident Michael J. Sweeney was on his way home from work that morning at about 4:00 AM when he saw the flames coming from the famous resort. He notified Officer David Cunningham, who was working desk duty that morning, and the fire department was promptly dispatched. The fire was too far advanced for the responding fire fighters to do anything other than stand by to prevent the fire from spreading to the other buildings on the grounds. Even if they had been able to attempt to put out the blaze, a lack of water pressure from a four inch main out of a Greenfield reservoir would have made knocking down the fire all but impossible.[32]

The building had recently been checked by the property manager and no issues were discovered. It was a shame that the fire consumed a recent addition to the main building that Nat Evans had spent $175,000 on. Police and fire officials conducted a joint investigation into the cause of the fire that started in the northwest corner of the building. It was determined that there were no active fireplaces in the building and the electricity had been turned off for the winter months.[33]

Despite the fact that no one was ever arrested for burning down the famous Brook, the insurance companies remained suspicious. After Nat Evans passed away in early February 1935, his son Jules had to sue seventeen different insurance companies to collect on the Brook fire.[34]

While the Brook was not the longest running of all the gambling joints in Saratoga Springs, it certainly was one the most important during its life of 17 years. The Brook bore Rothstein's signature, and his money, influence, and power ensured that no successful gambling raids were ever made against the place while he ran it, a feat even Richard Canfield could not match.

Endnotes

Chapter 11

1   Pietruza, David. *Rothstein: The Life, Times and Murder of the Criminal Genius Who Fixed the 1919 World Series.* Carroll and Graff. New York, 2003.

2   Pietrusza.

3   Katcher, Leo. *The Big Bankroll: The Life and Times of Arnold Rothstein.* Harper Press, New York, 1959.

4   Katcher.

5   Pietrusza.

6   Repetto, Thomas. *American Mafia: A History of its Rise to Power.* Henry Holt and Company LLC. New York, 2004.

7   Pietrusza.

8   Pietrusza.

9   "Describes Race Track Betting at Saratoga Meet," The Buffalo Courier, September 2, 1908.

10 "It's Not So Easy to Buy Chewing Gum Now," The Daily Saratogian, December 14, 1909.

11 "James H. King, Former Police Chief and Friend of the Boys, Dies at 68 After Active Life," The Saratogian, January 20, 1932.

12 "After Saratoga Gamblers," The New York Times, August 9, 1913.

13 "Madison Ave. House Raided by Police," The Saratogian, August 11, 1916.

14   "Crooked Roulette Wheel," The Mechanicville
      Mercury, November 25, 1916.

15   "Taylor Fails to Escape Twice," The Saratogian,
      August 12, 1916.

16   "Current Local Events," The Mechanicville
      Mercury, November 18, 1916.

17   Katcher.

18   "Rothstein Hoped to be Another 'Dick' Canfield," The
      Saratogian, October 4, 1920.

19   Katcher.

20   "Rothstein Hoped to be…"

21   Katcher.

22   "Rothstein Hoped to be…."

23   Pietrusza.

24   Katcher.

25   "Kummer and Fator will be Big Factors in Riding
      Brigade this Summer," The Brooklyn Daily Eagle,
      March 13, 1927.

26   Pietrusza.

27   "Raid on Church St., - Nothing Uncovered;
      Formel Discharged," The Saratogian. Thursday,
      July 31, 1919.

28   "Damon Runyon Says – Saratoga has
      Changed," Rochester Democrat and Chronicle,
      July 25, 1937.

29   "Fire Destroys Brook, Famous Saratoga Club,"
      The Schenectady Gazette, January 1, 1935.

30   "Tea Table Chat," The Saratogian. June 21, 1934.

31 Pietrusza.

32 "Brook Club, Exclusive Saratoga Night Club, Destroyed by Flames," The Saratogian, December 31, 1934.

33 Ibid.

34 Pietrusza.

Chapter 11

The Case of the Missing Evidence

Gambling raids should be a simple thing. Most often a tip is received by police that illegal gambling is going on at a particular place. Officers then set about gathering evidence to verify whether or not there is any truth to the information. They might send an undercover officer to the location to see what can be learned about the place and the people frequenting the location, or surveillance might be established, with the comings and goings of the place dutifully recorded.

Today, the use of wiretaps along with informants and undercover police officers would be expected in any major gambling investigation. Once enough evidence is obtained, officers then apply for a warrant to a judge who reviews the application and either signs the warrant or declines to sign the warrant if the police officer's application does not contain the requisite amount of probable cause that the laws are being violated.

A search warrant will direct the police to search a specified location for particular items of evidence. With a warrant in hand, the police may then enter the suspected premises and search for the evidence thought to be inside. Sometimes entry must be made by force, but a good raid plan will attempt to gain entry without resorting to the breaking down of doors.

In Saratoga Springs however, the serving of search warrants was not always such a simple task. One fateful night in late July of 1919 a search warrant at 210 South Broadway would set in motion an incredible series of events and expose the cancer of corruption - the likes of which hadn't been seen at the Spa since the bribery scandal of 1892 - and would not be seen again until the Kefauver Committee investigations in the early 1950's.

This one single raid would result in two separate state initiated investigations of conditions in Saratoga Springs, the exposure of links between local small time gamblers and national organized crime figures, the corruption and removal from office of local officials, and the theft of evidence from police headquarters.

It all started on Monday night, July 27, 1919, when a squad of police officers, led by Superintendent of Police Thomas J. Sullivan and Saratoga County Sheriff Austin L. Reynolds, quietly approached the house at 210 South Broadway in Saratoga Springs.

As they approached the front door they were met by a man who refused to open the door for them. The lawmen must have believed that they would not be quick enough to secure any evidence inside if they continued to negotiate with the man standing guard, so they promptly smashed in the front door. A marked difference in tactics from the "raid" that the two men conducted at the Brook around the same time.

Inside, several men were arrested. Their names were given as Aaron Burns (who was later thought to be Aaron Brunstein before he was finally identified as Rachel "Rachie" Brown), Frank Rosse, James Brooks, Samuel Anderson, and John Walker.[1] All of the five men found inside the house at the time of the raid were strangers to the Saratoga authorities. Arriving shortly thereafter was Jules Formel, who was known to the local authorities as a gambler. Formel announced that he was responsible for the property and the activity occurring therein. He was promptly arrested and brought to the police station with the others.

During the raid, the police seized two roulette tables, one of which had had the wheel removed prior to the entry of the officers. Sheriff Austin secured the ivory ball from the table with the wheel still attached and placed it in a bag, along with some gambling chips that were also seized. [2]

City Court Judge Michael McTygue and District Attorney Charles Andrus (son of Constable Eugene Andrus whose exploits as a constable are recorded earlier and was a former Village Justice who once signed a warrant for Richard Canfield and his Club House) were summoned for a late night arraignment for the gamblers. Neither had any knowledge of the raid before it happened and neither appeared to be too happy about that fact.

Judge McTygue criticized the police for obtaining the warrant from Justice of the Peace Elmer Freebern of Wilton rather than himself, and District Attorney Andrus proclaimed that he was not prepared to move forward with charges against any of the defendants except Formel. At that moment all that could be learned from Superintendent Sullivan was that he had been ordered by his boss, Commissioner of Public Safety William R. Milliman, to obtain the warrant from Justice Freebern. Each of the defendants was released after posting a small amount of bail.

It will be recalled that authorities used a similar tactic of applying for a warrant to an outside jurist during a raid on Richard Canfield around the turn of the century. Apparently local police who intended to have a successful raid thought it necessary to obtain their warrants from a judge outside of Saratoga Springs, the hope being that a judge without the Saratoga

Springs connection might not tip off the gamblers to the impending raid.

Superintendent Sullivan had stated that the information upon which he relied to obtain the warrant in the first place was received from Commissioner Milliman. Yet the following morning, when a hearing was held before Judge McTygue, neither Commissioner Milliman nor Sheriff Reynolds could be located by District Attorney Andrus. Andrus advised the court that without testimony from any of the officials involved in the raid he would be unable to produce any evidence against the five strangers arrested at 210 South Broadway and very little evidence against Jules Formel, admitted proprietor of the gambling operation.

Formel's attorney moved for an immediate dismissal of the charges against his client, but Judge McTygue would not agree, so Formel's bail was retained and a future court date was set. The others, however, were released immediately and their bail was refunded. All charges against them were dropped.

At the hearing, instead of examining evidence or attempting to ascertain the facts of the case, Judge McTygue seemed more interested in getting a statement on the record from Jules Formel that he, Judge McTygue, had never taken money from the gambler. In fact, since rumors that money had been exchanged between the two had been circulating in the city, Judge McTygue specifically called Formel to the stand to inquire if he had ever taken protection money from Formel. Formel, of course, denied on the record that he had ever paid Judge

McTygue any money and added (for good measure) that the subject had never come up between them. [3]

With that out of the way, McTygue focused his attention on the outrageous (in his mind) conduct of the local police who dared to circumvent his authority on the matter of the initial warrant. He issued subpoenas for Sheriff Reynolds, Commissioner Milliman, and Justice Freebern to appear before him the following day to explain themselves. [4]

Had this been all there was to the story everything could have gone on as usual in Saratoga Springs. The raid would have soon been forgotten. Small fines would have been paid or the grand jury would have failed to indict the gamblers during the fall term. Arrangements would have been made and everything put back in the proper order. But what happened next was beyond belief, even for those Saratogians who were used to gamblers having free reign in their town.

The gambling evidence that was secured by the police during the raid was brought to police headquarters and secured in one of the jail cells for the night. The five gamblers arrested during the raid at 210 South Broadway, not thinking that their deliverance from court with their bail refunded was enough, made a trip to the side door of the police department on Maple Avenue the following day with the intent to get their property back.

A Saratogian reporter, apparently tipped off that something was about to go down at police headquarters, stood watch from the news building across the street.

What happened next is so amazing that it could have come straight from a Hollywood movie script. The journalist recounted what he saw in the July 30, 1919, edition of the daily paper:

"The vicinity of police headquarters was a popular place with the alleged gamblers yesterday. Shortly after the noon hour the men who had been released on bail earlier in the day drove into Maple Avenue and drew up before the side door of the lower police headquarters on the floor above.

"One by one the men left the car and entered this door, emerging separately in a few minutes, glancing suspiciously around and with their pockets bulging.

"Two of the men left in the automobile and the rest separated in different directions but finally gathered again near High Rock Avenue, excepting two of their number who remained standing at the corner of Lake and Maple avenues, watching everything carefully.

"It was not long before one of the men reappeared bearing a small, heavy box under each arm, the shape of a shoe box, and wrapped in paper. He walked up the City Hall hill, preceded by the other two men.

"When in front of Martin Tierney's café, one of the parcels slipped from his grasp and fell to the sidewalk, a number of chips used in games of chance, being scattered on the ground. These were hurriedly picked up and the parcel rewrapped in a newspaper.

"Going on up Church Street, the man left the packages at the Franklin House and proceeded to the hack-stand where he engaged a truck for a later hour and then returned to South Broadway.

"Shortly after 10 o'clock last night the men again visited the vicinity of the lower City Hall, eight men leaving the house at 210 South Broadway in a touring car. They went through Circular Street, down Lake Avenue and stopped on the east side of Maple Avenue, immediately opposite the side door of police headquarters where they had been in the afternoon. They did not leave the car but in a minute or two drove slowly on about 100 yards where they stopped again for several minutes.

"It is believed that they became suspicious of being watched for they soon drove rapidly away out the Glens Falls road, stopping so suddenly in a quiet part of the road about half way to Wilton and all the men jumped into the road, that a car travelling in the same direction nearly ran them down."

Formel and his gang had not gotten all of their belongings back from police headquarters. It could have been an honest policeman who wouldn't go along with the plan (or got cold feet), or the inquisitiveness of the reporters might have tempered their arrogance.

Formel clearly did not enjoy the same level of protection that Rothstein did, even though they shared some of the same associates, Rachel Brown and Nat Evans, to name just two. Nor did Formel enjoy the bankroll that Rothstein did. He simply could not purchase a new set of roulette tables on a moment's notice; the profits hadn't accumulated yet, it being so early in the summer season. In any event, in order for the South Broadway house to open up again, they would have to re-acquire the remaining goods that were held in the police lock up.

Instead of another daring, daylight operation to remove evidence from police headquarters, the Formel group decided to bring a replevin action before Judge McTygue. A replevin action is a legal procedure seeking the return of personal property that is alleged to have been wrongfully taken or held by the person against whom the action is brought.

To do so, a man named George Remo from New York City stepped forward and claimed that the remaining gambling apparatus was his and that it was being held wrongfully by District Attorney Andrus.

The basis of Remo's claim was that since all of the gamblers arrested at 210 South Broadway had been released with their charges dropped and bail refunded, and since Jules Formel had been acquitted of the charges by Judge McTygue, there clearly was no probable cause to arrest the defendants and therefore no probable cause to indicate the property was used unlawfully at 210 South Broadway. George Remo, until now unknown as a Formel associate, claimed it was his right to recover his property that was unlawfully seized by police and was at that moment being unlawfully held by the District Attorney.

So on August 6, 1919, the replevin action was heard in City Court by Judge McTygue, who ordered the property returned to George Remo![5] At 7:30 PM the gambling paraphernalia that had not been previously removed from police headquarters by the gamblers was dutifully returned to George Remo by the City Marshall Rodney Van Wagoner acting on the replevin order issued by Judge McTygue. Despite the fact that the removal of the property was officially sanctioned, the gamblers, once in possession of the stuff, took great lengths to lose anyone who may have tried to follow them and discover the final destination of the gambling apparatus. [6]

In the days following the raid on 210 South Broadway, local officials made public statements that gambling was not to be tolerated. Each of the managers of suspected gambling joints in Saratoga Springs were called to police headquarters and given a specific warning that gambling was not going to be allowed going forward.[7] The warning was made by Commissioner of Public Safety Milliman at the suggestion of District Attorney Andrus.

Of course warnings had been given by authorities in the past and no one ever seemed to pay much heed to them. The gambling in Saratoga Springs over the years was so notorious that six times the governor or acting governor of the state itself warned local officials to put a stop to it. Adding to the general consensus that the gambling laws were not to be too stringently adhered to at the Spa, wasn't Arnold Rothstein now involved with the whole situation? And if he was, couldn't it be assumed that everything was in order for the gambling fraternity?

It is most likely that the warnings were merely public pronouncements by men whose duty it was to enforce the laws of the state in Saratoga Springs in order to give themselves public, political, and legal cover for their lax efforts. But for some reason, police made another raid during the summer of 1919. This time the date was August 16 and the place was 38 Circular Street, coincidentally not too far from 210 South Broadway. [8]

At 11:30 PM, Superintendent of Police Sullivan and Sheriff Reynolds again teamed up to lead a raiding party. At first approaching the wrong house, they quickly realized their error and threw a guard around the exterior of the correct residence.

Breaching the door and rushing into the first room to the left of the entrance, the police found chips laid out in front of five chairs set in front of a table that was evidently where a faro game had been in progress moments before. It was clear that the gamblers had been given time to dismantle some of the apparatus by the delay resulting from the earlier police mistake in approaching the wrong house. Indeed, a loud gong had begun to ring as police approached the correct door, giving advanced warning of the impending raid to those inside.

Apparently five gamblers had left their chips at the table before scurrying away from the scene while stewards and other employees of the house took away the roulette wheels from the tables. Evidence of betting in amounts ranging from $2 to $20 was found at the faro table where a raised platform for an observer was placed nearby to detect and deter possible cheating. The roulette wheels were located in the basement by Superintendent Sullivan.

Seven people were arrested during the raid. Like the raid on South Broadway, six players and the proprietor were all arrested. Henry Ragan was identified as the manager as he had the keys to the gaming room in his possession. The six others gave their names to police as Arthur Williams, Patrick Quinn, Charles Mitchell, Charles Koeskie, Peter Narrie, and John Johnson. All except Johnson were identified as players while Johnson was supposed to have been an employee of the place, responsible for the food and drink supplied to the patrons.

The little ivory ball, however, could not be located and this was again what was cited as the reason for the release of the prisoners. It will be recalled that the missing ball for the roulette wheel was the key piece of missing evidence that led to the release of the five gamblers arrested in the 210 South Broadway raid just a few weeks prior. The missing roulette ball, however, would not be the only fact linking the two raids.

At the time of the raid, Ragan protested loudly that he had been framed, claiming that he had been told that "everything was all right." He even went so far as to vow that he would start a newspaper to help the police locate other gambling places in Saratoga. The threat did not sit too well with Sheriff Reynolds who advised Ragan, "Young man, don't get me excited, for I am liable to do something."[9]

The threat worked, and Ragan was calmed for a short time. He was allowed to make a phone call from the residence and his half of the conversation was recorded in the Saratogian on August 18, 1919:

> "Hello, I want to talk to Julius"
> "Busy is he? Well tell him that I am the
>   busiest man in the state this minute."
> After a pause, "That you Julius?"
> "They just kicked in the front of this place."
> "Oh, it is, is it?"
> "Oh, all right, good-bye."

Ragan's call to "Julius" was the first indication that the two gambling places were being operated by the same group of gamblers. The second indication came when the seven men arrested required bail the following morning At their arraignment, bail was reduced by Judge McTygue to $100 each, down from the $500 initially set by the police desk officer. The bail was posted by Rachel "Rachie" Brown who had been arrested in the South Broadway raid and had given the name of Burns first, then Brunstein, before his real name was finally discovered.

Of course the men arrested had no reason to worry, as they each were discharged after the District Attorney was unable to produce evidence to convict them. Furthermore, the District Attorney, as in the South Broadway case, even refused to hold the defendants over for the fall term of the grand jury.

The final link between the two raids came when the roulette table confiscated at 38 Circular Street was discovered to bear markings similar to the table that had been seized at 210 South Broadway. In what must have been the ultimate insult to honest cops (if there were any) in Saratoga Springs, the police found themselves seizing the same gambling paraphernalia twice, within the span of three weeks, at two different locations.

As was the case in the South Broadway debacle, a mysterious stranger appeared before Judge McTygue to make a replevin action, as George Remo had during the first raid. This time, however, the stranger, Harry Oughton, was unable to obtain the gaming equipment and Judge McTygue had the good sense to ensure that the property stayed safely stored in the police station. [10] The security of the evidence at the police station could, of course, be questioned given the theft of the gambling equipment just a couple of weeks prior.

That the two houses raided were evidently run by the same people while other gambling places, like Rothstein's Brook and Arrowhead resorts, ran without interference for the entire summer must have seemed curious, even to jaded observers of gambling conditions at Saratoga Springs. With the exception of Jules Formel, all of the men were strangers to the Spa. Rachel Brown in particular had a reputation as a gangster associated with some of the most unsavory of New York City's underworld brotherhood.

For some reason the police raided the two places without notifying either the District Attorney or the City Court Judge who proceeded to brazenly allow all the suspected gamblers to go free. They didn't even pretend to go through the usual motions of sending the cases to the grand jury in October and having the grand jurors fail to bring indictments.

The raids on 210 South Broadway and 38 Circular Street in the summer of 1919 were just two of many events that shocked the good citizens of Saratoga since the arrival of Arnold Rothstein on the scene just a couple of years earlier. It was becoming increasingly apparent that the gangsters may indeed be all powerful in Saratoga Springs.

It wasn't just that the time honored arrangements between gamblers and authorities seemed to be fraying, but that local authorities were unable to stem the tide of increasing crime in general. As bad as things seemed with the gambling situation in 1919, many of the details of the raids would not become known until several months later when police officers and civilians testified in court about the raids. In the meantime, the situation was so bad that something had to be done, and the governor of New York agreed, appointing a special prosecutor, Wyman S. Bascom to investigate gambling at the Spa.

Endnotes

Chapter 11

1   "Police Raid House, Arrest Six, Take Gambling Apparatus," The Saratogian, July 29, 1919.

2   "Raiding Party on Stand in Saratoga Gambling Inquiry," The Schenectady Gazette, December 21, 1920.

3   "Five Taken in Raid Go Free; Officials Ordered Into Court," The Saratogian, July 30, 1919.

4   Ibid.

5   "Owner Gets Back Gambling Apparatus," The Saratogian. August 7, 1919.

6   Ibid.

7   "Warning Goes Out Against Gambling," The Saratogian, August 5, 1919.

8   "Another Gambling Raid; Seven Caught This Time; Everybody Freed Again," The Saratogian, August 18, 1919.

9   Ibid.

10 "Gamblers Wait All Night for Apparatus," The Saratogian, August 21, 1919.

Chapter 12

Bascom's Raiders

To say that Saratoga Springs was a gangster's paradise in 1919 and 1920 may not be too far from the truth. It appeared that everyone knew that gangsters and gamblers were in bed with local politicians, law enforcement, and the courts. Over and over again the local newspaper printed allegations of payoffs, identified locations where gambling and prostitution were carried on, and detailed violent crimes that went unsolved by police.

Thirty one serious felonies were reportedly committed during 1919-1920 without a single suspect apprehended. Over $13,000 in property was stolen by robbers and burglars during the same time frame. Even a burglary in City Hall itself went unsolved as $18 was stolen from the office of the City Engineer in February 1920.[1]

One burglary in 1919 was solved, however. Prominent local attorney and Republican powerhouse James Leary was the victim of a burglary in December of 1919 when $4,000 worth of liquor was stolen from the basement of the Algonquin Building on Broadway, which he owned.[2]

Louis Dematteo was quickly arrested for the crime but refused to cooperate with authorities. It was suspected that Louis had the assistance of several others and the police suddenly took an interest in a craps game occurring in the "Little Italy" section of the city that today is the area around the Beekman Street Arts District. Coincidentally, it was the same area of town where Dematteo lived.

The police were getting nowhere in their investigation into the burglary at the Algonquin Building and Louis Dematteo was able to post bail. But as soon as he did, he was rearrested by Police Sergeant (soon to be Superintendent of Police) Edward Carroll who also drew up complaints against Dematteo's brother, Gus Dematteo, and two associates of the siblings, Paul Smaldone and Genora Pompay, alleging their involvement in the aforementioned craps game.[3]

Unlike the raids at 210 South Broadway and 38 Circular Street earlier that summer, Sergeant Carroll apparently had all of the details of the operation in order before making an arrest. The Dematteo brothers were charged with being common gamblers, accused of having won $150 at 49 Beekman Street, a house allegedly owned by Smaldone. Pompay was charged with running the game.

Sergeant Carroll understood that where powerful figures in city politics and government were concerned, an ambitious police officer need not wait for orders to make the appropriate arrests or refrain from making appropriate arrests, to ensure everything was kept "in order." The larceny of liquor belonging to attorney Leary required a response. Other crimes might go un-noticed, un-investigated and linger un-solved, but the stealing of liquor from such a prominent resident, and friend of police and gambler alike, was over the line!

The cynical observer might note that without enough evidence to secure a charge of burglary, there were other ways to "skin a cat." In this case it might have been to arrest the suspects on other charges, charges that were much easier to prove, such as the running of a minor gambling operation that- until the liquor went missing- was allowed to run undisturbed.

Carroll may have been the beneficiary of local politicians who were looking for someone to head the police department who knew how to play the game. In June 1919, before the arrival of the likes of Rachel Brown, Jules Formel and company, and the summer raids on

South Broadway and Circular Street, Superintendent
of Police James H. King sought a medical retirement,
which was approved by Dr. Arthur J. Leonard. [4]

In 1919 Leonard was the City Physician but would
later preside as Public Safety Commissioner over
some of the most corrupt and wide open years in city
history. It should be noted that James H. King was
Superintendent of Police during a period that was
perhaps the cleanest decade in terms of the gambling
situation in Saratoga history before he was replaced by
Thomas J. Sullivan who served for less than one year
before Sergeant Edward Carroll took over as head of
the department.

Violent incidents also seemed on the upswing
during the time gamblers and gangsters were running
roughshod over the Spa. A violent black-jacking and
robbery on Broadway was reported to police and two
pistol shots were fired through the window of Harry
Green at his residence out Lake Avenue. Former
policeman Frank Buckett was shot five times and killed
by William DeMarco in Congress Park,[5] while Gertrude
Collins was murdered by George Thompson in July
1919.[6] All of these incidents of violent crime happened
while more and more gangsters flooded into the city
and local officials became more comfortable with their
presence.

Even the police were not immune from the
violence happening around Saratoga in 1919 and
1920. Superintendent of Police Carroll and Detective
Charles Ballou were investigating a racetrack worker

in the summer of 1920 for allegedly shooting at another worker's dog. When the two policemen approached the suspect, James Robinson, he told the men that he kept his gun in his bunk at the other end of the stable. Yet once they entered the room, Robinson suddenly pulled the gun from his shirt and shot Detective Ballou three times.

Thinking Ballou had been dispatched; Robinson pointed the gun at Superintendent Carroll's head and pulled the trigger. Ballou, though seriously injured, managed to recover his senses in time to knock the gun upward at the same moment Robinson pulled the trigger and the bullet grazed Carroll's forehead. Robinson was subdued shortly thereafter and charged with the attempted murder of the two officers. [7]

With the gambling situation thrown wide open, violence on the rise, a police department in turmoil and seemingly unable to deal effectively with criminal activity, Saratoga Springs was in a bad way. Even New York Governor Alfred Smith took notice. Receiving anonymous letters of the gambling situation, and with near daily press attacks on conditions of the summer resort, how could he not? Action was required and the governor appointed a special Deputy Attorney General to investigate the gambling and corruption in Saratoga Springs. The man he chose was Washington County District Attorney Wyman S. Bascom.

As an outsider, Mr. Bascom would have a difficult time working on his own and he enlisted the help of Saratogian and former State Senator Edgar T. Brackett to assist him. The addition of Brackett to Bascom's team brought three benefits.

First, Brackett lent considerable political power to the prosecution team and ensured that Bascom would not be left alone to face the likes of the popularly elected City Judge, District Attorney, and Public Safety Commissioner. If there was one thing Saratogians disliked more than anything else, it was "outsiders" calling attention to how things were run in town. This was something, it will be recalled, that Brackett himself railed against when New York City lawyers were causing search and arrest warrants to be served on his client, Richard Canfield, at the turn of the century. Nevertheless, Brackett would ensure that the local political wards wouldn't steamroll Bascom and was an effective counterweight to another politically powerful attorney, his former clerk James Leary, who would represent many of the defendants in the cases yet to come.

The second benefit that Bascom would receive with Brackett's help was access to the press. The Saratogian was essentially Brackett's newspaper and ever since Brackett's change of heart on the gambling question, the Saratogian had been the leading critic of conditions at the Spa.

Finally, Brackett gave Bascom an insider's view of how the gambling game was played in Saratoga Springs. As Richard Canfield's former attorney, Brackett could provide historical context for Bascom and make sense of the seemingly complex relationships between the public, the gamblers, and local officials. He knew everyone and everything about the gambling situation at Saratoga and was surely happy for the opportunity to bring to justice those who he believed were operating to the detriment of the City.

Additional help for Bascom would soon come in the spring of 1920. Two officers of the police department, Detective James Sullivan and Officer Hugh Dorsey both resigned before the summer of 1920 and joined Bascom's team.

James Sullivan, a detective for 15 years with the Police Department and brother of ex-Superintendent Thomas Sullivan, who had been replaced by Commissioner Gaffney in favor of Carroll in January, resigned from the force claiming that there was too much politics in the department. His claims were supported by local rumors circulating in the city that friction within the department was extreme and that the few officers who supported enforcement of the gambling laws were being forced out of the department by Commissioner Gaffney and Superintendent Carroll.

In fact, Superintendent Carroll had reportedly been harassing Detective Sullivan to the point that Sullivan appealed to Commissioner Gaffney seeking relief. After his meeting with Gaffney, Sullivan claimed that the harassment only worsened and left him no choice but to resign from the force. [8] Since Detective Sullivan was a clean officer and Superintendent Carroll was unable to bring forth any allegations of misconduct or neglect of duty against him, Commissioner Gaffney quickly

accepted his resignation and promoted Patrolman
Charles Ballou (a Carroll ally and an officer with less
than eighteen months experience) to fill the detective
position vacated by Sullivan. As an indication of just
how unbearable it must have been for poor Detective
Sullivan, his resignation came less than two years
before he would have been eligible for a pension. [9]

Hugh Dorsey, a well-liked and long serving
patrolman followed Sullivan in resigning from the
force in early 1920. And he did so in a much more public
manner than Sullivan. It was reported in the Saratogian
newspaper on May 12, 1920 that Dorsey resigned from
the police department after he received an anonymous
note at police headquarters the previous night asking
to meet him at the sundial in Congress Park.

Officer Dorsey claimed that he felt the note was
probably someone with information regarding criminal
activity who wanted to remain anonymous. When he
arrived at the sundial at the appointed time, he noticed
two figures hiding in the bushes nearby, two figures
whom he quickly recognized as Deputy Commissioner
of Public Safety Benjamin Wilson and newly appointed
Detective Ballou. [10]

Patrolman Dorsey was aware of a directive issued
by Superintendent Carroll the day after Detective
Sullivan's resignation that absolutely forbade any
officer of the department from investigating any matter
without approval from a superior officer and forbidding
all officers from discussing any police business outside

of the department. In addition, by walking to the sun dial in Congress Park, Dorsey had left his post.

The clear trickery used to trap Dorsey, who was closely associated with former Detective Sullivan, was unseemly. But even Patrolman Dorsey could recognize that Deputy Commissioner Wilson and Detective Ballou were in a position to testify to Dorsey's violation of department rules, namely being off post and undertaking an investigation without approval. Dorsey walked away and verbally resigned to the desk sergeant immediately, placing his gun and badge on the desk as he did so. [11]

Dorsey didn't simply resign, however, he went public. In his letter of resignation to Commissioner Gaffney, which was printed in the Saratogian on May 12, 1920, Dorsey echoed the sentiments of Detective Sullivan that conditions in the department were so bad that he had no other choice but to resign. Specifically, Dorsey claimed that since Carroll had been appointed Superintendent of Police by Gaffney on January 1, he had been "discriminated against and unfair methods and tactics had been used to such an extent that further service has become unbearable." Dorsey went on, "The department has got to such a state that it is no fit place for an officer who wants to do his duty, and has done it in the opinion of the public."

Dorsey told reporters that Detective Ballou had told him that Carroll had ordered him (Ballou) to meet Deputy Commissioner Wilson for a "job" on the night of May 11. He further explained that when he noticed

Wilson and Ballou near the sundial, Wilson appeared to be wearing a disguise, unusual clothes, and a hat that covered his face.

Neither Superintendent Carroll nor Commissioner Gaffney had any immediate comment other than Carroll stating that he knew of no complaints against Dorsey in the years that he had been with the department. Gaffney decided to think the matter over before commenting on the record.

The Saratoga Springs Police Department had gone through three heads of the department in less than eighteen months. After Superintendent King retired, James Sullivan replaced him during the fateful summer of 1919 when the open gambling conditions in the City were exposed by the raids on 210 South Broadway and 38 Circular Street and prominently reported on in the media. Upon taking office in January 1920, Gaffney replaced Sullivan with the much younger Sergeant Carroll. Shortly thereafter, Detective Sullivan resigned and by May 1920, Patrolman Dorsey was gone as well.

The Dorsey resignation must have been a difficult public relations problem for Gaffney and Carroll, as Dorsey, by all accounts, was an efficient and effective officer. He was the only member of the department to hold a certificate of standing from the New York State Civil Service Commission.

Dorsey and then-Detective James Sullivan had interrupted a robbery at the Thomas Cottage on Union Avenue and assisted federal law enforcement in apprehending a gang of human traffickers smuggling several Chinese nationals through Saratoga Springs via Montreal. Dorsey also was instrumental in developing the information that cleared a murder on Congress Street just a few years earlier. [12] With turmoil at the top of the department and the resignations of two long serving, effective, and respected officers, Gaffney and Carroll needed to respond, and they did so on May 13.

Commissioner Gaffney, in a letter made public accepting Dorsey's resignation, made the following statement, "Your resignation from the Police Department of this city received and I accept of the same. I wish to state, however, that the compromising position you were discovered in on the night of May 11, would have necessitated an investigation, and if the story reported to me was found to be true, your removal from office would have been necessary. However, you have chosen the best course, and thereby saved yourself from a public hearing."[13]

Superintendent Carroll went even further, claiming that Dorsey's presence at the sundial was not in response to supposed police business, but rather to rendezvous with a married woman. Carroll's letter, made public in the local newspaper accused Dorsey of being a less than efficient officer in that he had allowed a murder suspect to escape the previous year and that he had met repeatedly with married women while he was supposed to be doing police work.

Furthermore, Carroll mocked Dorsey's efficiency as an officer, claiming that he was fooled by Deputy Commissioner Wilson's "disguise" at the sundial that

Carroll said was a newly purchased hat but that Wilson told reporters was an old cap he wore around his home while working. [14]

Carroll's letter, published on May 13, 1920, on the front page of the Saratogian contained the following barbs, "A guilty conscience needs no accuser, and this is only too true in Mr. Dorsey's case. He violated the rules and orders of the department and then tried to use a smoke screen to shield himself, by saying 'I thought it was in reference to police matters.' How absurd! He may deceive some people, but those people are willing to be deceived." And, "Mr. Dorsey, you should use better judgement in selecting your companions and have them leave your notes at a place other than where you are employed." He made the whole public affair even more personal when he added, "...when Mr. Dorsey says conditions were 'intolerable' he must mean that engagements with women must be kept at times other than hours he was supposed to be doing regular police duty."

The resignation of Patrolman Dorsey was now a very public affair and Dorsey fired back the following day in a letter to Superintendent Carroll published in the Saratogian on May 14, 1920. In the letter Dorsey made six allegations against Carroll and Commissioner Gaffney.

First, Dorsey alleged that Carroll, in 1919 when he was still a sergeant, had stolen twenty pounds of coffee from Beyer's store in the Collamer Building. Dorsey alleged that Carroll had found the door unlocked and had requested Dorsey to assist him in securing the property. While inside Carroll, again according to Dorsey, took twenty pounds of coffee before locking the place up.

Next, Dorsey claimed that Carroll had frequented the gambling place at 210 South Broadway and other illegal gambling places in the City on more than one occasion prior to the raid. He also stated that Carroll associated with a known ex-convict named "Murphy" who started a small riot on Congress Street in 1919 after Murphy and a partner made off with $800 using crooked dice in a craps game above Foy's Restaurant.

This allegation was addressed by two men named Kobel and Foy who owned the place referred to as Foy's restaurant, but was really called Manhattan Lunch, in a letter to the Saratogian the following day. Kobel and Foy assured people that the cause of the riot was not a crooked dice game involving Murphy, since no African-Americans were allowed in the place, and to further weigh in on the controversy made reference to Dorsey frequently taking free meals there. [15]

The third allegation against Carroll was that he received letters from married women at the police station and as proof, Dorsey provided the local paper with a copy of a letter addressed to Edward T Carroll at the Police Department from "C" that he claims was found on the floor of the police station. The letter was clearly an amorous communication with a post stamp of Rome, NY, and was described as 'gilt edged' and smelling of violets.

Perhaps most shockingly, Dorsey accused then Sergeant Carroll of being the officer who unlocked the doors leading to the evidence being held in the police department after the raid on 210 South Broadway, thus allowing two gamblers to remove the ivory ball and crooked devices from headquarters.

Finally, Dorsey alleged that Commissioner Gaffney's associates were no better than Carroll's and offered to supply proof if called upon to support this claim. Dorsey agreed to an independent investigation of his personal and professional conduct provided that both Commissioner Gaffney and Superintendent Carroll did the same. [16]

These were serious allegations and marked the third consecutive day that the resignation of Patrolman Dorsey and the subsequent back and forth allegations had dominated the front page of the local newspaper. The following day Carroll flatly denied all of the allegations made by Dorsey and promptly filed a libel suit against Dorsey and the Saratogian, his attorney being City Court Judge Michael McTygue. [17] The libel suit would not be tried until the fall of 1920, but before that, much more action would transpire in Saratoga Springs.

Before the summer of 1920, ex-detective James Sullivan and ex-officer Hugh Dorsey would sign on to assist Bascom and Brackett in the campaign against the gamblers. They would move quickly, raiding four places simultaneously in the early morning hours of Sunday, August 15. They struck at two gambling houses, 75 Nelson Avenue and 60 Phila Street, one disorderly house at 238 Nelson Avenue, and a liquor dive at 40 Putnam Street. [18]

Approaching the 75 Nelson Avenue game, the Bascom agents nabbed the lookout before he could raise the alarm and broke into the house. The players and employees retained such concentration on their games that the raiders simply stood by and watched the play for a couple of minutes before Bascom himself had had enough. He reached over the roulette table and took possession of the ball in the middle of a spin. The forty patrons were lined up against a wall while the tables were dismantled and the employees arrested. [19]

At 75 Nelson Avenue, Rachel Brown again found himself being arrested as he had the year prior when he was arrested at 210 South Broadway. As was the case at 210 South Broadway, Jules Formel was thought to be the proprietor of 75 Nelson but was not present during the raid and a warrant was sought for his arrest.

The raid at 60 Phila Street moved with as much efficiency as the raid at 75 Nelson. Special Detective Sullivan led this raid, moving through the alley behind the place and catching the lookouts by surprise. There were fewer patrons present at this place but more employees. In all, nine workers in the place were arrested.

Arrested during this raid were John H. "Gold Tooth" Moore and Patrick Flynn who, like Rachel Brown and Jules Formel, apparently did not learn the lesson they should have when they were arrested the previous

August at 38 Circular Street. In addition to the familiar faces, among the plethora of evidence seized at 60 Phila Street was a crooked faro box that controlled which card was dealt, thus removing all luck and allowing the house to control the outcome of any given game.

At 40 Putnam Street, William Tolmie, the proprietor of the place, had all of his liquor seized but avoided arrest for the time being.

At 238 Nelson Avenue, Hugh Dorsey led a raid against a house of prostitution, making four arrests. Three of the ladies of the house taken into custody were charged with prostitution, while Grace Stillwater was charged with being the Madame of the house. [20]

For their part, the gamblers were shocked! Assurances had been made that they were in the clear as far as law enforcement was concerned. They felt they were double-crossed since they had been told that they had nothing to fear from Bascom. The apparent belief, even among local residents, was that Bascom's investigation was to be limited to conditions at Saratoga in 1919. [21]   And as everyone knew or assumed, the troubles of 1919 had been dealt with, for the most part.

The local police force, still under the command of Superintendent Carroll and Commissioner Gaffney, took note of the raids. Carroll's brother John, a motorcycle officer at that time, and a detective (probably Detective Ballou) watched the 60 Putnam Street raid from the sidewalk in front of the place. The detective was intent on entering the house during the investigation but was dissuaded by the stern warning given by Special Deputy Sullivan. [22]

Three uniformed police officers also watched the raid at 238 Nelson. They made no movement to interfere but simply stood across the street as Bascom's team went about their work, almost certainly taking mental notes to report to their superiors.

These initial efforts of the Bascom men produced 18 arrests and so much paraphernalia that several vehicles were needed to transport it all to headquarters. Perhaps embarrassed by Bascom's success, the local police quickly raided a place called the Spencer House on Woodlawn Avenue and arrested 12 people inside for gambling. They then moved to roll up a few men at a Congress Street venue. But they could not keep pace with Bascom and each of their prey was released within hours on $25 bail apiece. [23]

Those caught in Bascom's net, however, were not as lucky as those released by the City Court on bail. He had ordered all of his prisoners to be brought to the County Jail and placed into the custody of the Sheriff, to be held until they could be brought into a proper court. He further instructed that no one was to be allowed to visit with the prisoners without his being notified.

If the raids of the 15th were spectacular, the real fireworks would be in court and it began the day after the arrests were made. Bascom discovered that, despite his orders that the prisoners were to be held in jail, they had all been brought to City Court and arraigned before

City Court Judge McTygue with District Attorney Andrus appearing for the people. [24]

Bascom was incensed that his orders had been disregarded and that all of the defendants in the case had posted bail. Predictably, seven of the eighteen failed to appear when their cases were later called. Bascom wanted to know why he had not been notified that the prisoners had been moved and been allowed to post bail. All Andrus could say was that he was unaware that Bascom had superseded him and that he thought it was his responsibility to oversee the prosecutions.

That was, of course, a ridiculous position to take as District Attorney Andrus had clearly been removed from the gambling investigation when the Governor appointed a special prosecutor. Supreme Court Judge Van Kirk agreed and advised Andrus, on the record that the gambling cases belonged to Bascom and would remain so going forward. [25]

Despite the legal victory, Bascom was getting his first taste of the "Saratoga Way." He was upset that the release of the prisoners on such small bail (most having only to produce $100) by a City Court Judge in collusion with the District Attorney and obviously someone within the Sheriff's Department, amounted to a get-out-of-jail free card. He bemoaned the fact that the gambling fraternity was "all powerful in Saratoga Springs" and that they seemed to be even more powerful than the law in the city. [26]

Undeterred, Bascom continued raiding. During the early morning hours of Tuesday, August 24, he raided the Indian Head Tavern on Ballston Avenue with Sheriff Reynolds, Undersheriff Hovey, and Special Investigators Sullivan and Dorsey. The lawmen arrived while patrons of the bar on the first floor danced and drank the night away without a seeming care in the world.

Moving quickly through the dining room, they ascended to the second floor where the games were occurring. On the stairway they were met by John P. Denin, proprietor of the club who made an attempt to slow the raiders while trying to yell a warning to his brother of the approaching officers. [27]

The officials would not be hindered and entered the gaming room by breaking down the door to the room. Once inside they arrested three New York City gamblers who were running the games and seized a roulette wheel and all the paraphernalia. The Denin brothers were released to appear before the grand jury while the three New York men and a lookout were brought to the County Jail. [28] The efficiency of the Bascom men was evident by the fact that the patrons of the club remained unaware of what had happened.

Less than 24 hours later, Bascom was at it again, this time launching three simultaneous operations at poolrooms or "hand-books" as they were referred to in the local media.

Late in the afternoon of the 24th of August, James Fennell, Alfred Duval, and William Doherty, local men all, found themselves visited by the crusaders. Fennell, at 20 Phila Street, was the only gambler with some warning, as the team sent to his place arrived a couple of minutes after he had been warned. Fennell was unable to get rid of all the incriminating evidence as the officers arrived, while his employees were in the middle of destroying the evidence sought by the officers. The raiders did manage to retrieve some of the damning material once they put a stop to the efforts of Fennel's men.

Duval at 428 Broadway, and Doherty at 382 Broadway, were caught completely by surprise and the raiders made off with "a large number of racing charts, telephones, betting slips, ledger accounts of regular patrons, and sealed envelopes with debits and credits addressed not only to summer visitors but well known Saratogians."[29]

Bascom's next target was the nuisance small time book makers that had been allowed to run unmolested along the fence on Union Avenue just outside the race track. On August 26 Bascom's men approached by car but were spotted by a plainclothes police officer who, according to Bascom, yelled, "Here come the raiders!" causing a general scattering of the suspects before the lawmen had a chance to jump out and make their arrests. [30] The alleged officer in civilian clothes who shouted the warning was never identified.

Saratoga had never seen such a level of vice enforcement. Dozens of arrests and several raids during the course of the racing season was unheard of. The only comparable crackdowns on the gamblers that could be remembered were the raids of 1886 conducted by Anthony Comstock. In those days however, Comstock's raiders moved on after presenting the evidence to the local authorities with the predictable result that nothing would come of the cases once the grand jury convened in the fall. It was remembered that even Comstock himself made reference to the fact that his efforts would probably amount to nothing as he left town after his raids.

This time however, Acting Governor Harry Walker called for an extraordinary Grand Jury session to begin July 13, 1920.[31] The work of the grand jury would begin, even as the raiders were busy chasing down the gamblers during the summer of 1920. Bascom began calling witnesses almost immediately after the grand jurors were chosen and within just a few weeks witnesses had already begun testifying, including Saratoga Springs Police Officers and employees of the famous Brook nightclub. Additional evidence was presented as a result of the raids and the grand jury started issuing indictments by September.

With the raids concluded it was now time for Bascom and Brackett to get down to business. The first ten indictments became public on Tuesday September 7, 1920. If Bascom was looking to drop a bombshell with the first wave of indictments, he succeeded. Among those indicted by the extraordinary grand jury was District Attorney Charles Andrus!

It would have been big news in Saratoga even if the indictments had not included the District Attorney. Among those indicted in the first round were several

Corinth natives who were raided by Bascom during August, plus John Denin from the Indian Head Club on Ballston Avenue, and three people charged with operating disorderly houses.

Of the three brothel owners, the two local women (Alice Johnson of 17 Park Street and Marie Taylor of Crescent Street) along with Louis Butler (whose wife Corinne Butler was murdered two weeks prior to the indictment by George "Boots" Scroggins) from Ash and Beekman Streets, had been reportedly allowing prostitution to occur at their places during the summer of 1920. All three Saratogians were represented by local attorney and political power James Leary. [32]

But these defendants were afterthoughts. No one really cared about those indictments. The District Attorney was charged with neglect of duty and theft! Even though Andrus had been permitted to appear before the grand jury during its deliberations, he did not escape indictment.

The indictment against Andrus alleged that during his time as District Attorney he took no action against the gamblers in Saratoga County. The dates of the indictment covered January 1, 1918, through August 24, 1920, his entire term in office to that point. The basis of the indictment was that he was aware of, but took no action against, the open gambling conditions in Saratoga County during his entire tenure.

The charge of theft was based upon some liquor that had been seized by City and State Police from Mrs. John M. McNichols (who ran a speakeasy on West

Circular Street) on August 3, 1918. The $400 worth of spirits had been secured in the local police department where it was held until it "disappeared" in October. It was alleged that Andrus had paid for a truck to remove the seized liquor and kept it for his own consumption. Prior to removing the liquor, police officers were paid in 16 quarts of the stuff for their cooperation. Mrs. Adelle McNichols never was tried for the alleged crimes leading to the liquor seizure in the first place.[33]

The acrimony that would be ever present during the court battles to come was evident from the first court appearance of District Attorney Andrus. He was represented, at least initially, by County Court Judge Lawrence B. McKelvey who fired the opening shots by thundering, "These indictments are the result of a dastardly and wicked political conspiracy that has no equal in the annals of the state."

Referring to the district attorney's efforts to bring the gamblers to justice, Justice McKelvey said, "He (Andrus) has never been helped, he has always been hindered by the most powerful political influences here; when he secured a conviction he has been blamed for being unjust and when a man has escaped he has been accused of not doing his duty."[34]

McKelvey would go on, "He has been belittled and maligned by the foul press of the county." With tears in his eyes, the judge proclaimed, "he has been damned and cursed and dogged and ridiculed as no other public official ever was."

Before finishing his statement to the court McKelvey would go on to accuse Bascom and Brackett of persuading the Lieutenant Governor to convene the grand jury with the specific intent of going after Andrus for political reasons. Interestingly, no mention was made of the allegation regarding the theft of the liquor.

Of course Bascom disputed all of the allegations. He calmly appealed to Supreme Court Justice Charles C. Van Kirk to uphold the indictments. On September 10 Van Kirk did uphold the indictments without comment and, while the case was just starting to heat up, both the President of the Saratoga New York Racing Association,[35] Richard Wilson, and the local Boy Scout Troop No. 136 came out publicly in favor of the anti-gambling effort. They were joined by the local clergy and business leaders in the community who felt that the conditions of 1919 were detrimental to the economic and moral health of city residents.

For his part, Senator Brackett went on the offensive in the court of public opinion, penning a sharp retort for the papers to Judge McKelvey's statements in court. His diatribe was printed in the Saratogian newspaper on September 16. Taking the strongest stance against gambling in Saratoga in his long public career, Brackett said, "I have never had any illusions as to the wishes of a majority of the people of Saratoga Springs. They want it and they are firmly imbued with the notion that they are as much entitled to decide whether they shall, or shall not, have it, irrespective of the provisions of the Penal Law, as they have to decide on a system of street lighting or sewers. The person who would start an anti-gambling crusade here, as a political maneuver would find himself a candidate for the wildest ward in a lunatic asylum."

Reminding readers that the governor had warned the officials at Saratoga to put a stop to the wide-open gambling that had been going on the previous year, Brackett stated his position clearly, that the year of 1919 was despicable and he offered the opinion that no decent man or woman of the town would hesitate to support efforts to stamp out the plague of gamblers that appeared to be all powerful at that time.

In denying the accusation that the efforts being undertaken by Bascom and himself were politically motivated, Brackett acknowledged his dislike of the current county judge and Andrus' attorney. Referring to Judge McKelvey he said, "If it is thought a political move, I say, here and now, that as much as I abhor the present County Judge, if he will put himself in the position of leading a movement to drive out the poolrooms and gambling houses that are ruining Saratoga, I will fall in behind him with every ounce of support I can give him, hold my nose and work with him, and give him all the credit for its success when we are finished."

August and September had been good to Bascom and Brackett. Bascom's raids over the summer had resulted in many arrests and the seizure of much evidence. The prosecution had been successful in bringing initial indictments against not only a few gamblers but also the real evil (according to their thinking) of one county official who was seemingly powerless to confront the gamblers despite the authority of his office. They must have been feeling good going into the fall of 1920 as things looked like they were falling into place for some successful prosecutions.

But something happened on September 15th that was surely the cause of much consternation among the anti-gambling crowd. A primary election was held. And in that primary election, Charles B. Andrus, indicted just four days earlier for neglect of duty and theft, secured both the Republican and Democratic nominations for another two-year term as Saratoga County District Attorney. Defeating his opponent, John B. Smith, by 663 votes in a lightly attended Republican primary, Andrus was assured of reelection in November as the Democrats had no official candidate and the few write-in votes that were tallied were cast for Andrus, giving him the nomination. Nothing short of a miracle would prevent Andrus from winning another term in office, thus supporting Brackett's theory of the popularity of gambling in Saratoga Springs. [37]

By the time District Attorney Andrus was reelected in November, Bascom had been successful in bringing sixty indictments for various crimes related to his investigation of the vice conditions at Saratoga. [38] Bascom and Brackett were ready to proceed, but the criminal case of the People vs. Andrus would have to wait. First the libel suit filed by Superintendent Carroll against the Saratogian was going to be heard.

While Bascom's staff was gathering evidence and the grand jury was busy carrying out their solemn duties, the matter of the libel suit that Superintendent Carroll had filed against the Saratogian for printing the allegations of ex-patrolman Dorsey back in the spring was scheduled for trial. Carroll did not sue for libel on all of the allegations printed in March, he only sued on the basis that the theft of the coffee from Breyer's store was a lie. The other allegations of corresponding with a married woman, consorting with known ex-convicts, and participation in the removal of evidence from the police department after the 210 South Broadway raid, were not part of the suit. He sought $25,000 in damages.

Both sides dug in and the libel suit went to trial in October 1920 in front of a jury and Justice E.C. Whitmyer. County Court Judge McKelvey represented Carroll and Edgar T. Brackett appeared on behalf of the newspaper. The inquisition would be limited to the allegations contained in the printed editions of the Saratogian back in March, but there was no doubt that if Brackett could get anything on the record concerning the gambling conditions existing during Carroll's time as Superintendent of Police, he would.

The Saratogian's defense was simple. What had been printed in the paper was true. In order to defend the paper, Brackett would have an opportunity to go after Carroll on the stand and Carroll would have to prove that the allegations were false. It would be quite a grilling by the experienced Brackett as Carroll spent nearly two days being examined by the ex-senator.

When Carroll first took the stand he testified briefly to his job, when he was appointed, where he had lived during his life, a general denial of the allegations, and the usual preliminary testimony that one would hear at any trial when a witness first takes the stand. Immediately the issue of the articles penned by both Dorsey and Carroll back in March was brought up and Brackett referred to them as a "newspaper war," indicating that if there was to be a public fight between the two men Carroll wanted his side out to counter Dorsey. The term "war" was objected to by Judge Whitmyer who remarked, "I haven't heard anything about a war yet."

Brackett, displaying his sharp wit replied, "Cheer up your honor, you're going to." Whereupon Brackett opened his direct questioning by introducing letters of a romantic nature addressed to Edward Carroll from a woman who signed the letter "C." The letter was reportedly found in the police station and Carroll was ultimately forced to admit that the letter belonged to him and that it was from a married woman named "Nina" from Amsterdam, NY, where Carroll had spent about eight years of his life. Despite Carroll's assertion that he had never had an improper relationship with the married "Nina," he was not off to a good start.

Next Brackett addressed the allegation that then Patrolman Carroll had stolen ten pounds of coffee from Beyer's Store in 1919 when he found the door open. It was brought out that Carroll actually lived in an apartment above Breyer's Store in the Collamer

Building on Broadway. Despite some harsh initial questioning, Carroll maintained that he never stole the coffee as alleged and that he did not know where the bags were kept in the store even if he had wanted to.

Brackett quickly moved to the night of the raid on 210 South Broadway back in July of 1919. Carroll insisted that he had never been in the house at 210 South Broadway in response to Brackett's specific question, "Will you swear that you were not in that house twice after dark in July, 1919?"

Brackett's effort to get Carroll to admit that he knew 210 South Broadway was a gambling house was met with Carroll's answer that he had his suspicions but he did not know for sure that gambling was carried on there. He knew Jules Formel but he claimed to have never seen Formel inside the building although he saw him near the place in the summer of 1919.

It was brought out that the reason Carroll had had suspicions that the house at 210 was used for gambling was that he had been assigned in 1918, the year prior to the raid, to watch the front of the house. He was assigned there by Superintendent King and Commissioner Milliman as it was suspected that there was gambling being conducted there. It was further learned that Carroll had met Rachel "Rachie" Brown in 1918 although he could not recall what the notorious gangster did for a living.

In addition, Carroll admitted that he did, in fact, know the African-American man named "Murphy" who was alleged to be an ex-convict. Carroll further admitted that he had probably spoken to the man on Congress Street but offered no details of either the mysterious man or their relationship.

Question after question was lobbed at Carroll by Brackett and time and again, Carroll's answers were vague. He didn't recall being certain places at certain times. He "might have" seen Formel, Brown, and other gamblers in the station during the night of the 1919 raids. He was particularly evasive when answering questions about whether or not he had let the gamblers in the station to retrieve their apparatus and if he had been the one to unlock the cell door. He was so equivocal that he was twice directed by Judge Whitmyer to answer with either a "yes" or "no" to questions that required such a simple answer. He was even forced to admit that in the winter of 1920 he had met with Jules Formel and failed to arrest him even though he knew an indictment against him had been found. It was not looking good for Carroll, especially once Brackett began calling his own witnesses.

Sheriff Austin Reynolds was the first witness called to defend the paper. He told of the raids at 210 South Broadway and 38 Circular Street. He recounted the raid, the lawmen being denied entry and having to break down the door at the Formel place, and the seizure of two roulette wheels, a faro layout, a few poker chips, and other paraphernalia. He specifically recalled placing the ivory ball from one of the roulette wheels in a bag with some of the poker chips. The Sheriff remembered seeing the evidence in a jail cell after 1:00 AM on the night of the raid.

Upon cross examination, Judge McKelvey brought a line of questioning that consisted of trying to show that the district attorney had frequently met with the Sheriff and discussed the gambling situation. Perhaps aware that the district attorney was, at that very moment, under indictment and that McKelvey was involved with his defense, Judge Whitmyer did not allow the line of questioning to proceed further than having the Sheriff acknowledge that, despite the assumption that he was supposed to work with the district attorney and had frequent meetings with him, he had little to offer. If McKelvey had planned to get detailed information in defense of District Attorney Andrus on the public record before his upcoming trial, he was not successful.

Hugh Dorsey was sworn next and, after the usual preliminary background questioning, Brackett got right into the alleged theft of the coffee by Carroll. Dorsey recounted meeting Carroll at the corner of Lake and Maple and accompanying him to Breyer's store which Carroll had found unlocked. While inside, according to Dorsey, Carroll helped himself to a bag of coffee. The two then left the building, with Carroll heading to his apartment after telling Dorsey he would come back and lock the door. Dorsey admitted that he never reported the theft to anyone at the time.

Next Dorsey testified to the night of the raid at 210 South Broadway. He was assigned as the desk sergeant on that night and recalled the gambling apparatus being brought into the station and secured in the jail cell. He further recalled seeing Carroll, Judge McTygue, and District Attorney Andrus at the station that night when bail was fixed for the prisoners.

Dorsey swore to the following encounter in the corridor outside the jail cell, "I saw Carroll, Brown and Walker in the cell room. They came out and as they passed me, Carroll said, 'Oh, he's all right.' As they went out Walker was holding his coat which was bulged out considerably. As they got to the street someone said to Walker, 'What's the matter; getting weak; brace up.'" He further claimed that Carroll had in his possession the keys to the cell block.

Dorsey also recounted that during July, 1919, prior to the raids, he was assigned to watch 210 South Broadway. He stated that Carroll had been in the place two or three times when he, Dorsey, had been posted there. Carroll had visited the place late at night, once staying for about forty-five minutes. He also claimed that during the summer of 1919 he had seen Carroll meeting with "Murphy," an ex-convict, on Congress Street several times.

Dorsey was next asked about the "Nina" letters and he claimed that he had found them on the floor of the locker room and that he had kept them in case he needed them in the future. He explained that since Carroll had been appointed Superintendent their relationship had been frosty and he felt the letters might come in handy someday if he were to be set up.

Dorsey would face cross-examination by McKelvey next. He freely admitted, under McKelvey's questioning, that he kept the "Nina" letter so that if he ever got in trouble with the department he would "have something" on Carroll. Dorsey would also admit that he destroyed the letter that he says directed him to the sundial and that he regretted doing so when McKelvey suggested that the letter was actually from a paramour. Dorsey admitted to playing poker in McNaughton's garage while he was supposed to be on patrol once and that he had played "penny ante" winning and losing small amounts, no larger than two dollars.

Detective James Sullivan was called next. His testimony, although less in detail when compared to Dorsey's, was just as damaging to Carroll. He testified that, like Dorsey, he was on duty the night of the 210 South Broadway Raid and the following day. He claimed that he had spoken with then Sergeant Carroll in the police station before the gambling evidence had turned up missing. He said that Carroll told him that he was going to wait until then Superintendent Thomas Sullivan went to dinner, at which time he planned to help the gamblers get their stuff back. James Sullivan told the court that he had told Carroll not to do it since it was "pretty dangerous business."[39]

Carroll, according to James Sullivan, said that he was going to risk it anyway and that later he (James Sullivan) heard a commotion in the area of the rear of the station after Carroll had come through and took possession of the jail cell keys. A few moments later, his suspicion aroused, Sullivan walked back to the rear of the station and saw Carroll watching the gamblers walking down the stairs and out of the police station onto Maple Avenue. [40] From there it can be presumed that the story continues with the accounts given by the Saratogian reporters recounted earlier.

The Carroll libel case was supposed to have been strictly about the theft of coffee. The removal of gambling apparatus from the police station, the vice conditions in existence during his tenure as Superintendent of Police, and the love letters to "Nina" were never even mentioned by Carroll in his lawsuit. The judge, however, allowed questions about vice conditions during Carroll's tenure to be admitted into evidence, with some restrictions. Direct accusations of public officials would be forbidden and any such evidence would need to be strictly related to questions of Carroll's character.

Brackett was obviously aware that there were on-going criminal gambling cases and any evidence brought out publicly concerning the gambling conditions then in existence in Saratoga Springs would be beneficial to both he and Bascom as they processed the criminal cases in court. Even if they could not get direct testimony into the court record about sitting officials, namely District Attorney Andrus and City Court Judge McTygue, Bascom and Brackett would have certainly been glad to have the freedom to at least highlight the vice conditions, knowing that the public would be following the newspapers very closely.

Public pressure would surely make it more difficult for officials to conduct business in the manner that they had always done. With the pending criminal cases undoubtedly in mind, Bracket called two young boys to the stand to testify that gambling was so prevalent that even they, as children, were able to place bets in town without difficulty. The boys, George Beyer and Joseph Stapleton, ages 16 and 15 respectively, testified that in 1919 they had no trouble placing bets on the races at 60 Church Street where Ms. Anna Rosselle was the proprietor of a grocery store. [41]

He also called a Mr. George Waring who testified to betting at Tolmie's, Duval's, Doherty's, and Fennell's in 1919. Finally he called Joseph Guido who was a summer patrolman for the police department in 1919 when he was assigned to watch the Leffler place on the way out to Saratoga Lake.

He testified that during the course of performing his duties one summer night, a car pulled up and told the people inside to "close up tight"." A flurry of activity was observed and after a few minutes Sheriff Reynolds and District Attorney Andrus arrived with a squad of deputies. They found nothing and shortly after they departed, gambling implements were moved back into the house from a barn at the rear of the property. [42]

The jury would have to determine simply whether or not they believed the Saratogian had printed a fact when the issue went to press that contained Dorsey's allegation that Carroll had stolen coffee. If they believed Dorsey, then the paper had an iron-clad right to publish the truth. If the jury decided that Carroll's denials were to be believed, then the matter of damages would be the only issue that needed to be determined.

It seemed that Brackett had gotten the better of the opposition throughout the trial. Much information was brought forward outside of the simple question of the theft of the coffee that Carroll's lawyer seemed unable to counter. Carroll's evasiveness on the stand did not serve him well either and it was not a surprise to objective observers when the jury deliberated for only about 90 minutes before deciding that the Saratogian had printed the truth about Superintendent Carroll. [43]

With the Saratogian vindicated, the publisher and president of the company, John K. Walbridge, demanded that Carroll be removed from office. In the October 29, 1920, edition of the Saratogian the newspaper listed the items upon which Carroll's removal from office was demanded.

First, he had stolen coffee from J.A. Breyer's store while he was on duty. Second, he allowed gamblers to remove the People's evidence from the city jail. Third, he was associated with the ex-convict Murphy. Fourth, that he had received love letters from married women. Fifth, he had frequented gambling houses during all hours of the night.

Although the verdict in favor of the Saratogian in the libel case was not a criminal conviction, Walbridge (a Brackett ally) sent the following letter to Commissioner of Public Safety John Gaffney on October 28, 1920:

To John E. Gaffney,
Commissioner of Public Safety
City of Saratoga Springs, NY

Sir: You are hereby called upon and required, forthwith, to remove Edward T. Carroll from the position held by him as Superintendent of Police of the City of Saratoga Springs, to which you appointed him about January 1st 1920, and from which you can remove him at any time.

Your attention is recalled to the record in the action brought by him against the Saratogian, recently tried at Ballston Spa, at which trial you were present much if not all of the time, as showing his unfitness for the position he holds as requiring his removal.

Unless you forthwith act in the matter, we shall prefer charges against you for gross neglect of official duty on your part.

Yours truly.
The Saratogian
John K. Walbridge, President 44

Carroll had reportedly left town shortly after the verdict had been delivered and reporters from the Saratogian made inquiries as to his whereabouts in the days following the verdict. At first they were told by Deputy Commissioner Benjamin Wilson that there was no record of Carroll's having requested or been given a leave of absence. When a reporter later spoke with Commissioner Gaffney and asked if Carroll was in town Gaffney replied that he was not. Whereupon the following exchange between the reporter and Gaffney was recounted:

Reporter: "Has he (Carroll) been given a leave of absence?"
Gaffney: "Yes."
Reporter: "For how long?"
Gaffney: "Until he gets back."[45]

Carroll later explained that he had taken a couple of days of vacation immediately after the verdict. His leave of absence was made official on November 2, 1920. On that date Carroll officially requested a leave of absence from Commissioner Gaffney in a long letter that was published in the Saratogian on November 4, 1920.

In his letter requesting the leave of absence, Carroll expresses his confidence that he would not have been found guilty of stealing coffee and that losing a libel suit was not unusual, even if the facts were on the petitioner's side. Furthermore, he explained that District Attorney Andrus had presented the same evidence to a grand jury that failed to indict him (although he does not mention how he knew this since grand jury proceedings are supposed to be secret). Carroll includes in his letter his estimate that ninety percent of the population of Saratoga Springs did not agree with the libel verdict. Referring to the accusation that he had stolen the coffee from Breyer's store and addressing the calls for his removal by the Saratogian he writes, "…as I am not guilty of that offense I do not feel that it requires any action on your part toward my removal."[46]

Interestingly Carroll made no mention of any of the other allegations that were made during the trial. Could his specific statement that he was not guilty of "that offense" indicate that there might be other offenses that he may be guilty of?

He explains in his letter that he would not appeal the decision as his lawyers advised him that it would be too expensive to pursue that course. In addition he states that he had been told that he was going to be indicted in the near future, although he could not image what for. To spare the department and Commissioner Gaffney any further difficulty, the leave of absence was requested until the pending indictment was disposed of.

Gaffney authorized the leave of absence and made a public reply of his own. Even after the verdict in the libel case, Commissioner Gaffney's loyalty to Carroll remained strong as he wrote, "While I have confidence in your ability and integrity as an officer, and while I would not think for a moment of convicting you of any wrongdoing upon the testimony of former patrolman Dorsey, I think you are right in your suggestion that there might be criticism of your continuing in office during the time the indictment was pending."[47] Expressing his hope that the pending criminal case would be resolved quickly, Gaffney authorized the temporary leave of absence.

With the Carroll libel case settled, Brackett could turn his full attention to assisting Bascom with the prosecutions of those arrested during the summer raids. The first to go to trial would be Jules Formel and the drama in the courtroom rivaled anything seen in Saratoga Springs history to that point.

Endnotes

Chapter 12

1   "Too Busy to Protect City," The Saratogian,
    October 5, 1920.

2   "Whiskey worth $4,000 Stolen from Algonquin Block,"
    The Saratogian, December 24, 1919.

3   "Police Round Up Four Italians on Gambling Charges,"
    The Saratogian, December 26, 1919.

4   "King to Retire as Police Chief," The Saratogian,
    June 21, 1919.

5   "Demarco Planned Suicide After he Killed Buckett,"
    The Saratogian, June 24, 1919.

6   "Thompson Sought by Saratoga Police," The Schenectady
    Gazette, July 25, 1919.

7   "Ballou Shot by Negro at Racetrack; Close Escape
    for Carroll," The Saratogian, July 30, 1920.

8   "Sullivan Forced out of Department," The Saratogian,
    April 1, 1920.

9   Ibid.

10 "Patrolman Dorsey Resigns; Says He Was
    'Framed Up,'" The Saratogian, May 12, 1920.

11 Ibid.

12 Ibid.

13 Woman in the Dorsey Case, Declares Carroll, Challenging
    Ex-Officer," The Saratogian, May 13, 1920.

14 Ibid.

15 "Deny Crooked Game," The Saratogian, May 15, 1920.

16 "Carroll Burglarized Beyer's Store While on
    Duty, Charges Dorsey," The Saratogian, May 14, 1920.

17 Lawsuit Sequel to Police Charges," The Saratogian,
    May 15, 1920.

18 "Bascom Raiders Round Up Gamblers Over Heads of
    Police and District Attorney," The Saratogian,
    August 16, 1920.

19 Ibid.

20 Ibid.

21 The Daily Saratogian, August 17, 1920.

22 "Bascom Raiders…"

23 Ibid.

24 Ibid.

25 Ibid.

26 Ibid.

27 "Indian Head Tavern Raided for Gamblers," The
    Saratogian, August 24, 1920.

28 Ibid.

29 "'Hand Books' in City Raided by Bascom Officers,"
    The Saratogian, August 25, 1920.

30 "Police Prevent Raid on Bookies," The Daily Saratogian,
    August 27, 1920.

31 "Walker Calls Extraordinary Grand Jury to Investigate
    Gambling Here Last Summer," The Saratogian,
    July 2, 1920.

32 "Andrus Indicted by Grand Jury," The Saratogian,
    September 7, 1920.

33 "Grand Jury Finds Police Shared in Stolen
    Whiskey," The Saratogian, September 8, 1920.

34 "Andrus Indicted…"

35 "Racing Association Endorses Effort to Drive
    Out Gambling," The Saratogian, September 10, 1920.

36 "Gambling Opposed by Boy Scouts," The Saratogian,
    September 13, 1920.

37 "Andrus Defeats Smith by 600 for District Attorney,"
    The Saratogian, September 15, 1920.

38 "Work of Extraordinary Grand Jury at an End,"
    The Saratogian, November 20, 1920.

39 "Dorsey Repeats Story of Carroll's Theft of Coffee,"
    The Saratogian, October 25, 1920.

40 Ibid.

41 "Young Boys Swear to Betting on the Races," The
    Saratogian, October 27, 1920.

42 Ibid.

43 The Saratogian, October 27, 1920.

44 "The Letter to Mr. Gaffney," The Saratogian,
    October 29, 1920.

45 "Removal of Carroll from Office Demanded of Gaffney,"
    The Saratogian, October 29, 1920.

46 "Carroll Granted Leave of Absence," The Saratogian,
    November 4, 1920.

47 Ibid.

Chapter 13

The Trials of Jules Formel

As the year 1920 came to a close, the situation was looking better than it ever had in Saratoga Springs for the anti-gambling forces. Bascom's raiders had made multiple investigations and arrests during the summer months. Not even the bookmakers at the racetrack had escaped their attention. The grand jury had been handing up indictments as the cases made their way through the court system. The libel case against the Saratogian newspaper filed by ex-Police Superintendent Edward Carroll was unsuccessful. Newspapers across the state were filled with commentary praising the crusaders in their efforts to stamp out the evil scourge of gambling at the Spa.

In all, it seemed that the momentum had shifted to the Bascom-Brackett forces and although the outcome of a criminal trial is never a certain thing, Bascom and Brackett must have been feeling confident in the final months of 1920 that their efforts and those of their associates would eventually bear fruit. Their first order of business would be to put on trial Jules Formel, the alleged proprietor of the house at 210 South Broadway that had been raided in the summer of 1919.

Even though 43 people had been indicted by the extraordinary term of the Grand Jury, Formel's case was to be the first criminal case tried as a result of the raids made by authorities during 1919 and 1920.[1] Fifteen defendants had already pled guilty prior to Formel's trial and undoubtedly some of those would have agreed to provide testimony to Bascom in exchange for avoiding jail time.

Almost every Saratogian was sure to have known about Jules Formel and the 1919 raids at 210 South Broadway and 38 Circular Street. They would have recalled the allegation that Formel had taken responsibility for all of the goings-on inside the South Broadway joint. They would surely have heard about the release of the prisoners on low bail, and could there be any doubt that the removal of the evidence from police headquarters was not a topic of conversation throughout the city, county, and state during that time?

And so it was that on Friday, December 17, 1920, a jury was selected to hear the case against Julius Z. Formel on charges of being a common gambler. Seven of the twelve jurors selected were farmers and none of the jurors lived within the city of Saratoga Springs. [2] The trial began the following Monday.

The Formel trial started, as all trials do, with the prosecution presenting its evidence. In this case, Deputy Attorney General Bascom began with the testimony of two associates of District Attorney Charles Andrus who testified to events on the night of the 210 South Broadway raid.

J.M. Cavanaugh and Harold Corbin both testified that on the night of the raid, shortly before the police made entry to the building, District Attorney Andrus had a conversation with Jules Formel about the pending raid. Both witnesses recalled Formel making the statement that, "If they get in there they will have to break in."[3]

Interestingly, the testimony of Cavanaugh and Corbin was not challenged by the defense counsel. Apparently they felt it was not at all unusual for a sitting District Attorney to meet with the subject of a police investigation prior to a gambling raid, on the street, in close proximity to the location of the pending police action.

What was slightly unusual was the testimony from Corbin that he had been riding in a car with Andrus from Ballston Spa to Saratoga at the time of the raid and conveniently saw a shadowy figure in a yard nearby that he decided to investigate. It was only after he turned around (never making contact with the suspicious person) and went back to the District Attorney's car that he noticed Formel and Andrus having a conversation, with the only part that he was fortunate enough to overhear being the comment about breaking into the place.

After establishing the connection between Andrus and Formel prior to the raid, Bascom called Arthur Berg of Binghamton, whose testimony sent shock waves through the gamblers in Saratoga, not to mention a couple of public officials.

Arthur Berg, a travelling corset salesman, told the court that he met "Rachie" Brown at the Grand Union Hotel and, with Brown as his escort, he had no trouble entering 210 South Broadway despite the fact that he was not generally well known in Saratoga Springs. He said that on the night of August 1, 1919, he had played roulette at 210 South Broadway and quickly lost $260. He then traded three pieces of jewelry (one diamond stick pin and two rings) for a $400 credit that he also quickly lost to the house at the faro table. [4] He was consoled on his way out with a gift of a cigar from the house, which according to Berg, he was told were the "kind John W. Gates smokes," in an apparent reference to the legendary gambler who frequented Saratoga regularly while in his prime.

Suspecting that he had been the victim of unfair practices on the part of the Formel syndicate, Berg later confronted Formel and Brown, who politely declined to return any of the money or jewelry to the unlucky player. Berg was persistent, however, and advised Formel that "if you want to run the whole month you had better return my jewelry."[5]

Getting no satisfaction from Formel, who was certainly not in the habit of giving players their money back when they lost, Berg went to police headquarters and asked for a warrant. He was told to see the judge.

The next day he met City Judge Michael McTygue, District Attorney Andrus, and Detective James Sullivan and asked, again, for a warrant. A warrant was not issued but the next morning at about 11:00 A.M. Sullivan met Berg and returned his jewelry along with a receipt that read, "Received from R. Brown one diamond ring, one diamond solitaire ring and one diamond cluster pin. Signed, A. Berg."

Glad to have his property returned to him, Berg promptly left town.

To support Berg's testimony, Bascom called a reporter for the New York Sun, Don Lyons, who testified that he had been in the 210 South Broadway gambling house in the later part of August, 1919, and had seen two roulette wheels and one faro bank table set up inside. He did not claim to have seen anyone playing, nor did he claim to have seen Formel at the place during that time.

Next to be called for the prosecution was James Sullivan, who in 1919 was on the payroll of the police department, but most recently had worked as a special investigator for Mr. Bascom. Sullivan corroborated Berg's recollection of the meeting with McTygue, Andrus, and himself.

Sullivan further testified that he had received the jewelry directly from Jules Formel himself on the Sunday after Berg had played and lost at Formel's place. Sullivan tracked down Formel at his room at 210 South Broadway and informed him, Formel, that he had been sent by Judge McTygue and District Attorney Andrus to "get the jewelry Berg lost" in Formel's place.

According to Sullivan, Formel told him that, "he was sorry it had to be returned for he had one selected for Mrs. McTygue," wife of Judge McTygue. He then returned the jewelry to Berg at the Grand Union Hotel and identified the receipt in open court as the one given to him on the date in question.

Acting Superintendent of Police Thomas Sullivan was then called to produce the police blotter showing the date of Mr. Berg's complaint that he had lost the jewelry at 210 South Broadway. A few other witnesses were called to solidify dates and times along with some other minor details.

In the eyes of the prosecution it was a simple enough case. Two men testified that Formel and Andrus had met and talked shortly before the raid at 210 South Broadway in 1919. A police officer testified that he had returned jewelry to a loser at the gambling tables run by Jules Formel and furthermore, the City Judge and District Attorney were linked to the whole situation.

The prosecution team of Bascom and Brackett

would have surely not fired all of their ammunition in the first trial of a gambler who faced a mere two years in prison if convicted of the charge. After all, they had public officials to later try on their own indictments and therefore probably presented just what they believed would be enough to convict Formel. They certainly would have wanted to withhold evidence that might be damaging to the public officials in later cases and they would definitely have realized that the attorneys for Formel, McTygue, and Andrus were having frequent discussions during the trial.

The defense, led by local Attorney Burton D. Esmond, never even bothered to deny that his client was a gambler. His defense was predicated solely on attacking the character of the prosecution witnesses, saving his most vitriolic attacks for the gambler Berg and the ex-policeman Sullivan.

Claiming that James Sullivan was a drunkard and a wife-beater who once shot at his spouse, Esmond attacked not the facts of Sullivan's testimony, but the man's character. Under heavy grilling, Sullivan admitted that he often was drunk, though never on duty, and that he frequently played poker and bet on the horse races, placing his bets and receiving his winnings (if any) on Broadway.

As far as shooting at his wife was concerned, Sullivan claimed that he had once accidentally discharged his revolver while cleaning it. He said that he was alone in his home at the time. He also denied ever having been drunk while on duty and claimed to have been involved in about ten gambling raids during his police career.

As for Mr. Berg, Esmond was successful in bringing the salesman's past criminal record into court. It was brought out that Berg had been arrested on more than one occasion and convicted three times during his life. The last time Berg was arrested, it was for assaulting a lawyer trying to serve a subpoena on him at Berg's Binghamton home.

As with Sullivan, the facts of Berg's testimony were not addressed by the defense, only the character of the witness. In his closing statement Esmond went so far as to tell the jurors that Berg was not a credible witness, calling him a perjurer and criminal.

After just one day of testimony, Justice Van Kirk charged the jury. It was a simple enough case he told them; they had only to consider two questions, "was 210 South Broadway a gambling place, and was Formel owner, agent or manager of the place?" [6]

Justice Van Kirk quickly outlined the case and instructed the jury on several points of law before the twelve men retired to the jury room around 10:40 on the morning of December 22.

After deliberating for seven full hours, the jurors reported to the judge that they had become hopelessly deadlocked. According to the Saratogian on December 23, 1920, the jurors had agreed that 210 South Broadway was indeed a gambling place and that Formel was a gambler. However, they could not come to a consensus on whether or not Formel was the proprietor of the joint. It was reported that the jurors finally stood at 8 to 4 for acquittal. They were described as looking rather haggard and worn out at the end of the day.

Justice Van Kirk then met behind closed doors with the jury foreman and the attorneys involved in the case. Upon emerging from the conference, Justice Van Kirk declared a mistrial and announced that Formel would be tried again and the second trial would start the following Monday.

If the first trial of Jules Formel was sensational, the second trial would be even more so. To begin with, the Formel legal team would be headed by perhaps the greatest legal mind of the era, William "Bill" Fallon, otherwise known as "The Great Mouthpiece."

Fallon was a New York City lawyer and courtroom giant with an exceptional record of defending high profile murderers and gangsters who invariably would be freed after some legal maneuvering or courtroom theatrics by Fallon. His courtroom style was to endlessly bait judges and prosecutors. His audacity at the bar would often leave judges exasperated, prosecutors steaming, and the gallery amused. He found himself often on the edge of a contempt of court charge and other lawyers admired his skill and daring, if not his ethics. [7]

He was Arnold Rothstein's attorney and often defended Rothstein associates like Nicky Arnstein, who was gunned down by associates of Rachel Brown, and probably, though it was never proven, on the orders of

Rothstein himself.

He later represented Rothstein's confidant Abe Attell at the Chicago Grand Jury investigating the fixing of the World Series in 1919. Fallon also defended Rothstein when he faced undisputed charges that he had shot three policemen during a raid of a card game in New York City that Rothstein was taking part in. That Rothstein was acquitted of the charges despite the overwhelming evidence served only to solidify the public's impression, if not the reality, that Rothstein was indeed the all-powerful criminal mastermind the press made him out to be and that Fallon was the greatest defense attorney of his time.

Fallon had a knack for delivering hung juries in his murder cases. The count was often 11-1 for acquittal. How such an amazing record of acquittals with the same vote count could be explained without suspecting some untoward behavior was difficult. Against all odds, Fallon could deliver a hung jury and many suspected that he was adept at simply bribing jurors.

At Saratoga, Fallon played his usual games during the second trial of Jules Formel and two stories illustrate his theatrics in court. Both stories are recounted by Gene Fowler in his biography of Fallon, *The Great Mouthpiece*.

First, Fallon would routinely parade a stream of well-dressed lawyers in front of the jury, each stopping to give advice in hushed whispers to Fallon or to sit during particular sections of testimony. Often there would be a phalanx of lawyers sitting at the defense table. The impression was created that the defendant had a powerful defense team and that they were constantly at work on the most important legal case of the century in that very courtroom.

Senator Brackett, no slouch himself when it came to delivering a courtroom performance, sought to highlight the difference in the legal teams by arranging to sit all alone at the prosecution table. He seemed to be sending the unspoken message of "look at me, all alone against all of these slick New York City lawyers."

He even managed to inch ever closer to the jury box until Fallon noticed the Brackett play and raised an objection in the middle of the trial. He asked that a mistrial be declared by the judge on the ground that in all his years he had never faced a jury with more than 12 members, but here he had a jury of 13. He was alluding to Brackett, who by this time had positioned himself at the corner of the jury box! The objection was overruled but for the rest of the trial Fallon referred to Senator Bracket as "juror number 13." [8]

His games were not limited to verbal jousting with the prosecution. Fallon was enjoying the nightlife of Saratoga Springs and was repeatedly late to court. When he was chastised by the judge, he could provide only the meager explanation that his hotel was a long distance from the court in Ballston Spa, as he was staying at the United States Hotel in Saratoga Springs.

The judge replied that he was staying at the same hotel and from then on would instruct the bell boy to wake both Fallon and he at the same hour to ensure

Fallon could make it to court on time as he, the judge, seemed to manage to get there before the appointed hour each morning.

Fallon would have none of it, and the following day he paid the bell boy to wake the judge one half hour later than usual. Fallon, of course, promptly arrived in court on time that morning, looking impatient as the judge entered late that day, surely with a scowl upon his face.

With Fallon conducting the defense now, the prosecution was sure to need a stronger case than was presented to the first jury. They would not disappoint.

The jury was picked during the week after Formel's first trial closed. The court then took the customary Christmas break and Formel's second trial began in earnest on December 29, 1920.

The majority of the first day of testimony was basically a re-telling of the raid at 210 South Broadway. Lawmen described the raid, witnesses again testified to the conversation between Formel and Andrus outside the place, and of Formel taking responsibility for the activity inside the house.

Fallon wasted no time in engaging in his customary theatrics by repeatedly objecting during Bascom's opening statement, each time being overruled. He spent thirty minutes cross-examining a Saratogian reporter who had been called to the stand to corroborate Mr. Corbin's testimony during the first trial that he had seen Andrus and Formel meet, and Formel say that the police would have to break into the place.

Sheriff Reynolds was then called to recount the events of the raid yet again. Fallon, despite his best efforts to bamboozle Reynolds, was unsuccessful in tripping up the Sheriff. Fallon repeatedly asked Reynolds if he had made any effort to stop the gambling at the racetrack to which the sheriff replied that his attorney, James Leary, had advised him that what was occurring at the track was not illegal. Fallon's questioning of the betting at the racetrack, he said, was an attempt to show that the law in Saratoga County permitted one form of gambling while pretending to enforce the gambling laws against other places. All of his questions about the racetrack were objected to by Brackett as irrelevant, and all were sustained.

Acting Police Chief Thomas Sullivan was called next and told of the raid almost exactly the same as Sheriff Reynolds had and the same as he had testified to during the first trial. He added that about ten days after the raid, Formel had met him at the police station and asked him to reassign the officers who had been stationed outside of the house during that summer. According to Sullivan's testimony, after he replied that he could not reassign the officers, Formel remarked, "If I wanted to give a nice gold watch to a fellow it would be nobody's business but his and mine."[9] Sullivan claimed to never have taken a watch from Formel and the subject never came up again.

Fallon's cross-examination consisted of questioning Sullivan about whether or not he had ever worked at a gambling house. Sullivan said that he had. He had worked at Caleb Mitchell's place on Broadway as a doorman and at the United States Club for a short time during the 1890's.

Fallon then asked if Sullivan had ever seen Brackett at the United States Club. Brackett immediately objected to the slanderous suggestion and was sustained by the court. Fallon claimed that he was - innocently enough - trying to show that the prosecution was being undertaken in bad faith. His not-so-subtle message was that Brackett had instigated the prosecution as a method of damaging his political enemy, District Attorney Charles Andrus, rather than as an honest effort to rid the city of vice. Fallon conveniently forgot to mention that Bascom had been appointed a special prosecutor by the governor.

Saratoga Springs Police Detective George Mason was the next prosecution witness and testified to his participation in the raid at 210 South Broadway. The new detail that he provided was that during the raid the telephone of the house rang and he answered it. The person on the other end of the line asked for Formel and Mason handed the phone to Formel, after which he only heard the Formel side of the conversation.

Mason was asked if he recognized the voice on the other end of the line and he said that he did. The importance of just who was calling the house during the police raid was evident when Fallon practically jumped out of his shoes to object to the question as not competent evidence. Like so many times before, he was overruled and Mason was allowed to answer. The person on the other end of the line, he said, was District Attorney Andrus! [10]

Fallon cross examined Mason and of course attacked his character. He managed to have Mason admit that he had gambled occasionally himself and that he had been assigned to the racetrack on numerous occasions but was unable to get evidence against suspected bookmakers. Brackett again was sustained in his objections to Fallon's line of questioning regarding the policeman's efforts at suppressing gambling at the race track.

To this point in the trial, Fallon made no effort to object to the facts or to fight over the evidence. He never bothered to deny that Formel had made the statement that he was responsible for the activity at 210 South Broadway, that the conversation took place between Formel and Andrus outside the place just after the raid had commenced, that Formel had made the offer-in-not-so-many-words of the watch to Superintendent Sullivan, that it was Andrus' voice on the other end of the phone, or any of the other facts that had thus far been presented by the prosecution.

Next up for the prosecution were Police Officer Edward Morrison and Deputy Sheriff Clarence Hovey. Morrison testified, as he had during the first trial, that he was positive that Formel had stated, "I will be responsible for what is going on here."[11]

Deputy Hovey told of his participation in the raid. One of his jobs was to disassemble the faro and roulette tables for transport. In this task he was assisted by none other than Jules Formel himself, who told officers taking apart the tables to be careful as "it was valuable furniture."[12]

Hovey was also the deputy sheriff assigned to bring Formel back from New York City where he had been arrested on the indictments stemming from the Bascom investigation. According to Hovey, during the trip to Saratoga, Formel was quite talkative.

He said that Formel again stated that he was responsible for 210 South Broadway and bragged that the profits from the first night alone were $18,000. The deputy also remembered that Formel talked of the Brook and the Arrowhead clubs. He was interrupted by attorney Fallon who asked, "Did he mention the name of Mr. Leary?"[13]

Deputy Hovey could not recall if he had mentioned Leary or not.

An attempt was made to put the doorman for 210 South Broadway on the stand but this was successfully objected to by the defense. The gambler Arthur Berg was again called to the stand and recounted the same story of his gambling at 210 South Broadway, his losses, and the return of his jewelry. This time he also testified to how he gambled at the racetrack and where he would meet the bookmaker the following day on Broadway to collect his winnings or to pay for his losses.

Berg was in for an even more intense grilling about his past than during the previous trial. Fallon was pulling no punches with Berg. He produced the man that Berg had been charged with assaulting a few years earlier for dramatic effect.

The man weighed about 125 pounds and had a withered arm.[14] Berg claimed the man had entered his home without permission during the night and he only later found out that the man was serving court papers for an attorney. Once again, the facts weren't important to Fallon, only the image of a bully (Berg) who assaulted a frail man.

Fallon continued his assault on Berg's character, suggesting that Berg had once threatened a Binghamton gambler with having him raided if the gambler did not return money Berg lost in his establishment. Fallon brought out that Berg had served a couple of days in jail on a bounced check charge. He accused Berg of gambling while his wife was at home and in such poor medical condition that a collection was being taken for her at the same time. Berg, with as much rage as he could muster, screamed, "that's a damned lie!"[15]

Berg was forced to explain his betting activities at the track and Fallon was having so much fun at Berg's expense that he made a great show of covering his face with his hand to conceal his laughter. Brackett objected to the actor in the court and chided Fallon, saying that he saw no humor in the proceedings, to which Fallon retorted that that was probably because Brackett had no sense of humor.

Of course, none of this had anything to do with 210 South Broadway or the man on trial and Judge Van Kirk had all he could handle in keeping Fallon under control, the proceedings focused on the facts, and the attorneys from verbally attacking each other.

The next phase of the trial consisted of Bascom and Brackett introducing several checks that were shown to have come from gambling at 210 South Broadway. The paper trail was somewhat confusing but Bascom and Brackett patiently walked through the process of identifying checks that were paid to cover gambling losses that eventually ended up in the bank accounts of Jules Formel and one of his partners in the venture.

The only surprise was that Bascom had called Mrs. Formel as a witness for the prosecution as she had cashed some of the checks. Fallon made a few objections to having certain checks entered into evidence but, on the whole, he offered virtually no defense to the paper trail.

With the testimony of the first trial basically recounted and the methodical introduction of the paper trail completed, it was time for the prosecution to call its star witness, Abraham "Rachel" Brown. But before Brown's testimony is recounted, an examination of the man should be made, for he is much too interesting a character and deserves particular attention.

Aaron Braun, Abraham Braunstein, Rachel Brown, or more commonly known as "Rachie," was an active and well known gangster in New York City. Originating in St. Louis, Brown made his way to New York City and partnered with William "Bridgie" Weber during the time when the "Tenderloin" district was in its glory days under the protection of the prolific grafter and Tammany Hall associate New York City Police

Lieutenant Charles Becker. [16]

Brown and Weber ran gambling joints in the early days of their partnership on Broadway and on 28th Street in New York City. They were once arrested for attempting to bribe three police sergeants sent to their place to check up on things soon after it opened up. They offered the sergeants five dollars each to not harass any patrons desiring to enter their establishment. [17] The two novice gamblers soon figured out the precinct Captain was the one who needed to be bribed and enjoyed relative success in their gambling adventure thereafter.

Brown's association with Weber had him on the fringes of organized crime and big-time gamblers in New York City. When he learned that rival gamblers were planning to kill him behind some dubious dealings, Brown fled to Europe, eventually turning up in Spain.

A month later the gambler Herman Rosenthal was killed for "squealing" and when Brown return to America he was promptly thrown in jail on suspicion of having some connection to the Rosenthal murder. [18] Most likely the suspicion of Brown was the result of his timely "vacation" to Europe and his association with Weber, who was reportedly seen running from the scene of the murder.

Both Weber and Brown turned state's evidence and it was documented in the newspapers of the day that Brown had been making frequent visits to the office of the Manhattan District Attorney. Eventually Lieutenant Becker and several of his associates would be put to death after being convicted of the murder of Rosenthal, their convictions being partly based on the testimony of Weber and Brown. [19]

By this time Weber and Brown had a falling out and Brown was on his own running a saloon. One night, shortly after the Rosenthal murder, he was visited by a local thug around closing time and assaulted. After a customer beat off the assailant with a cane, Brown became fearful and appealed to the New York City Police for protection.

Two detectives were sent to hide in the bar and soon Brown was visited again by local thugs. This time four gangsters stood look-out as two associates entered the business and tried to pull Brown through a back door. The hidden police officers burst forth and fought off the tough guys, charging them with felony assault. [20]

After his split with Weber and when things quieted down after the Rosenthal murder, Brown realized that he did not have the skill set needed to run gambling joints himself and so began a career as a steerer and political fixer. Brown joined the Arnold Rothstein camp and became the go-between for public officials and gamblers in New York City, Nassau County, and Saratoga. It was "Rachie" who could be seen any night during the Saratoga summer seasons of 1918-1920 along Broadway or in the lobbies of the fashionable hotels, plying his trade of matching customers and resorts. [21]

Summer visitors during that time could be led to any number of gambling places that Brown was connected with, including the Brook, the Arrowhead Inn, 210 South

Broadway, 38 Circular Street or 75 Nelson Avenue, depending upon the player's preferences. When the heat was too hot in the city of Saratoga Springs, Brown could easily arrange a visit to gambling joints in nearby Lake George or Lake Luzerne.

Finally it was the same Rachel Brown who spun the wheel at 210 South Broadway who was indicted by the Cook County Grand Jury in Chicago for his part in fixing the 1919 World Series. While some authorities on the "Black Sox" scandal have had difficulty in identifying the mysterious Rachel Brown, the press coverage of Brown's involvement in both the Jules Formel trial and the indictments in Chicago that occurred at nearly the same time made it clear that the Rachel Brown in both cases was one and the same.

The editorial board of the Saratogian made no secret of its distaste for Rachel Brown. In a scathing editorial in the October 5, 1920, edition of the paper they let loose the following commentary: "If there has been any crookedness and dirty work, or shady transaction that he has not been connected with during his career they have escaped him because his hours have already been filled and he couldn't take on any more."

Describing Brown as the fixer between the gamblers and local public officials, the paper asks, "Isn't he a fine type of manhood for us to cater to? Have we got so low down on the ladder that we must depend for our prosperity on a crooked gambler, and friend of gunmen and thieves like "Rachie" Brown?"[22]

Thus it was on the third day of Jules Formel's second

trial in October 1920 that the notorious "Rachie" Brown took the stand for the prosecution. Of course Brown was facing his own charges after being caught by Bascom's raiders earlier in the year at 75 Nelson Avenue, but by now he had a signed immunity agreement with Bascom and with this in hand, he took the witness chair.

Rachel Brown's testimony was immediately recognized as being the most important to date. After all, Brown was a self-confessed partner in the 210 South Broadway venture and his testimony, while somewhat reluctantly given, was nevertheless protected by his immunity agreement. He should have had nothing to fear as he testified in open court. He had been in the grand jury just the day before and was reported to have been a willing witness at that time.

But in open court there were a couple of burly looking strangers in the room on the day of Brown's testimony. When the court took a recess after Brown's initial testimony he refused to leave the library claiming, "I won't go out, some of those big guys will knock me on the head. They killed a guy in New York the other day."[23] He was persuaded to return to the courtroom in the company of one of his lawyer's associates.

As reluctant a witness in open court as Brown may have been, his testimony was damning. He claimed that he, Formel, Cornelius Fellows, Bennie Russell, and J. R. Ward (alias Dr. J. Kennedy) had agreed in the spring of 1919 to open a gambling enterprise in Saratoga Springs that summer and to share in the profits. Brown produced a piece of paper that he said he had picked up from the floor of 210 South Broadway during the summer of 1919 and saved. On the paper were the names of "Boss," "Russell," "Rachie," "Jules," "Fellows," "Steerer," and "Ward."

The only person who Brown would not, or could not, identify on the paper was the person referred to as "Boss."

"The Boss" was believed to be District Attorney Charles Andrus as newspaper accounts relayed that during the summer of 1919 either Brown or Formel had once held up $4300 in cash and yelled, "this is for the _____ (naming a county official)!"[24] But Brown was unwilling to name the District Attorney in open court and instead answered questions about the identity of "The Boss" flippantly saying, "We were all Boss."[25]

Brown was useful to discredit Mrs. Jules Formel and to help establish that gambling had occurred at 210 South Broadway but he provided few specifics in his testimony in open court. He did not identify the "Boss," he did not admit to running the roulette wheel, he could not recall any other gambling at 210 South Broadway other than some small games of hearts, and he could not withstand the withering cross examination of Attorney Fallon. He did not remember Berg being at the gambling house but did recall meeting him along Broadway.

Fallon had gotten hold of Brown to the point that many of his questions were met by Brown asserting that to answer he would risk his own rights if he were to answer. Judge Van Kirk had to repeatedly reassure

Brown that his rights were protected. Fallon pushed Brown's buttons to the point that Brown in desperation answered one question with, "You keep picking at me until I don't know where I am at."[26]

Fallon tried desperately to show that Brown had been offered money to testify and asked several questions of Brown suggesting that through intermediaries Brackett had offered Brown $20,000 to testify against Saratoga County officials. Brackett and Fallon again engaged in verbal sparring with Fallon getting under the Judge's skin once more.

It was nearing the end of the trial now and Judge Van Kirk had just about had enough of Fallon declaring, "When I make a ruling it is to be observed, and when you are rebuked, you are not to reply." [27]

This was all typical Fallon stuff. Attack witnesses, play to the jury, insult, and antagonize the court. There was no real defense of the gambling. No denial by Formel on the stand. No defense of the paper trail that clearly showed money won by the proprietors of the gambling house ending up in the bank account of Jules Formel. Perhaps Fallon was waiting to deliver a secret witness. His defense would be detailed and thorough. He would stop playing around and get to the business of emphatically denying that Jules Formel was a gambler.

The case against Formel seemed open-and-shut, based on the evidence given during the first three days of the trial. After a few minor witnesses were recalled for clarification purposes, the court adjourned with the anticipation that Formel's grand defense would be delivered on the next day court was in session which would be on Tuesday, January 4, 1921.

On the morning of January 4, Fallon rose to present his witnesses and defense. Everyone in the courtroom was surprised when Fallon offered no defense. Instead, Fallon offered only his summation in defense of Jules Formel.

Fallon began by attacking the credibility of Detective Sullivan and the witness Arthur Berg. He ridiculed the paper that Rachel Brown had produced on the stand. He pointed out that the paper had no date and there was no proof that the paper had come from 210 South Broadway in any case.

He derisively referred to Brown as "$20,000 Brown" insinuating that he had taken that sum in exchange for testimony Brackett wanted against Andrus and other local officials, of course leaving out the fact that Brown never did say anything against any Saratoga officials.

Fallon pointed out that the prosecutors of Formel had made little to no effort to stamp out gambling at the racetrack and questioned whether or not the whole affair was the result of bad faith politics.[28] He, of course, failed to mention the little incident at the racetrack when an officer yelled a warning to the gamblers as Bascom's raiders approached the Union Avenue location.

That was it. Other than pleading with the jurors to acquit the upright and honest man, Jules Formel, the Great Mouthpiece, had rested his entire defense on his summation of just a couple of hours.

Brackett was chosen to sum up for the prosecution. He started by appealing to the duty of the jurors to give a fair and honest consideration of the evidence. He pointed out that while Fallon attacked the credibility of Berg and Sullivan, he never did call any witnesses to dispute what they had said regarding the jewelry Sullivan claimed to have returned to Berg.

Bracket went over the paper trail again linking gambling losses at 210 South Broadway to the Formel bank accounts and again the testimony of two witnesses that Formel and the District Attorney had met and conversed in the area on the night of the raid.

Fallon ridiculed the suggestion that the District Attorney, having knowledge of the raid, would have tried to warn Formel in the manner described. But Bracket countered that the prosecution did not think that Andrus had foreknowledge of the raid, recalling that the authorities had gone out of their way to have the warrant signed by the Wilton Town Justice and the execute it with secrecy. Besides, Brackett asked the jurors, if this was the case why hadn't District Attorney Andrus been called to the stand to deny it?

Brackett closed with a summation of the evidence presented and an appeal to the jurors to show the world that Saratoga Springs would no longer be a gathering place for criminals, gangsters, and gamblers and that, in fact, justice could be done in Saratoga County. [29]

Judge Van Kirk charged the jury and they then

retired to the jury room around 3:00 PM where they deliberated for about three hours. When they returned to the courtroom it was reported that, just as in the first trial, the jurors were hopelessly deadlocked. Even though the evidence was much stronger during the second trial of Jules Formel, the result was the same, another hung jury. [30] Predictably the jurors were deadlocked at 11-1, consistent with Fallon's record.

It was time for the prosecution to regroup. Surely Fallon's appearance on the scene smacked of Rothstein influence. Fallon had been representing Rothstein for some time and it was no secret that Fallon was "The Brain's" attorney. Why Fallon appeared as Formel's lawyer was the big question for the anti-gambling forces. In their view it could only be that Formel's place was connected somehow to Rothstein and the other New York City gangsters.

In fact, it was probably more likely that Rothstein recognized that of all the gamblers arrested by Bascom, only Formel had an apparent direct connection to local officials. Defending Formel, in Rothstein's view, was good for business since he would have wanted to protect the public officials whom he had reportedly paid to operate with a free hand. If Formel was guilty and it was established in a court of law the connection between the gamblers and the Saratoga officials, it could only be bad for Rothstein's own business.

Bascom and Brackett had not come this far to quit now. They had thus far led the most successful attack against illegal gambling in Saratoga history, which was certainly no small achievement. Two hung juries did not mean that Formel was innocent and their evidence was certainly strong. They decided to try Formel a third time, but before they did, they would need some time to move through many of the other gambling cases that were still pending.

January 8, 1921, was a big day in Saratoga County Court. Many of the gamblers that had been caught in Bascom's net during the previous summer were sentenced by Judge Van Kirk. They were:

Fred Smith, John Quinn, and John Regan: maintaining a gambling house at the United States Bowling Alleys. $500 fine.

James C. Fennell and Matthew Byrnes: Bookmaking at 20 Phila Street. Suspended sentence.

Alfred and Ernest Duval: Keeping a room for gambling at 428 Broadway. $500 fine.

William R. Tolmie: Common gambling and bookmaking at 36 Putnam Street. $1000 fine and three months in jail. Jail term suspended.

Michael J. Sweeney: Keeping a room for gambling at 446 Broadway. $500 fine.

Jeal Smith and Clarence Bird: Keeping a room for gambling at 83 Henry Street. $100 fine.

Thomas Brophy: Keeping a room for gambling at 388 Broadway. Suspended sentence.

John P. Brown: Common Gambler. $500 fine. Nine months in jail suspended.

During sentencing the attorneys for the men made

some interesting remarks. The capable attorney and one time Brackett protégé James A. Leary represented Smith, Quinn, and Regan and did his best to clear up the name of the United States Bowling Alleys. He wanted the court to note that even though there had been testimony that minors had gambled there, Leary insisted that no one under the age of eighteen was ever allowed inside. Leary went on to remind the judge that, "Handbooks are looked upon in Saratoga Springs as being as legitimate as grocery stores" and that his clients had "acted, lived and operated in that environment."[31]

Bascom had proven that the Duval brothers had made a profit of about $27,000 over two years with Alfred getting about ninety-five per cent of that. The attorney for Fennell and Byrnes argued for leniency based upon the young men's military service during World War I. Judge Van Kirk looked kindly on the argument and suspended sentence, not wishing to tarnish the former soldier's records on Fennell and Byrne's promises that they never engage in the gambling profession again.

Thomas Brophy was warned to stay out of the gambling business for the sake of his wife and two children. He promised the court that he would.[32]

Michael Sweeney's lawyer, William Lannon, explained to the court that Sweeney was a well-respected member of the community, having been twice elected village trustee, and deserved leniency from the court. How then, the court asked, did Mr. Sweeney explain a previous conviction on his record?

Mr. Lannon offered the excuse that Mr. Sweeney had

been the unfortunate victim of bad luck when he was once travelling to New York City and a car in front of him broke down near Albany. Mr. Sweeney left his own car and entered the broken down vehicle at apparently the exact moment that the police arrived and arrested Sweeney and the owner of the car for smuggling the liquor found within. At the time, Mr. Sweeney could not afford to fight the case and agreed to pay a fine of $100 to settle the matter.

In the interest of full disclosure, however, Sweeney did admit to being involved in the liquor trade, just not on the day he was arrested and he declared that he had stopped smuggling booze the previous fall any way.[33]

Jeal Smith and Clarence Bird offered that they had a small get-together at their place above a blacksmith's shop on Henry Street when they were interrupted by the authorities. They claimed that the only profit they kept from the games was to pay their expenses to heat the place and buy sandwiches for the players. Bascom interrupted to claim, "there wouldn't have been enough sandwiches in Saratoga Springs to use up that money."[34] They were fined $100 each.

Finally the operators of the houses of prostitution, known as disorderly houses, were sentenced. James Leary represented the madams, Marie Taylor, Frankie Hamilton, and Alice Johnson.

Marie Taylor had been a nurse at the front in World War One and Frankie Hamilton was an elderly woman and was having considerable emotional difficulty handling her arrest. They both had their sentences suspended by the court. Alice Johnson was fined $250.00.[35]

With these cases out of the way, Bascom could return to the third trial of Julius Formel. William Fallon would not be able to attend this trial and Burton Esmond of Ballston would return as attorney of record for Formel, as he had during the first trial.

Trial number three was laid out much the same as the previous two trials. Police officers testified as to the raid at 210 South Broadway. The so-called "divvy sheet" that Rachel Brown had produced during the second trial was reintroduced. The paper trail was traced from 210 South Broadway to the banks. Formel again declined to testify and Attorney Esmond again insinuated that the whole prosecution was out of the ordinary and based upon a political grudge that ex-Senator Brackett held against District Attorney Andrus.

The only noteworthy occurrence of the third trial was comments made by Supreme Court Justice Borst in regard to the handing over of the gambling apparatus to George Remo through his replevin action.

The matter was brought to the attention of the court during the testimony of Officer Edward Morrison. Justice Borst, upon hearing the testimony of Officer Morrison, asked, "You don't mean to tell me that a city judge of Saratoga Springs would issue a writ of replevin for gambling apparatus seized by the police?"[36]

When Attorney Esmond produced the paperwork indicating that it was in fact true, gambling equipment had indeed been returned to George Remo, an alleged gambler himself, Justice Borst noted, "It is a strange performance on the part of any official who had regard for law and decency."[37]

For the third time the fate of Julius Formel was placed in the hands of the jury. This time they needed only one hour and forty minutes to find Formel guilty of being a common gambler. [38] The verdict seemed an anticlimactic end to the saga that began so many months ago at 210 South Broadway. Jules Formel was sentenced to one to two years in prison at Dannemora despite his desperate pleas for leniency.

Ironically, his sentence was announced on the same day that his partner in the 210 South Broadway endeavor, Rachel Brown, was indicted as part of the investigation into the fixing of the 1919 World Series. Indeed, the March 26, 1921, edition of the Saratogian ran adjoining stories reporting the sentencing of Formel and the indictment of Brown.

The verdict was a victory for Bascom and Brackett. They now had many convictions of the gamblers and were showing a great deal of success for all of their efforts at cleaning up the City.

The convictions of the "little fish" were all well and good but everyone knew that any lasting accomplishment would only come with convictions of the local officials currently under indictment. Bascom and Brackett, along with all of Saratoga, would now turn their attention to the first public official to go before a jury, the duly elected District Attorney of Saratoga County, Charles B. Andrus.

Endnotes

Chapter 13

1   "No Saratogians on Formel Jury Panel," The
    Saratogian, December 18, 1920.

2   Ibid.

3   "Formel Fails to Take Stand in His Own Defense,"
    The Saratogian, December 21, 1920.

4   Ibid.

5   Ibid.

6   Ibid.

7   Fowler, Gene. *The Great Mouthpiece*, Bantam Books,
    New York. 1951.

8   Fowler, Gene.

9   "Formel Talked to Police Head About Gift of
    Gold Watch," The Saratogian, December 29, 1920.

10 Ibid.

11 "Formel Prosecution Springs Surprise With Two
    Mysterious Checks," The Saratogian, December 30, 1920.

12 Ibid.

13 Ibid.

14 Ibid.

15 Ibid.

16 Dash, Mike. *Satan's Circus: Murder, Vice, Police
    Corruption and New York's Trial of the Century.*
    Crown Publishers, New York. 2007.

17 "Police Turn Down Bribes," The Sun, July 22, 1908.

18 "Rachie Brown, Saratoga Gambler, Flees to
    Europe," The Saratogian, October 5, 1920.

19 Dash, Mike...

20 "Halt Attack on Rosenthal Chum," The New York Press,
    March 26, 1914.
21 "Rachie Brown, Saratoga Gambler..."
22 "A Friend of Our Officials Leaves Us," The Saratogian,
    October 5, 1920.
23 "Bank Accounts of Formel and Wife Placed in Evidence,"
    The Saratogian, December 31, 1920.
24 "A Friend of Our Officials..."
25 "Bank Accounts of Formel..."
26 Ibid.
27 Ibid.
28 "Formel Case Given to Jury at 3. P.M. No Defense
    Entered," The Saratogian, January 4, 1921.
29 Ibid.
30 "Second Formel Trial Ends in Disagreement,"
    The Saratogian, January 5, 1921.
31 "Gamblers Fined by Court; Agree to Quit Game for Good,"
    The Saratogian, January 8, 1921.
32 Ibid.
33 Ibid.
34 Ibid.
35 Ibid.
36 "McTygue Scored by Borst for Freeing Gambling
    Fixtures," The Saratogian, March 25, 1921.
37 Ibid.
38 "Formel Convicted," The Saratogian, March 25, 1921.

Chapter 14

The Trial of District Attorney Charles Andrus

While the Formel verdict was certainly a victory for the prosecution, the real big fish were still to be tried. Formel was a gambler and he was indicted along with many other gamblers as a result of the Bascom raids in 1920. But three public officials were also indicted at the same time as those nickel-and-dime gamblers during the extraordinary term of the Grand Jury. District Attorney Charles Andrus would have his case heard first. The prosecution then planned to try Superintendent of

Police Edward Carroll (on leave) and City Court Judge Michael McTygue. With any luck, the gamblers and the officials would all be brought to justice and the scourge of wide open gambling and vice in Saratoga Springs would be stopped forever.

The case against District Attorney Andrus was pretty straightforward. The sum and substance of the prosecution's case was that there was a considerable amount of gambling in Saratoga Springs, that District Attorney Andrus knew it, and that he did nothing about it. Bascom began by presenting a map of Saratoga Springs. On the map, alleged gambling locations were noted: 20 and 60 Phila Street, 85 Henry Street, 40 Putnam Street, the corner of Phila and Putnam, 2 Maple Avenue, 60 Church Street, The US Bowling Alley on Railroad Place, 16 Congress Street, 446, 428, and 390 ½ Broadway, 38 Circular Street and 210 South Broadway.[1]

Andrus's defense would be simple. He would claim that the prosecution was charging him not with neglect of duty, but for not being a policeman. According to the defense theory, even if there was open gambling occurring in Saratoga Springs, District Attorney Andrus was not responsible for leading criminal investigations and making arrests, but rather for prosecuting the cases brought to him by law enforcement officials. His defense team, headed by County Judge Lawrence B. McKelvey, was joined on the second day of the trial by William Fallon. Judge McKelvey would continue the questioning of witnesses but Fallon would assist at the defense table and the two held frequent conferences regarding the case. [2]

Fallon's antics during the Formel trial would have been still fresh in the mind of the local populace. It was impossible not to have escaped the public's attention that Fallon was also Arnold Rothstein's attorney and he had recently appeared with Rothstein at the Grand Jury during the Chicago Black Sox Scandal. Only in Saratoga Springs could the same man defend the most notorious organized crime figure of the day and the sitting District Attorney of the county. What a place; what a time.

The Andrus trial was every bit as spectacular as the Formel trials had been. By the end of the second day of testimony Bascom had witnesses testify that gambling was happening in the open at several places around town. The testimony of witnesses was limited to 1919 and 1920 through July of that year on the orders of Judge Borst. Newspapermen from New York City and Schenectady testified that they had found open gambling at several places around town and that several boys were playing in a couple of establishments for small stakes. One gambler testified to losing between $30,000 and $40,000 at Formel's 210 South Broadway place in 1919 while the notorious Rachel Brown spun the wheel. [3]

James Fennell, proprietor of a place raided by Bascom on Phila Street, told the jury that he had no difficulty in running his gambling room, even while police officers were stationed outside. Ernest Duval testified that City

Judge Michael McTygue had placed bets at his place, although he was sure the bets took place outside of the time period that Justice Borst had established as being relevant to the present trial.[4]

A private detective, George Young, testified that he was employed by Cornelius Fellows in 1919 and that he was hired to protect the gambling establishments at the Arrowhead and 210 South Broadway. He had provided an armed guard at the Arrowhead during that summer in response to several robberies in the area and the presence in town of some rather nefarious fellows that year including, according to Young, "Chink, the Italian" and "Jerry, the Cuban."

Fallon, unable to help himself interjected, "If the people want to show that there were armed guards so the District Attorney couldn't get in, that's all right." Justice Borst quickly admonished him.[5]

Many of the gamblers who had already pleaded guilty to their charges testified as to the details of their various operations. All claimed that they encountered little, if any, resistance from the local law men. They all noted that token visits were sometimes made but that the officers were easily seen coming in plenty of time to hide any gambling paraphernalia lying about. All testified that the only time they were arrested was when they were raided by Bascom and his men.[6]

Finally, the most important testimony of the second day of the trial came from Detective George Mason. After thoroughly recounting the story of the raid at 210 South Broadway, Mason took the stand and told for the third time in open court that during the raid the telephone of the place rang and he answered.

But unlike the previous two times that he testified, this time he insisted that he could not recall whose voice he heard on the other end. This was directly contradictory to Mason's previous testimony that he recognized the voice of the District Attorney on the phone. Bascom was clearly upset by Mason's lack of recall about the voice on the other end of the line and Borst would not allow into the record Bascom's statement that Mason had previously testified three times as to the identity of the caller. [7]

"Benny" Russell, supposed partner of Formel at 210 South Broadway and Shaughnessy at the Arrowhead, testified that prior to opening the gambling joints he was brought to Saratoga to scout possible locations for the operation. Russell was investing $9000 in the endeavor and in April 1919 he and Formel, along with another partner, John R. Ward, went to the office of the District Attorney to make sure everything was all right, meaning that they had the approval of local officials to operate a gambling house during the summer. Russell also testified that he heard Formel tell Andrus that, "these men are coming up here with me this summer," before the two went into a private office. Andrus reportedly came out of the private talk with Formel shaking hands with the gamblers and wishing them good luck for the coming season. [8]

Russell purchased some essential supplies for the gambling places in preparation for the profitable summer the partners expected. Three roulette wheels, a hazard table, chips, liquor, and cigars were all provided by Russell to the house. All was in readiness when Russell and his partners had a falling out. Assuming that the District Attorney had the most power in the city, Russell went to Andrus and asked him to get back the $9000 he had invested with Formel and the others. [9]

Andrus arranged for a meeting the next afternoon in his office. Present for the meeting were Formel, Russell, and Andrus. A settlement of $6000 was mediated and Russell soon left town, no longer having a financial interest in any Saratoga gambling place. Interestingly, the defense for Andrus never denied the meeting took place or that the settlement meeting was held in his office. Fallon cross-examined Russell and generally attacked his character and had a little fun with the witness but never did deny the fact that the meeting happened or that it was for any other purpose than what Russell had alleged. [10]

As if the testimony of Russell were not damaging enough for the defense, the next witness called should have terrified Andrus's attorneys. John R. Ward, the mysterious "Dr. Kennedy" referred to in the Formel trial as being responsible for renting the 210 South Broadway building, was placed on the witness stand by Bascom. He testified that he attended the meeting in April of 1919 between Formel, Russell, Andrus, and himself. He verified Russell's testimony that Formel told Andrus that the two others were going to be with him that summer, that Formel and Andrus met privately, and that Andrus wished them good luck with their plans. Ward, however, added that after the meeting Formel went to the bank and returned to the building where Andrus' office was located but entered alone. [11] The reader is left to decide the implication of this particular statement.

The testimony of Ward was recounted in the Saratogian newspaper of May 14, 1921. Ward testified that 210 South Broadway continued to operate, even after the raid. Bascom attempted to enter into evidence the so-called "divvy sheet" that Rachel Brown had produced at the Formel trial, over repeated objections by Mr. Fallon. Ward helped put an end to their bickering over the paper by offering to explain the division of the profits without looking at the sheet.

He explained to the court the split of the profits that was detailed on the now famous slip of paper. His account was the same as Rachel Brown's was during the Formel trial except for his wording when it came to the 25 per cent allegedly earmarked for "the Boss." Instead of saying the share belong to "the boss," Ward said the 25 per cent went for "ice."

When Bascom asked Ward to explain what he meant by "ice," Ward stated that, "Ice in the gambling game means money paid for the privilege of operating." [12]

Ward went on to relate that 210 South Broadway continued operation after the raid and that about the middle of August he again visited Andrus because he was concerned about the police officers who had been stationed outside the place since the raid. He wanted to know if there was a problem with local authorities and explained to Andrus that they did not want to keep the place going if everything wasn't all right. Ward said that Andrus replied by telling him, "I'm getting no money from your place."

Ward, surprised at the statement, asked if it was true that Andrus had received $1360 from Formel. Andrus told him that he received only $360.62 and pulled out his ledger book to show Ward his accounts related to the supposed payoff. The figure $1360 that Ward had assumed Andrus had received would have been the District Attorney's share of the house profits that Formel was supposed to have delivered. Profits made by the house after the raid had been conducted and the gambling apparatus returned to the gamblers.

At this point Ward realized that Formel had probably stiffed Andrus on his cut (assuming that Andrus was indeed "the boss" and entitled to "ice" from the gamblers) and that things were not "all right" with the local authorities. Before departing his meeting with Andrus the District Attorney warned Ward that the police would eventually make another raid if they stayed in business. Ward testified that he went immediately to 210 South Broadway, packed up his gambling equipment, and left town. Ward stated that in all, Andrus had received payments from the 210 South Broadway house totaling over $2500 in the summer of 1919 before things went sideways.

Before being cross examined by Fallon, Ward provided one more bit of information by fingering

Rachel Brown as one of the gamblers who stole some of the gambling equipment from the police department and that he had seen the stolen equipment in operation later that summer.

Fallon wasted no time in attacking Ward. Accusing him of being a party to crooked gambling and a lifelong degenerate gambler, Fallon would refer to Ward as nothing more than a "common thief."[13]

Again without bothering to deny the charge of bribery and outright corruption that the District Attorney had just been accused of in open court, Fallon attacked the character of Russell and Ward, both convicted gamblers. He never denied that the meeting of Formel, Ward, Russell, and Andrus before the summer of 1919 took place or what was said. He never denied that Andrus had taken money but rather asked Ward if he had ever paid protection money to Detectives Sullivan and Dorsey. Ward denied that he ever had.

Bascom defended the decision to use Ward and Russell as witnesses against the District Attorney. After all, who other than gamblers and officials would be in a position to testify about protection payoffs in Saratoga? Andrus was not about to offer up any evidence against himself and Formel was in Dannemora prison. At this point Bascom had one other witness to call, F. G. Robinson, whose wife was a half-sister to Jules Formel.

Robinson had apparently testified before the grand jury that he had a conversation with Andrus during which Andrus admitted to Robinson that Formel had paid him $3800 in the summer of 1919 but that Formel owed him another $4000. This was a pretty damaging statement but Robinson suffered from the same type of amnesia that afflicted Detective Mason earlier in the trial. Where Mason could not remember recognizing the voice of Charles Andrus when he picked up the phone during the raid at 210 South Broadway despite his testimony on three prior occasions that he did, Robinson could not recall the conversation that he swore happened before the grand jury. [14]

All in all, despite the fading memories of Detective Mason and Mr. Robinson, it was a pretty strong case presented by Bascom. Now the defense team of McElvey and Fallon would have a chance to convince the jury that their client, the duly elected District Attorney of the County, was innocent.

The defense was rather simple, and had been hinted at throughout the trial. McKelvey and Fallon would argue that Andrus was the District Attorney, not a police officer. According to the theory offered by the defense, the District Attorney was dependent on the police to bring him evidence and it was his responsibility to prosecute the crime, not to actively investigate criminal matters. Charles Andrus was not an investigator, but he was a prosecutor, and he had never failed to prosecute anyone for a gambling offense when evidence was brought to his attention.

Fallon used a similar defense strategy as he did during the second Formel trial. He presented few witnesses on behalf of the defendant and instead relied mostly on his summation to try to sway the jury's opinion. Only four witnesses were called by the defense. Andrus' secretary was called and testified that she never saw Ward in Andrus's office.

Mr. Van Wagoner, the man who returned the gambling equipment pursuant to the replevin action approved by Judge McTygue testified that he notified Andrus only after the implements were returned to the gambler George Remo.

The defense also called the prosecutor himself, Wyman Bascom, who was asked a few questions about the grand jury proceedings that resulted in the indictment of Andrus. [15]

Only one of the witnesses offered any testimony that would be considered of interest, if only for the light it shed on the gambling conditions of 1919 in Saratoga Springs. Former Commissioner of Public Safety William B. Milliman was called to the stand and testified to two seemingly contradictory points.

On the one hand he testified that he had almost daily communication with Sheriff Reynolds and District Attorney Andrus regarding the gambling situation and urged cooperation between the three of them. Furthermore he stated that the gambling dens at the Arrowhead, 210 South Broadway, Rothstein's Bonny Brook, Riley's Lake House, and the Leffler Cottages were all visited regularly by police officers who never were able to find any gambling going on.

On the other hand he testified that officers were all posted outside the gambling houses in order to, "warn people that they were gambling houses and to take everyone's name going in or coming out."[16] He added that he conducted the raid at 210 South Broadway without notifying the District Attorney or the City Judge because, in his words, "if it was a matter of public knowledge, what chance would we have?"[17]

The Andrus defense team apparently did not consider it unusual that the Commissioner of Public Safety, the elected civilian head of the police department and who was in daily contact with the District Attorney about the gambling situation in Saratoga Springs, would find it necessary to keep that same District Attorney in the dark about a pending gambling raid. They never addressed the question of how it was even possible that the police could find no gambling evidence against any of the gamblers who were operating in town, and yet still post police officers to warn people that they were about to enter a gambling house, taking their names as they came and went for good measure.

After calling their witnesses the defense moved on to the summation of their case, which was delivered by Judge McElvey rather than William Fallon. This was a curious play for the defense as Fallon was widely regarded as a great legal orator who was at his best in front of the jury, delivering a summation. Nevertheless, McKelvey delivered the speech and, rather than address the specific charges that Andrus faced, McKelvey attacked the motives behind the prosecution as well as the cost to the taxpayer of the investigation.

The charges against Andrus were characterized by McKelvey as being, "filed with politics and aimed solely with the purpose of destroying the defendant."[18] Could McKelvey have been accurate? While Bascom was not involved with the politics of Saratoga, locals might have recalled the heated exchange between Brackett and Andrus on the steps of the town hall in 1901 when Andrus had dared to sign the warrant for the arrest of Richard Canfield, "Prince of the Gamblers" and at that time, a client of attorney Brackett. Was it possible that the Brackett-Andrus feud had grown to such fury that a state investigation was called for by the Governor and Attorney General of the State and, as a result, dozens of gamblers had been caught up in the crossfire? Was it possible that Brackett had waited twenty years to make good on his threat that Andrus would be sorry for issuing the warrant against Canfield?

Whatever the case may have been, McKelvey's defense was basically that. According to him, politics had been the driving force behind the prosecution and this was evident by the fact that not a single witness had seen District Attorney Andrus ever take a dime from any gambler. And with that, McKelvey closed his defense of Charles Andrus.

Wyman Bascom, as he had in the three Formel trials, closed the proceedings by patiently laying out the people's case during his summation. Dispensing with the theory of a political conspiracy being behind the prosecution of the District Attorney, Bascom reminded the jury that two State Supreme Court justices, the attorney general, and the governor had all had a hand in approving the special investigation that he led and which resulted in the charges the jury was soon to consider. [19]

He then moved on to ask the questions he had asked at the start of the trial. Was there gambling in Saratoga Springs in 1919, was the District Attorney aware of it, and being aware of it, did he do anything to stop it?

The answer to the first question was an undeniable yes. There was gambling in Saratoga Springs in the summer of 1919. The second question was answered by Bascom when he pointed out that the testimony of Ward and Russell had gone unchallenged by the defense. The defense had failed to call the one person who probably could have testified to the whole affair, Jules Formel. That the defense did not call Formel, according to Bascom, indicated that Formel's testimony would be unable to assist the defense in showing that he did not know gambling was happening during his watch.

Finally, Bascom reminded the jurors that rather than seeking methods to suppress gambling in Saratoga Springs, the District Attorney failed to prosecute the admitted gambler, George Remo after he was successful in getting the gambling apparatus of 210 South Broadway back during the replevin action approved by Judge McTygue. Bascom explained that Andrus never intended to prosecute Jules Formel and he reminded the jurors that Andrus assisted the gambler Benny Russell in getting back $6,000 that he felt he was owed from his failed dealings with Formel. [20]

Bascom closed by acknowledging the seriousness of the jury's task by reminding them, "Every mother of a boy, every father of a girl, every family in the county looks to you to prevent these conditions. The eyes of the county, of the State, and, of the nation are upon you."[21]

Indeed it seemed as if all eyes in the county were upon the jurors and at 8:00 PM on May 17, 1921, the men of the jury retired to the jury room to conduct their solemn duty of determining the guilt or innocence of Charles Andrus, duly elected District Attorney of the County of Saratoga, charged with neglect of duty.

After a full ten minutes of deliberation, the jurors notified the court that they had reached a unanimous decision and were ready to render the verdict. A packed courtroom waited in silent anticipation as Justice Borst cautioned the members of the gallery to remain silent when the verdict was read. He would allow no outbursts regardless of the verdict.

He then turned to the foreman and asked what the jury had decided. The foreman, a man named Patrick C. Ryan, dutifully reported that the members of the jury had found Charles Andrus, NOT GUILTY![22]

The crowded courtroom immediately burst into applause despite Justice Borst's earlier warning to the crowd to receive the reading of the verdict with the decorum appropriate for a court of law. Edward Burns was singled out for his wild celebration upon hearing the news and narrowly escaped being thrown in jail for contempt when Judge McKelvey pleaded with Justice Borst on behalf of the overly excited man.

Edward Burns was not the only friend of Andrus and the gamblers who was overjoyed at the verdict of not guilty. In fact, a mob formed and rioted throughout the night in celebration of the jury's decision.

Dozens of people raced their cars up and down Broadway in celebration of the verdict. The homes of people aligned with the prosecution were visited by the mob and had their porches and doors defaced. The lawless group even came up with the creative insult of rolling dice on the front porch of one of the anti-gambling men. Young trees were torn up by their roots on Huestis Court. False fire alarms were pulled by the jubilant crowd. Ex-Senator Brackett had a bonfire lit on his front yard and several windows broken on the first floor of his home. The churches on Washington Street were not even spared as the group made a point to shout insults and jeer at the houses of worship along that street, though they refrained from doing any property damage there. [23] The police made no apparent attempts to stop the marauders and no arrests were ever made.

As if the outbreak of lawlessness was not enough, the Saratogian reported that there were several city officials among the crowd of lawbreakers. Deputy Commissioner of Public Safety Benjamin Wilson, City Judge Michael McTygue, Superintendent of Police Edward Carroll, and City Physician Dr. R.H. McCarty were all counted among the rioters. Wilson, Carroll, and McCarty were all appointed to their respective positions by the Commissioner of Public Safety at that time, John E. Gaffney. The paper speculated that perhaps this was the reason that the police did not make a move to stop the demonstrations. [24]

While McCarty and McTygue publicly denied any involvement in the mob's actions, the Saratogian stood by its reporting of the incident. Brackett wrote a letter to Commissioner Gaffney asking for a full investigation of the matter and requested that those responsible be held accountable. [25]

Brackett got a detective assigned to the case who was never able to make any headway in the investigation and ultimately no one was ever charged with any crimes related to the celebration of the verdict by some of the good citizens of Saratoga Springs.

The acquittal of Andrus was not the first time that the forces of law and order had been checked in Saratoga Springs and it wouldn't be the last. The verdict was seen by everyone as a victory for those who believed that the conditions that existed in Saratoga Springs in 1919 and 1920 were as they should be. Open gambling was beneficial for the city, supporters believed. Over time, a wide-open village had become as natural a part of Saratoga Springs as the mineral water flowing from beneath it. So natural a state of affairs, in fact, that city officials, then under indictment themselves, felt compelled to riot in celebration of the acquittal of one of their co-defendants.

The opinion of the law abiding citizens of Saratoga Springs was represented by an editorial appearing in the May 19th edition of the Saratogian which read, in part, "It was proved by the prosecution - and no attempt was made to disprove it by the defense - that gambling has brought to this city the lowest class of visitors. It was proved during the trial - and again no attempt was made by the defense to disprove it - that gambling has flourished in Saratoga Springs wide open. Gamblers, who have pleaded guilty to operating the lowest kind of dives, where no patron had a chance for his money, told how they operated openly while a police officer was stationed outside their doors. Young boys have explained in the court room to men thrice their years how easy it was for them to gamble. A clergyman testified that he became alarmed over the gambling going on among the boys of his Sunday School."

Quoting Justice Borst, the editorial went on, "'Judging from the testimony this vice fastened itself on youths and followed them all through their lives. Some of the youths in Saratoga Springs were being educated in crime.'"

The anti-gambling forces had been dealt a blow, but if recent history was a sign of things to come, they could take heart that the Bascom-Brackett team had shown considerable stubbornness in trying Jules Formel three times. Indeed, Bascom had given no indication that he was anything but committed to conducting his duties diligently and thoroughly. Therefore, on the Thursday following the Andrus acquittal, Bascom dutifully appeared before Justice Borst once again and announced that the prosecution was ready to make motions regarding the remaining charges against the other officials.

Unfortunately, Bascom's announcement was that the prosecution was ready to dismiss the remaining indictments against the officials Andrus, McTygue, Gaffney, Wilson, and Carroll. In addition to the neglect of duty charge that he had been acquitted on, Andrus had still faced charges of grand larceny, bribery, and conspiracy to defeat justice. Those indictments were dismissed after Bascom had consulted with the Attorney General of the State and had determined that it would be a "waste of time, effort and money to try the defendant upon any of the remaining indictments in view of the conclusion reached upon the last trial in the face of the evidence presented."[26]

Commissioner of Public Safety John Gaffney, Deputy Commissioner of Public Safety Benjamin Wilson, and Superintendent of Police Edward Carroll all faced indictments for neglect of duty. Bascom consented to the dismissal of those indictments as he did with the remaining Andrus indictments because essentially all of the evidence presented during the first Andrus trial would be presented against the others and Bascom, along with the Attorney General, did not believe any convictions against the officials could be obtained in Saratoga County. [27]

Bascom indicated that the people might have been willing to proceed with the charges against Edward Carroll but that since he was no longer associated with the police department, it was decided that his charges would be dismissed along with the others. Carroll had been on leave from the department since his indictment and Thomas Sullivan had been acting Superintendent in his absence. Sullivan was appointed officially to the position on May 1, 1921, and this satisfied Bascom that Carroll would no longer be a part of the police force in the future. [28]

Just a couple of days after the indictments were dismissed however, Commissioner Gaffney made the surprise move of reinstating Edward Carroll to the position of Superintendent of Police, and with a pay raise no less!

Almost before the ink was dry on the paperwork for the acquittal of Andrus, Sullivan requested, and was granted, a disability pension and Carroll reinstated to his former position. At the same time, Detective Mason was promoted to the rank of Sergeant. Everyone remembered that it was detective Mason who had a seeming case of amnesia during the Andrus trial as he could not recall that he had heard the District Attorney's voice on the phone during the raid at 210 South Broadway, even though he had testified to that very fact on at least three different occasion under oath. [29]

As for Judge McTygue, despite the dismissal of the indictment against him, he still had a pending misconduct and disbarment proceeding before the Appellate Division. The opinion of the prosecution was that the Appellate Division was better suited to consider evidence against the judge "where bias, passion and prejudice of local opinion and political feeling can have no influence."[30] McTygue would survive the Appellate Division inquiry and go on to win re-election as City Court Judge in November by over 1,000 votes.[31]

If Bascom could have had the benefit of their counsel, the gamblers of old Saratoga would have certainly warned him that it was useless to seek truth and justice in Saratoga County where gambling was concerned. Surely the likes of Ben Scribner, Chris Schaffer, and Robert Gridley would have advised against disrupting the honored traditions of the Spa. After them, John Morrissey would have explained the gamblers' position of power and influence over the local populace and their representatives. The gamblers caught up in the Comstock raids of 1886, including the then sitting President of the Village poor old Caleb Mitchell, would have shown him how the game was played. Commissioners Knapp and Gailor, along with the "Prince of the Gamblers" himself, Richard Canfield, could have demonstrated how the system of token arrests followed by mere slaps on the wrists for the gamblers was conducted. But in 1921 Bascom was just the last in a line of crusaders, pursuing the noble cause of justice in Saratoga Springs, to see all of his efforts come to naught.

What chance did Bascom really have anyway? National figures in organized crime had taken hold of the city by 1919. Arnold Rothstein had more money and more influence than any of them. The Brook ran straight through all of the Bascom raids in the summer of 1920.

The greatest lawyer of his time, coincidentally on the payroll of Mr. Rothstein, managed to show up at the defense table of a small time gambler running a small time operation on South Broadway, and then appeared by the side of the duly elected District Attorney of the County during his trial for neglect of duty. Gamblers were stealing their equipment back from the custody of the police. City Judges were dismissing charges and handing over gambling paraphernalia on a highly questionable and unusual replevin action. Officers were stationed outside the doors of gambling joints while inside the games were running full tilt. A lawless mob was celebrating the acquittal of one of their own, creating a general disturbance and harassing those who favored a law and order town.

Despite all of his success in making raids and gathering indictments, despite all of the guilty pleas obtained from the small time gamblers, and despite the assistance of one of the most powerful individuals who also happened to be the ex-state senator of the district, Bascom, just like all the others who had come before him, really had no chance to make a lasting impact on the community by obtaining meaningful convictions of those most responsible for the wide-open conditions of the Spa in 1921. The "facts-on-the-ground" as the saying goes, went unchanged. Gambling reform, at least in Saratoga Springs it seemed, was a lost cause.

Seven months after he was acquitted, District Attorney Charles Andrus was re-elected by the good people of Saratoga County.

Endnotes

Chapter 14

[1] "Jury Box Filled; Prosecution Opens in Andrus Trial," Saratogian, May 11, 1921.

[2] "Witnesses Testify There Was Plenty of Gambling in Saratoga," Saratogian, May 12, 1921.

[3] Ibid.

[4] Ibid.

[5] Ibid.

[6] Ibid.

[7] Ibid.

[8] "'Benny' Russell, Formel's partner, Links Andrus with Place at 210 S. Broadway," The Saratogian, May 13, 1921.

[9] Ibid.

[10] Ibid.

[11] "Andrus Admitted He Shared Gambler's Profits, Formel's Partner Testifies," The Saratogian May 14, 1921.

[12] Ibid.

[13] Ibid.

[14] "Attorneys Summing up in Andrus Trial; Defendant Fails to Take the Stand," The Saratogian, May 16, 1921.

[15] Ibid

[16] Ibid

[17] Ibid

[18] "Jury Acquits Andrus of Neglect of Duty Charge After Brief Deliberation," The Saratogian May 17, 1921.

[19] Ibid.

20   Ibid.

21   Ibid.

22   Ibid.

23   "Lawlessness breaks Out in Demonstrations that Follow Andrus' Verdict," The Saratogian, May 17, 1921.

24   City Officials in Lawless Parade," The Saratogian, May 18, 1921.

25   "Question Gaffney Regarding Action Against Paraders," The Saratogian May 19, 1921.

26   "Indictments Against Officials Dismissed," The Saratogian, May 20, 1921.

27   Ibid.

28   "TJ Sullivan New Police Dept. Head," The Saratogian, May 17, 1921.

29   "Carroll Reappointed Police Department Head with Raise in Salary," The Saratogian May 21, 1921.

30   "Indictments against officials...."

31   "Result in the City," The Saratogian, November 10, 1921.

Epilogue

With the acquittal of District Attorney Andrus, Saratoga Springs seemed on the verge of total surrender to the gangsters. With prohibition in its infancy, great power and wealth was on the horizon for organized crime groups and Saratoga Springs would not escape their reach.

More reform efforts would continue throughout the 1920's in Saratoga Springs. Another state directed investigation, led by Justice Thomas Heffernan, would expose more corruption among Saratoga Springs politicians and police officials. Law and order candidates would win seats on the city council and several raids would be conducted. Yet the liquor continued to flow and the gambling dens remained open throughout the decade. The gangsters would find a friend in Dr. Arthur "Doc" Leonard who was just emerging as the dominant political power in Saratoga Springs during the 1920's. "Doc" Leonard would serve as Public Safety Commissioner, controlling the police and working with the gangsters through the 1950's.

The 1930's was a decade that would see increasing violence amongst the gangsters vying for control of the lucrative summer liquor and gambling markets. There would be running shoot-outs on the streets of Saratoga

Springs. Men with bullet holes in their bodies would be dumped at the hospital. More corruption and crime throughout the city would mark the decade of 1930-1939.

The most memorable unsolved murder in Saratoga Springs history would occur in 1936, when native Saratogian Adam Parillo was gunned down. Was his murder the result of a disagreement with a local criminal or a revenge assassination by former international gangland associates?

Both the gangsters and the "Doc" Leonard political faction would see their power solidify through the 1930's and lead to the golden age of the Lake Houses during the following decade. The Arrowhead Inn, Newman's Lakehouse, Riley's, the Piping Rock Club, and others would have their heyday as local and national organized crime figures enjoyed the official protection of the local police.

Eventually it would all end. The Kefauver Committee would expose the corruption in Saratoga Springs to a national audience. Where Trask, Bascom, Brackett, and Heffernan may have been successful in closing gambling places for short periods of time, the investigation into the wide open gambling that was exposed following the Kefauver inquiry would permanently change the gambling situation at the Spa. Saratoga would be changed forever and the days of wide open gambling, crime, and corruption would come to an end.

It is true that Saratoga was, and still is, a wonderful resort destination. From its earliest days, Saratoga Springs was a summer destination for the rich and famous. The grandest hotels and most fashionable people dominated the Saratoga scene every year. Presidents, entertainers, international royalty, and the wealthiest men and women of society all flocked to Saratoga for over one hundred years.

If John "Bet-A-Million" Gates and "Diamond Jim" Brady came to Saratoga each summer, so did Jere Dunn and Rachel "Rachie" Brown. High society and Saratoga fit together like hand in glove. And so did some of the most questionable elements of low society. Saratoga attracted men with large bank accounts and sometimes, men with large body counts. It drew men involved with finance and industry and men involved with murder and vice. Regardless of their station in life, it seemed everyone was drawn to Saratoga.

This history of Saratoga Springs focuses on the darker side of Saratoga's past. The Saratoga Springs of the past was a place far different than the vibrant and relatively crime-free city that it is today. No longer are places like Willow Walk and Searing's Alley producing routine violence and despair. No longer are gamblers and gangsters openly plying their trade, paying off local officials for the pleasure of doing so. No longer do the residents of Saratoga Springs elect officials who openly declare their allegiance to peddlers of vice. Men like Pat Brady, Jules Formel, Rachel Brown, and Arnold

Rothstein would likely find the Saratoga Springs of today far less welcoming than they found it years ago.

All of what is written in these pages can be summed up in this simple statement: from the very beginning, the situation in Saratoga Springs was exactly the way the people of Saratoga Springs wanted it. In the end, no matter what the gamblers and gangsters wanted, they would need public officials who they could rely on to keep the town open. It was the citizens of the city who elected such officials time and again that made this part of the history of Saratoga Springs possible.

From Police Commissioners Knapp and Gailor through Jim Leary and "Doc" Leonard, gamblers and gangsters certainly did pay off local officials. Corrupt and or inept police officers like Edward Carroll definitely played a role in how powerful organized criminals became in the first half of the 1900's. Yet all these men enjoyed the support of the average voter and essentially the will of the people was reflected in what Saratoga Springs eventually became, a haven for gambling and vice.

The stories recounted in this book are all true. There are, without doubt, descendants of the men and women whose activities retold in these pages may not cast the heritage of the surnames mentioned herein in a very flattering light. I have tried to be objective and understanding in re-telling the tales of Saratoga past. I have intended no offense and as a native Saratogian with questionable ancestors of my own, I am certainly not casting any stones toward those who lived at a very different time and in a very different reality than that which exists today.

I did not seek out any family legends or conduct any interviews while researching this book. Only publicly available sources were utilized and, in doing so, I recognize the drawbacks that must attach to such an approach. Any speculation in these pages is mine and mine alone. I am solely responsible for any inaccuracies contained in these pages and offer an apology in advance for any shortcomings.

Local legends and oral histories passed down through generations would make this narrative a much more colorful story. Such recollections may have been able to fill in missing pieces that newspaper accounts of the day certainly left out. My hope is that this book, as an historical record, will encourage my fellow Saratogians to continue to keep their family histories and local legends alive by stimulating discussions among family and friends of what can be recalled from days long ago. As a community we must keep those legends and stories alive, passing them down to Saratogians yet to come.

Whether native born or recent arrival, Saratoga residents have intense pride in the history of the place. We may not know all the stories or recall all of the details, but one thing is for sure, Saratoga has a history like no other place and that is something that Saratogians truly appreciate. We recognize that we can celebrate our past without condoning it. We can understand the realities of yesteryear and still feel amused and ashamed by it at the same time.

Our history belongs to all of us, and whatever we may feel about it, we must understand that in the end, the history of Saratoga Springs is how the people of Saratoga Springs wanted it. I doubt very much that if Saratogians could go back and do it over again, that we would do anything differently.

Index

About The Author

Greg Veitch is a fifth generation Saratogian. A lifelong resident, he currently serves as the Chief of Police for the Saratoga Springs Police Department. Greg holds a Master's Degree in Leadership from SUNY Plattsburgh and teaches in the Criminal Justice program at SUNY Adirondack. He attends New Life Fellowship Church in Saratoga where his wife, Jennifer is Director of Family Ministries. Greg and Jen have five children, Rebekah, Rachel, Elizabeth, Luke and Nathan.

CPSIA information can be obtained
at www.ICGtesting.com
Printed in the USA
BVOW08s0234061017

496872BV00004B/4/P